Mapping Early Modern Japan

ASIA: LOCAL STUDIES / GLOBAL THEMES

Jeffrey N. Wasserstrom, Kären Wigen, and Hue-Tam Ho Tai, Editors

Mapping Early Modern Japan

Space, Place, and Culture in the
Tokugawa Period (1603–1868)

Marcia Yonemoto

UNIVERSITY OF CALIFORNIA PRESS
Berkeley · Los Angeles · London

University of California Press
Berkeley and Los Angeles, California

University of California Press, Ltd.
London, England

Library of Congress Cataloging-in-Publication Data

Yonemoto, Marcia, 1964–
  Mapping early modern Japan : space, place, and
culture in the Tokugawa period (1603–1868) / Marcia
Yonemoto.
    p.   cm. — (Asia: Local studies/global themes ; 7)
  Includes bibliographical references and index.
  ISBN 0–520–23269–0 (Cloth : alk. paper)
    1. Japan—Civilization—1600–1868.   2. Na-
tional characteristics, Japanese.   3. Ethnopsychol-
ogy—Japan.   I. Title.   II. Series.

DS822.2.Y665   2003
915.204'25—dc21   2002013902

Manufactured in the United States of America
12   11   10   09   08   07   06   05
10   9   8   7   6   5   4   3   2

The paper used in this publication is both acid-free
and totally chlorine-free (TCF). It meets the minimum
requirements of ANSI/NISO Z39.48–1992 (R 1997) ⊚.

For my parents
James Mitsuru Yonemoto
and
Mary Shoji Yonemoto

Contents

Illustrations

Notes to the Reader

Throughout this book Japanese names have been rendered in Japanese style, family name first. Well-known literary figures and artists, however, are often referred to by their pseudonyms and not by their family names (e.g., Hiraga Gennai is "Gennai," Ishikawa Ryūsen is "Ryūsen"). Edo-period authors often used several pseudonyms; in this case, alternate names are bracketed or given in the endnotes.

All dates have been converted to the Gregorian calendar from the lunar calendar and *nengo* (era-name) system. To avoid using misleading Gregorian names of the months I have left months and days in their lunar calendar numberings, as in "the twelfth day of the eighth month of 1763."

Commonly used Japanese terms (shogun, daimyo, Shinto) and place names (Kyoto, Tokyo, Kyushu) do not bear diacritical marks, nor are they italicized.

All translations from Japanese materials are the author's, unless otherwise indicated.

The following are equivalents for Tokugawa-period weights and measures that appear in the book:

1 *sun*	3 cm.	1.2 inches
1 *bu*	3 mm.	0.12 inches
1 *shaku*	30 cm.	1 foot

1 *ken*	1.7 m.	5.5 feet
1 *ri*	3.9 km.	2.4 miles
1 *koku*	180.4 liters	47.7 gallons

Acknowledgments

I have been extremely fortunate over the years to benefit from the counsel and criticism of a great many teachers, colleagues, and friends. Mary Elizabeth Berry introduced me to the study of Japanese history, and some years later supervised the dissertation upon which this book is based. Without her inspiration and guidance I would not have begun this project, much less finished it. Irwin Scheiner and Thomas C. Smith first sparked my interest in the early modern period, and I have profited greatly from their encouragement and judicious criticism. Kären Wigen has been an extraordinarily generous colleague and friend whose responses to this and other projects have shaped my thinking in important ways. In Tokyo, Watanabe Kenji of Rikkyō University guided my research, and his readings of Edo literature and culture have influenced my own.

During the long process of revision, parts or all of what has become this book passed through many hands. I am very grateful to Beth Dusinberre, Robert Eskildsen, Mack Horton, Lionel Jensen, and Kären Wigen, all of whom read the entire manuscript in draft form and gave extremely helpful comments and corrections. Svetlana Alpers, James Ketelaar, Randolph Starn, Carlton Benson, Susan Glosser, Mark Halperin, Keith Knapp, Chris Reed, Henry D. Smith II, and Tim Weston read and critiqued parts of the dissertation. Sumie Jones was generous with her time and offered astute guidance on researching Edo literature. Anne Walthall, Takashi Fujitani, and an anonymous reader for the University of California Press all gave extremely thoughtful and thorough criticisms on the penultimate version of the manuscript. My editor, Sheila Levine, took an interest in the project from early on and she, along with Mary Severance and Sharron Wood, efficiently guided it through the publication process. Nancy Mann provided expert last-minute proofreading. Parts of chapter 1 appeared as "The 'Spatial Vernacular' in Tokugawa Maps" in *The Journal of Asian Studies* 53, no. 3 (Aug. 2000); thanks are owed the *Journal*'s editor at that time, Anand Yang, for his support of the special issue "Geographies at Work in Asian History," in which the article appeared. I have also received countless helpful suggestions and comments from colleagues, especially those in the Department of History and the Department of East Asian Languages and Civilizations at the University of Colorado at Boulder, and from audiences at talks and presentations in various venues; I hope I have adequately expressed my gratitude to them personally or in print elsewhere.

Much of my research on Tokugawa maps was made possible by access to the Mitsui Collection in the East Asian Library at the University of California, Berkeley; several of the Mitsui Collection maps are reproduced here. I would like to thank the library's former directors, Donald Shively and Thomas Havens, its present director, Peter Zhou, and its staff members, especially Hisayuki Ishimatsu, Tomoko Kobayashi, and Bruce Williams, for their help and patience. The National Diet Library in Tokyo and the Tokyo Metropolitan Central Library both gave permission for the reproduction of illustrations from books in their collections. In Boulder, Taku Sekine volunteered his skills in computer graphic design to make the book's outline maps, and Ogihara Saeko efficiently handled copyright issues and last-minute logistical matters.

Research and writing was supported at various stages by generous funding from the Japan Foundation, the Social Science Research Council, the University of California, Berkeley, and various research and travel grants from the University of Colorado at Boulder; from the latter, I wish to acknowledge in particular the IMPART grant program, the Junior Faculty Development Award, the Council on Research and Creative Work, the Graduate Committee on the Arts and Humanities, and the Dean's Fund for Excellence. Receipt of the Eugene M. Kayden Manuscript Prize from the University of Colorado for the year 1999–2000 provided a subvention that helped underwrite the production of the book. In spite of this abundant assistance, no doubt many errors and infelicities remain, and for these I assume sole responsibility.

My immediate and extended family has long supported my scholarship and my career, even though both have taken me away from them in many ways. My parents, James and Mary Yonemoto, have always taken to heart the Japanese aphorism "send a treasured child on a journey." I owe them more than I can begin to say, and for what it is worth, I have dedicated this book to them. The Yonemoto, Shoji, Hamaguchi, Noguchi, Mamiya, Weston, and Bergmann clans have my deepest appreciation. Tim Weston has been my best companion, colleague, and critic and has enriched my life in countless ways. And lastly, to our daughter, Leah, who arrived just in time to supervise the final revisions of this book: I promise the next one will be for you.

Boulder, Colorado
May 2002

Introduction

By the middle of the Tokugawa period (1603–1868), literate people had
access to a vast and varied selection of maps and geographical writings.
As a result, those with the means to borrow or buy printed media could
readily conjure up images of and information about an entity called,
alternately, "Japan" (Nihon), "Great Japan" (Dai Nihon), "our realm"
(honchō), and "the entire country" *(zenkoku)*.[1] They could also find
maps, guidebooks, and travel accounts describing Japan's cities and
provinces, and the roads and sea routes that linked them together. They
might even come across one of many depictions of the "myriad [foreign]
countries." But while such texts proliferated because of the growth of
commercial publishing in the seventeenth and eighteenth centuries, formal geography education was limited and the science of cartography remained poorly developed. And, like most people in the early modern
world, the Japanese had no singular concept of "nation" or "state"; indeed, even highly educated people had very malleable notions of what it
meant to call oneself "Japanese."[2] The wide diffusion of various forms
of spatial knowledge and representation in the absence of a definitive notion of geography or national identity is not as contradictory as it might
seem. Rather, it is reflective of the flexible nature of geographic consciousness in the early modern period. In broadest terms this book,
which examines the texts that shaped and spread geographic consciousness, examines the elusive processes by which people came to name, to

know, and to interpret the natural and human worlds in which they lived.

Since the act of naming is central to this study, one might properly begin by explaining or, as Clifford Geertz would have it, "unpacking" the three principal terms of the title *Mapping Early Modern Japan*. In the first instance, this book is a history of mapping as an idea; it is not a history of cartography. Until fairly recently, histories of cartography tended to create fixed and supposedly universally applicable categories ("world maps," "national maps," "road maps") and to chart their technological development over time in all parts of the world in a linear fashion and on a timeline determined by the experience of the West. But as recent, more critically informed work by historians of cartography has argued persuasively, there is more to the history of cartography than a narrative of Western-centered progress, and more to mapping than maps alone.[3] This recent scholarship has shaped my approach, as I have attempted to write a history that comprehends not only officially and commercially produced maps, but also travel narratives and fiction on geographic and cartographic themes. As it is construed here, mapping is as much about the processes of perception and representation as it is about the material products of those acts.

A broad definition of mapping is particularly important in studying the early modern period, for as subsequent chapters show, writers and artists "mapped out" imaginary or discursive spaces just as mapmakers did actual places.[4] Both sources and theory thus conduce to a study that, rather than moving forward at the pace of progress, moves "out and about" to show the linkages between various spatializing practices and situates those practices in their historical contexts.

By defining mapping broadly, we might begin to perceive how a history of mapping is imbricated in the history of the early modern period. Indeed, scholars of early modern Japan recently have done groundbreaking work in proving, as Kären Wigen has put it, that "history 'takes place' in a spatial as well as a temporal dimension; by the same token, places are not merely geographically given, but historically constituted as well."[5] More specifically, the present study contends that spatial and geographic discourses inhered in the political practices and cultural forms of the early modern period. In the realm of politics and institution building, for example, the Tokugawa shogunate from the earliest years of its rule put considerable resources into measuring and mapping "the realm" *(tenka),* meaning not only its own lands—which amounted to only about one-quarter of the total land in Japan—but the entire country. Between the early seventeenth and the early nineteenth centuries, the shogunate repeatedly ordered daimyo to make maps and gather cadastral records of land under their control, and this information ultimately allowed the Tokugawa to assemble what was up to that time the most comprehensive store of spatial information ever compiled by a Japanese government.

Spatiality inflected political thought as well; in the late seventeenth century Confucian scholars like Kaibara Ekiken (1630–1714) began to articulate the notion that a model for political order might be found in the natural and physical world. For Ekiken and his followers, travel, direct observation, and recording of one's findings were the ways to discern that order. Intellectuals like Ekiken utilized forms of mapping to identify and maintain the class, status, and gender distinctions that defined early modern politics and society.[6]

But in contrast to the ways in which modern cartography and geography promote the understanding of sameness that characterizes the nation-state, in the early modern period the plural practices of mapping functioned as a means of discerning, categorizing, and preserving difference.[7] As Tessa Morris-Suzuki argues, the early modern definition of difference itself had a distinctly spatial inflection, for in the manner of the "civilized vs. barbaric" *(ka-i)* view of the world originally devised in imperial China, physical distance from the putative center determined the relative level of civilization of all places and peoples. Unlike their modern counterparts, early modern rulers not only tolerated difference, they emphasized it as a marker of the subordinate status of marginal people on the geographic peripheries such as the Ainu in Ezo and the people of the Ryūkyū Islands.[8] Nor was this "logic of difference," as Morris-Suzuki calls it, limited to the political center; as Herman Ooms's work on Tokugawa "village practice" shows, class, status, legal, ethnic, and gender differences structured fields of power in rural areas as well.[9]

And yet, although these forms of mapping established durable epistemological categories and lasting cartographic images, as we shall see, neither the shogunate, its officials, nor intellectuals monopolized the control of map images or spatial information. The shogunate depended upon the cooperation of daimyo and local officials to map Japan, and its struggles to enforce compliance with its orders reveal both the strengths and the limitations of the regime's "parcellized sovereignty." [10] The mix of authority and autonomy inherent in the early modern system of governance manifested itself in spatial politics at other levels of the political and cultural hierarchy as well. For in spite of the energy invested in administrative mapmaking, neither the shogunate nor daimyo regarded most cartographic information as confidential, and in at least one notable case, the shogunate allowed its official maps of Edo to be adapted, reproduced, and published by the commercial press.[11] The free flow of geographic information had the unintended effect of leaving the discursive field of mapping open to the innovations and interpretations of nonelites. Ultimately, then, it was not the shogunal government or local officials but artists, writers, mapmakers, and their commercial publishers who were most effective at spreading the texts and images of mapping to the public.

The commercial and public nature of early modern mapping compels a focus on the development of publishing and of "print culture," the social world encompassing and engaging the public dissemination of words and images. Both were functions of the growth of the economy and increases in commoner education and literacy in the seventeenth century.[12] A distinctly early modern phenomenon, the culture of print encouraged the spread of an unprecedentedly vast store of knowledge, geographical and otherwise, to a reading public of diverse class and regional origin. Most of the maps and geographical writings analyzed in this study were printed by publishers in the major cities of Edo, Kyoto, and Osaka and sold, often in considerable volume. In mapping's transformation from official to popular discourse—the latter defined here as texts published in and for the commercial marketplace—mapping took on new and unanticipated meanings as the visual and textual culture of mapping inspired a vivid geographic imagination.[13]

Printed maps and comic fiction on geographical themes provided an alternative and sometimes critical perspective on the substance and structure of the very political and cultural norms that, in their official guises, maps helped construct. Among the norms constructed (and deconstructed) in maps and other geographical texts was that of Japan as a territorially and culturally integrated entity. For in many ways, both more and less obvious, the history of early modern mapping is also a history of the changing representations of Japan itself. In general terms, the appellation "Japan" has a long (and contentious) history, as do the various spatial entities to which that name has been applied.[14] In the early modern period, Japan was depicted in many ways, visual and narrative, and for many purposes. Although the combined efforts of official and commercial mapmakers resulted in the establishment of a geographical model in which the three main islands of Honshu, Kyushu, and Shikoku comprised the country, these boundaries were by no means hard and fast. The northernmost island of Ezo appeared and then disappeared from shogunal and printed maps according to political necessity and cartographic or artistic exigency. Travel accounts, gazetteers, and encyclopedias, for their part, struggled to establish neat categories in which to place Japan and its many "others," but even these narratives' declarative prose betrays considerable ambiguity and uncertainty about who and what belonged within the domestic sphere. The result is that "Japan" was at the same time both a thoroughly mapped and narrated space *and* a profoundly elusive and impressionistic amalgamation of places and peoples. The perceived porousness of geographic and cultural boundaries gave room for discursive play with the categories of "insider" and "outsider." As the chapters on the satirical uses of maps and geographies in early modern fiction show, in the hands of the sharp-witted writer the amorphousness of boundaries lent itself readily to the identification and manipulation of forms of exoticized otherness within the domestic sphere.

For the reasons I have tried to explain above, I see the history of mapping early modern Japan as an investigation of texts, cultural practices, and intellectual processes. To put it in more general theoretical terms: as Henri Lefebvre contends, no space that is subject to human apprehension simply exists; space is always and in all places the result of productive processes.[15] Therefore, my methodological task at hand is not to define early modern mapping in putatively objective or absolute terms (did maps and travel accounts show places as they really *were?*), but to try to understand what purposes mapping served, for whom, and how. To borrow the words of the geographer David Turnbull, the goal here is to "recognize that all maps, indeed all representations, can be related to experience and that instead of rating them in terms of accuracy or scientificity, we should consider only their 'workability'—how successful they are in achieving the aim for which they were drawn—and what is their range of application."[16]

In the following chapters, I show how mapping "worked" at two transitional historical moments, and in three principal genres of text. The first of the temporal transitions dates from the mid- to late seventeenth century to the early eighteenth century. During this time mapmakers and travel writers began to produce new articulations of spatial order, and to disseminate them through the commercial press. The detailed depiction of Japan and its cities in both administrative and commercially published maps (chapter 1), the development of a new type of travel writing based on direct observation (chapter 2), and the prolifer-

ation of Chinese-style encyclopedias containing information about the
outside world (chapter 4) all work to categorize—though never to
erase—cultural difference through the imposition of spatial frameworks
of order.

The second mode of mapping dates from the mid-eighteenth through
the early nineteenth century. In this period, writers of travel accounts began to embellish their descriptions of the landscape in order to conjure
up for the reader visions of unknown places and exotic customs in Japan's hinterlands (chapter 3). Writers of illustrated comic fiction went
one step further, taking the spatial frameworks and categories established in maps and travel accounts and putting them to decidedly playful uses. Fictive accounts of foreign travel and satirical mappings of the
pleasure quarters (chapters 4 and 5) parody or otherwise subvert received
spatial knowledge by applying "serious" mapping tropes to seemingly
frivolous subject matter. Unlike their predecessors, they are documents
of *dis*order. Despite the seeming irrelevance of mid-eighteenth-century
fiction, however, it had a critical edge, for it revealed spaces, places, and
subcultures that were often kept hidden in official, or officious, forms
of mapping. Texts like Hiraga Gennai's faux travel account *Fūryū
Shidōken den* (The tale of dashing Shidōken, 1767) and satirical takes
on encyclopedic knowledge such as Akatsuki Kanenari's *Akan sanzai
zue* (The insatiable illustrated three assets, 1821–50) were works of
elaborate parody that showed the topsy-turvy erotic underworld that
existed within the apparently orderly realm. These texts represent what
I call an "antipolitics of pleasure," which celebrated frivolity at a time
when Japan was facing serious challenges on both domestic and international fronts in the form of diplomatic entanglements with Russia and
popular uprisings in urban and rural areas.

By the turn of the nineteenth century mapping in Japan had begun to
diverge from the Western models of geography and cartography. But by
this point both images and narrative descriptions of Japan had become
commonplace and conventionalized. When the Tokugawa shogunate set
out to compile a representative list of maps and geographical writings
in 1821, it accumulated more than nine hundred titles, the majority of
which were commercially printed and published.[17] Even as the science
of cartography gained in importance, and accuracy in mapmaking became increasingly prized, the multivalent cultural practices that comprised mapping continued. Imaginative and satirical maps, as well as
printed versions of older, technically "flawed" maps, were produced and
reproduced well into the late nineteenth century. Early modern mapping

thus constituted a vernacular language that continued to be employed even as geography and cartography became the standardized spatial discourses of modern Japan.[18] Although late nineteenth-century geographers and historians placed early modern Japan at a precise developmental stage—a stage of incomplete modernization, civilization, and empire—the persistence of mapping is one indication of the overstatement inherent in the modern rhetoric of progress. Far from being a stunted pseudo- or proto-scientific practice, mapping allowed for and even encouraged the endless arrangement and rearrangement of multiple spatial, cultural, and political identities whose protean nature reflected the possibilities as well as the limitations of being Japanese in the early modern period. The subsequent chapters focus on texts that captured, at distinct historical moments, those identities and show how they changed, through space and over time.

CHAPTER I

Envisioning the Realm

*Administrative and Commercial Maps
in the Early Modern Period*

The cartographer Phillip C. Muehrcke has observed that even a map of a "real" place can be seen as a "controlled fiction," an act of creation as well as replication.[1] This is an apt description of the administrative and commercial mapping of Japan in the Tokugawa period. For the shogunate as well as for the many commercial mapmakers and publishers, maps envisioned, created, and ultimately enshrined a new geographical, political, and social order. And insofar as nearly all types of maps were constantly updated and revised throughout the early modern period, they not only chronicled important changes in the spatial definition of Japan, its boundaries, regions, and cities, but also charted shifts in power relations across time. This chapter explores the relationship between the two main forms of early modern mapmaking: administrative and commercial. It argues that although early modern mapmaking was born of the shogunate's attempts to impose spatial order on its newly conquered realm, makers of printed maps and their publishers—most of whom were urban dwellers of the merchant class—provided the new perspectives and creative energies that fueled the unprecedented expansion and diversification of mapmaking in the Tokugawa period.

ADMINISTRATIVE MAPMAKING
UNDER THE TOKUGAWA SHOGUNATE

Although administrative mapmaking became a standard practice only in the Tokugawa period, maps have been used as tools of governance throughout Japan's recorded history. Evidence shows that Japan's early imperial governments began ordering provincial governments to submit cadastral maps in the seventh century.[2] At about the same time the imperial court initiated the compilation of gazetteers, or *fudoki*.[3] Sometime after 745, the legendary Tendai priest Gyōki (688–749) is said to have mapped the entire country after traveling its length and breadth gathering alms for the building of the Tōdaiji in Nara.[4] In the medieval period, the military governments (shogunates) used maps to adjudicate land disputes on private estates, or *shōen*.[5] And in the late sixteenth century, Oda Nobunaga began surveying lands under his control, a process continued much more extensively and systematically by Toyotomi Hideyoshi; the latter also began to map his lands for purposes of administrative control, albeit in a limited manner.[6]

External influences also shaped mapmaking practice. World maps and globes brought to the archipelago by European missionaries and traders in the late sixteenth century may have inspired the Tokugawa to remap Japan in its entirety.[7] Certainly the ongoing influence of cadastral mapmaking by the Chinese imperial state, with its syncretic mixture of ritual and administrative functions, shaped the content and form of Tokugawa official maps. Under the Chinese imperial state, the ordering of territory through mapping and the writing of gazetteers went hand in hand with cosmic ordering of the heavens discerned through astronomy and astrology.[8] Both Chinese and European models combined with Japan's indigenous geographic and cartographic legacy to bequeath to the early Tokugawa shogunate the motives and the methods for mapping its realm. The Tokugawa in turn built on these precedents but took them to new heights by transforming mapmaking into a systematic and ritualized practice.

The Tokugawa government generated five complete sets of provincial maps *(kuniezu)* and from this and other data compiled four maps of Japan *(Nihon sōzu)* in the course of its long reign. The provincial mapmaking projects were begun in 1605, ca. 1633, 1644, 1697, and 1835. Two maps of Japan were likely made in the 1630s (neither is extant), a third was completed in 1670, and the fourth was completed in 1702.[9] The shogunate also made maps of cities and castles. The available evidence seems to suggest two very different narratives of official mapmaking under the Tokugawa shogunate. One narrative emphasizes innovation: it sees maps as a novel form of the exercise and display of power by a regime seeking to stabilize and extend its rule in unprecedented ways.[10] The other narrative emphasizes continuity: the Tokugawa elaborated upon existing cartographic and geographic practices and, like its predecessors, saw the exercise of its political authority as necessarily limited by competitors for power (in the case of the Tokugawa, these competitors were the daimyo).[11] The most likely scenario, if the more complicated one, lies between these two poles.

In the case of provincial maps, it is true that the shogunate attempted, and in part succeeded, in gradually increasing its direct control over the administrative mapmaking process. In general, the shogunate seems to have used its mapmaking projects as one of many forms of indirect control over the daimyo. Its repeated demands that daimyo make and render to the government detailed local maps and cadastral records compelled the daimyo to expend time, energy, and financial resources to provide the shogunate with valuable geographical information. Moreover, from 1605, when the shogunate first issued edicts to the daimyo to submit cadastral registers and "maps of all the provinces" *(kuni-guni no chizu),* through its last large-scale mapping effort in the Tenpō era (1830–44), the shogunal government steadily increased its investment of resources in its mapmaking projects.

The first provincial mapmaking edicts of 1605 were confoundingly vague, requiring only that each map contain a clearly written notation of the productivity (in rice) of each district, or *gun,* and that it depict the provincial *(kuni)* boundary.[12] In response to the confusion this caused the shogunate dispatched its own inspectors *(junkenshi)* to supervise the collection of data and the making of maps for the second round of provincial mapping in the 1630s. It also put some of its highest-ranking officials, the *rōjū* (senior councilors), in charge of collecting the finished maps.[13] For the third provincial map project in the Shōhō period (1644–48), two shogunal police inspectors *(ōmetsuke)* were charged with crafting detailed instructions and standards for the making of maps; in all, more than a dozen regulations specified the content and structure of the new maps and registers, and a fixed scale of measurement was established: six *sun* on the map was to equal one *ri* on land or sea.[14] Moreover, in addition to the provincial maps and their accompanying land registers, the bakufu also requested in the Shōhō edicts the submission of castle maps *(shiro ezu),* which were to include detailed information on the size of each enceinte, the depth and width of moats, and the topography immediately surrounding the castle.[15] The shogunate's fourth provincial mapping project, which began around 1697, took five years and resulted in the collection of eighty-three maps. It was overseen jointly by a quartet of powerful officials: the *ōmetsuke,* the *jisha bugyō* (magistrate of shrines and temples), the *machi bugyō* (city magistrate of Edo), and the *kanjō bugyō* (finance magistrate). To further regulate the process, the shogunate also established a map clearinghouse *(ezugoya)* in Edo for the inspection of all maps and cadastral registers.[16] Finally, in the Tenpō era the shogunate attempted to manage the mapmaking process directly from start to finish, requesting that daimyo submit only the productivity figures for villages in their own domains; shogunal officials would then calculate the overall productivity figures and construct the maps themselves.

This portrait of steadily increasing shogunal control over the provincial mapmaking process, however, obscures the recurring problems the shogunate had in getting daimyo and other local officials to comply with its orders. These conflicts stemmed from the fact that, in most cases, provincial boundaries did not correspond to domain boundaries; provinces usually were comprised of several domains or, less frequently, a single daimyo oversaw territory in more than one province. Because of this, the making of provincial maps often required the cooperation of several daimyo and cadres of local officials, and disagreement among them over province, domain, or district boundaries was not infrequent. For example, during the making of the Shōhō *kuniezu,* the shogunate admonished officials in Saga domain not to provoke their neighbors into conflict over boundary issues. In Bizen and Sanuki provinces, the domains of Kagoshima and Shiogama argued over possession of three islands located between them, in the Inland Sea. The shogunate finally had to intervene, awarding the islands to Bizen. A dispute between domains in Bungo and Higo provinces provoked officials from those domains to lead a procession of local people all the way to Edo, where shogunal officials in charge of the mapmaking project were compelled to hold a special hearing to adjudicate the matter.[17]

But more often than not, mapping failed to resolve boundary disputes, and contested territory appeared on the provincial maps as "disputed land" *(ronchi)*. In the Genroku period, in order to forestall further disputes, the shogunate identified provinces comprised of more than one domain and ordered the daimyo in these provinces to submit geographical information concerning provincial, district, and village names directly to the province's map intendant, who would presumably rectify the ambiguous boundaries on his own.[18] Despite this measure, however, eighteenth-century local records show that the provinces of Chikuzen, Higo, and Iga had, respectively, six, eight, and five ongoing boundary disputes. Of these nineteen disputes, only five were settled at the time the Genroku *kuniezu* were being made.[19] One of the six disputes in Chikuzen involved a ten-kilometer stretch of the boundary dividing Chikuzen and Chikugo provinces and Akitsuki and Kurumae domains. This conflict proved so intractable it took the shogunal courts until 1854 to finally resolve it.[20]

But perhaps the most serious setback for shogunal mapmakers occurred at the outset of the Tenpō provincial mapping project, when the financially strapped shogunate attempted to utilize a new measure of land productivity: the so-called "true productivity figure," or *jitsudaka*. Daimyo were to arrive at this figure by taking the productivity of their lands (as previously estimated), and adding to it any produce from new or enlarged lands.[21] Many domains refused to do this, seeing in it the obvious threat of more onerous demands, fiscal and otherwise, by the shogunate. Although the shogunate issued threats and established deadlines for the submission of the new maps, most daimyo stubbornly held out for more than two years. In the end the bakufu was forced to make do with what information it had and to construct the maps on its own. In sum, despite the general impression that the successive provincial mapmaking projects proceeded steadily down a path toward increasing standardization and centralization of the mapmaking process, the continuous battles to define provincial boundaries and the persistence of local proprietary concerns revealed the shogunate's less-than-complete control over the spatial politics of its realm.

As fitful as the evolution of the shogunate's efforts to map the provinces was, the Tokugawa nevertheless managed to produce the most comprehensive and detailed local administrative maps and cadastral records ever made by a Japanese government, military or imperial. In addition to this significant accomplishment, the shogunate also drafted at least four large-format maps of all Japan. Judged solely in technological terms, these maps are quite flawed; errors in surveying and drafting caused significant skewing of the outlines of the main islands of the archipelago. From the perspective of political symbolism, however, the maps succeed in conveying in bold and dramatic fashion the broad geographical and political dimensions of the "Tokugawa peace." More than anything, they are testaments to the ambition and imagination of the early Tokugawa rulers who were able not only to conceive, but also to construct maps of such unprecedented detail, size, and scope. Indeed, as we shall see, the impressive appearance of the map of Japan, combined with the relative simplicity of its representational scheme, contributed to its utility for both official and commercial mapmakers.

The map most scholars agree best represents the first attempt to comprehensively map Japan is the so-called Keichō map, begun in 1605, completed around 1639, and revised in 1653.[22] It is notable for several characteristics that would serve as the template for all the shogunate's later maps of Japan: it is huge, measuring approximately twelve by fourteen feet, and shows the islands of Honshu, Shikoku, and Kyushu. The most visually dominant geographical entity is the province, each of which is set off by the use of color. Sea routes, rivers, roads, castle towns, post stations, and harbors also appear on the map, as do traveling distances by land and sea. Place-names of individual villages and towns, however, are few.

Later maps of Japan compiled by the shogunate in the 1670s and in the early eighteenth century extended the boundaries of the realm to include parts of the northernmost island of Ezo, and shortcomings in surveying and drafting were also corrected. But precision was not as important as symbolism in determining the workability of the map. Magisterial in their sweeping visions of an integrated polity, the shogunate's maps of Japan constituted a splendid, if largely invented, image of the seamless unity of a country that in actuality was quite profoundly divided by regional, administrative, class, and status differences. In great part because the shogunate was remarkably laissez-faire in controlling access to its maps, the shogunate's view of Japan influenced the work of artists and mapmakers who copied and emended administrative maps for commercial publication; in this manner, official maps shaped the geographic imagination at large. Although the dissemination of map images to the reading public was not part of the shogunate's original agenda, the transformation of the map from local administrative tool to a replicable "logo" of a unified polity was the Tokugawa shogunate's most durable legacy to early modern mapmaking as a whole.[23] The shogunate's attempts to envision the ideal polity effectively—if unintentionally—spread map images and mapmaking techniques throughout the realm, where they were adopted and adapted in ways the government could not have foreseen.

COMMERCIAL MAPS OF JAPAN AND EDO

By the end of the first century of Tokugawa rule artisan mapmakers were leading the way in reinventing the map of Japan. Since few of them had formal training in cartographic techniques and they thus did little original surveying, commercial mapmakers borrowed images and textual information from earlier maps, including (but not limited to) those made by the shogunate. In doing so, they inherited and transformed spatial concepts and map visions. In maps of Japan commercial mapmakers continued to emphasize the provinces, districts, and roads, and they tended to depict the archipelago in isolation from neighboring countries. These features were characteristic not only of shogunal maps but of Gyōki-style maps and gazetteers as well. In the case of city maps, the level of detail in official shogunal maps was increased significantly in commercially printed maps. Not content simply to replicate official visions of Japan, its cities, and its roads, commercial mapmakers took the spatial frameworks provided by models from the recent and distant past and layered upon them information pertaining to the culture and politics of their own time. In general, commercial maps tend to show traveling distances on roads, sightseeing venues, historical sites, markets, commercial districts, temples, and shrines; they also contain information about daimyo, including the value of their lands and the locations of their residences. The type of information conveyed in commercial maps, unlike official maps, was determined by the demands of the publishing market, which emphasized novelty and innovation, and maps were often reprinted several times in "revised" forms. This process of repeated emendation made the printed map a truly hybrid text, combining influences past and present, official and commercial. In order to fully understand printed maps, however, we must understand the broader context in which they were produced and sold.

Print Culture, Map Culture, and the "Vernacularization" of Space

In the last two decades or so, Japanese scholars have amassed a formidable body of research on the history of printing and publishing in early modern Japan.[24] In recent years, non-Japanese scholars have made this topic more accessible to an English-language readership.[25] Both the English- and Japanese-language research make it clear that the rapid development of commercial publishing beginning in the mid-seventeenth century was an economic, political, and cultural process of enormous historical significance. While the elite in classical and medieval Japan always had been highly literate, they constituted a tiny minority of the total population. Most of the texts they read were not published, but were circulated in manuscript form. This changed significantly in the early modern period, as rising literacy rates and the growth and diversification of the market economy in the first century of Tokugawa rule made possible a vast expansion in the number and types of people constituting the reading audience.[26]

Printing technology itself predated the Tokugawa period by several centuries. It began to develop in medieval Kyoto among a small community of copyists of religious manuscripts who used carved wood blocks to make multiple prints. After a brief experiment with movable type in the late sixteenth century, woodblock printing was deemed a more efficient mode for reproducing Japanese script, and it became the dominant printing technique in the first decades of the seventeenth century. Once established, the printing and publishing industry grew rapidly, first in Kyoto, then in Osaka and Edo.[27] By the mid-seventeenth century Kyoto had more than a hundred shops of varying size that published books, and in the same period approximately five hundred titles appeared on the market. In the first fifty years of the seventeenth century the fledgling industry had produced more books than had been printed in Japan in the previous two centuries.[28]

In the late seventeenth century and especially in the eighteenth century, publishing spread to other cities, and also to the provinces. By the Kanbun era (1661–72) publishers had established themselves in Osaka, and the first directories of publishing guilds and their output were compiled. Whereas early publishing had focused on religious and educational texts, by the early eighteenth century books aimed at a general reading audience, such as picture books and illustrated tales, comprised a significant proportion of total book production. Over the span of the entire Tokugawa period, it is likely that on average well over three thousand titles were published per year; ninety percent of these were commercial (as opposed to official or private) publications.[29] This figure bears little relationship to actual readership, however, which was almost certainly significantly larger than the number of books published because of the significant role of book lenders *(kashihon'ya),* who functioned as mobile libraries, loaning out books for fixed periods at quite reasonable prices, and sellers of used books *(furu hon'ya).* By the late eighteenth and early nineteenth centuries, books—new, used, and borrowed—were readily available to a wide range of consumers. As Peter Kornicki writes, "print culture in the Tokugawa period matured rapidly into a phenomenon with all the complexity and variety that is customarily associated with only the most advanced Western countries before modern times."[30]

Although the scholarship on publishing tends to focus on the book trade, other types of printed goods proliferated as well, especially in the largest cities. By the late Edo period "society was flooded with printed ephemera," as Henry D. Smith II has put it, ranging from elaborate multicolored *surimono* prints to inexpensive handbills for advertising new stores or products.[31] Within this varied and expanding realm of published material, maps occupied a distinct niche. In the early Tokugawa period, many printed and published maps were virtual reprints of official maps. As we shall see later in this chapter, in a remarkable example of the shogunate's nonproprietary attitude toward cartographic information, commercially published versions of official maps of Edo began appearing as early as the late seventeenth century. In similar fashion, a woodblock-printed atlas-style version of the shogunate's Keichō provincial maps was published in 1666.[32] And world maps, although they came from a different source, circulated in much the same way. The Jesuits used copies of Matteo Ricci's world maps to teach geography at their academy in Kyoto from 1605, and by 1645 printed copies of world maps based on Ricci's 1602 edition were being published in Nagasaki.

The growing diversity in the form and function of maps by the turn of the eighteenth century went hand in hand with popular demand for what Mary Elizabeth Berry has called "public information."[33] Publishing houses in the major cities produced a variety of encyclopedias, guidebooks, directories of the warrior houses *(Bukan)*, and geographical primers *(ōraimono)*, all of which comprised the source materials from which artisan mapmakers fashioned their visions of Japan. Once published, maps joined this corpus of published information and became themselves the basis for embellishment, revision, and outright copying by other mapmakers. The market mechanism fostered innovation, for up-to-date, detailed information and novel images were key selling points. By the eighteenth century, travelers could purchase numerous different scroll-format picture maps of the main highways of Japan and of sea routes encircling the archipelago. City dwellers could obtain "new" and "revised" maps of particular neighborhoods within Japan's larger cities. Sightseers could buy maps and illustrated guides of the innumerable *meisho* (famous places), whose number expanded in the early modern period to include not only temples, shrines, and sites famous for their natural beauty, but also shops, outdoor markets, teahouses, theaters, and the ubiquitous pleasure quarters. Throughout the Tokugawa period, it appears that maps were one of the few types of print goods for which there was a consistent and sizable audience; as old maps became outdated, publishers amended and reprinted new versions and variations. Maps comprised a good proportion of the output of the prominent publishing house of Suharaya Mohee in Edo, and they contributed significantly to its economic prosperity. The many uses to which maps could be put enhanced their marketability and thus insured their consistent circulation.[34]

Envisioning Edo in Printed Maps

Print culture not only affected the content of map images, but also changed the dynamic of mapmaking and map reading, as the producers and the consumers of maps found themselves living in an increasingly commodified world of goods. At the same time, commercial mapmakers remained, to varying degrees, influenced by the administrative maps drawn by the shogunate. In some instances one can place printed maps of both Japan and its cities in a direct line of descent from the shogunal maps upon which they were modeled; this is most evident in the case of printed maps of the city of Edo, which began to appear in the late seventeenth century. Edo was a small village of several thousand inhabitants when the Tokugawa took control of it in 1590, but by the time the first population survey was taken in 1678, there were 570,361 commoners listed in the urban registries. To this figure one must add a conservative estimate of a few hundred thousand samurai and a floating population of about 50,000, for a total urban population of around 900,000.[35] Comprehensive censuses in the 1720s indicate that Edo's total population was just over one million around the turn of the eighteenth century, making it one of the largest cities in the world at that time.

The shogunal capital's constant growth was chronicled in a series of regularly updated and revised large-format maps.[36] The oldest surviving printed map of Edo dates from 1632, but it was in 1657 that significant changes were made in the way the city was represented cartographically. In that year a disastrous fire engulfed the capital, destroying nearly two-thirds of Edo in a matter of days. In the aftermath of the conflagration, the shogunate assigned Hōjō Ujinaga, the surveyor who had compiled the Shōhō era (1644–48) map of Japan, the task of surveying and re-mapping the entire city to aid in the reconstruction process. The manuscript map that Hōjō ultimately submitted to the government around 1658 became the template for many subsequent printed and published maps of Edo.[37] The castle appears as a blank in the map's center, a convention that was followed rigorously on all castle-town maps for security reasons. Daimyo estates *(yashiki)* spiral outward from the castle's environs. Roads, rivers, canals, ponds, and reservoirs were depicted and labeled, as were the regular rectangular blocks that formed commoner neighborhoods. Either Hōjō himself or his assistant Fujii Hanchi (who later assumed the pseudonym Ochikochi Dōin, under which he published many maps and road guides) revised the manuscript map to produce the first printed and published map of Edo based on surveying, the *Kanbun go-mai zu* (Five-page map from the Kanbun era, 1661–73).[38]

From the late seventeenth century on, variations of the Kanbun-era map began to appear. Ochikochi Dōin's revision of the *Kanbun go-mai zu*, entitled *Shinpan Edo ō-ezu* (Newly published large map of Edo, 1676), hews fairly closely to the original's unornamented and highly detailed depiction of the city space. Slightly smaller than the manuscript map, the *Shinpan Edo ō-ezu* carries a table listing place-names that marked the outer boundaries of the city: Itabashi to the north, Meguro Fudō to the south, Kameidō to the east, Hyakunin-chō to the west. Another table lists traveling distances (in *ri*) within the city measured from the official city center at Nihonbashi. The map also bears a legend that explains the map symbols and gives the date and the names and seals of author and publisher.[39]

Other adaptations of the Kanbun map, like Ishikawa Ryūsen's *Edo zukan kōmoku* (Outline map of Edo, 1689) (fig. 1), departed significantly from the shogunal model. Ishikawa Ryūsen (active ca. 1680–1720) became fairly well known during the Genroku period as a writer and illustrator. Like his contemporary, the great Osaka-based writer of parodic fiction, Ihara Saikaku (1642–93), Ryūsen published works that were for the most part light and humorous fiction on the themes of love and money, aimed at a commoner audience. In addition to his work as artist and writer, Ryūsen also produced many maps of Edo, of Japan, and of the world throughout his career.

Ryūsen's life is relevant to his maps in that the latter reflected the knowledge and interests of the social group to which Ryūsen himself belonged: the literate, fairly prosperous, most likely urbane city dweller. In Ryūsen's map, unlike the official map upon which it was based, the space of Edo is densely layered with text. Every space on the map is labeled and marked, from large daimyo *yashiki,* which are labeled with the names of their occupants, to the commoner quarters whose streets and neighborhoods are named and numbered. In the map's lower left

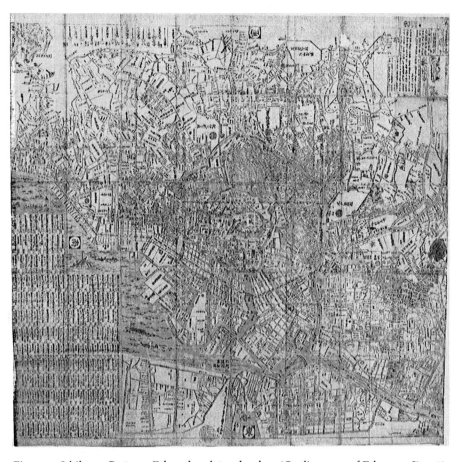

Figure 1. Ishikawa Ryūsen, *Edo zukan kōmoku, kon* (Outline map of Edo, part I), 1689. Courtesy of the East Asian Library, University of California, Berkeley.

corner, in the space where Edo Bay should be, is a large table listing 240 daimyo, arranged in order of political status (gauged by the daimyo's relationship to the Tokugawa house) and by wealth (in *koku* of rice).[40] Beginning at the top right-hand corner of the table and reading in vertical columns right to left, each rectangular section lists the name of the daimyo, including his official title, followed by the *kokudaka* of his lands, the name of his domain, and the location of his residence *(yashiki)* in the capital. By perusing this table one learns, for example, that the high-ranking daimyo "Owari *dainagon* Mitsutomo" (Tokugawa Mitsutomo [1625–1700], who held the office of *dainagon,* or senior councilor) was lord of the domain of Nagoya, controlled lands valued at

209,000 *koku,* and maintained a residence in Edo at Ichigaya. Further down on the list is "Kuroda Kai no kami Nagashige" (Kuroda Naga-shige [1659–1710], daimyo in the province of Kai), who controlled the domain of Akitsuki; his lands were valued at 50,000 koku, and he main-tained his Edo residence at Shiba. Lesser daimyo like "Oda Yamashiro no kami Nagayori" (Oda Nagayori, daimyo of Uda in the province of Yamashiro) rounded out the list; Oda's lands were valued at 31,200 *koku,* and he maintained his residence in the capital at Shitaya. Later versions of this map contain further embellishments, such as the family crests *(mon)* for all daimyo listed in the table at lower left, and a table stretching along the map's bottom edge that lists, by location, all the temples and shrines in the city.[41]

This sort of detailed information about daimyo wealth and residences at first seems anomalous on a map intended for a largely commoner audience. But the information found in the tables on Ryūsen's Edo maps was of the sort readily available in other published materials, most notably the *Bukan,* or registries of the military families. *Bukan* were printed, updated, and reprinted numerous times and in numerous forms throughout the early modern period. First published in the Kan'ei era (1624–44), the *Bukan* was subdivided into sections for daimyo, *hata-moto* (shogunal vassals), and other bakufu officials or workers. Each en-try in the *Bukan* gave the daimyo's family name, traced the recent fam-ily genealogy in chart form, listed the fief lands, and gave the location of the daimyo's Edo residence. Accompanying illustrations depicted the family crest and forms of distinctive weaponry or symbols used by the clan in warfare. By the late 1650s, variations on the *Bukan* began to ap-pear, and such texts proliferated in the Genroku period. Like other sorts of guidebooks and gazetteers, these vast compendia seem to have ap-pealed to an audience outside the warrior class, drawing the interest of readers eager for details about the lives of the elite. By the eighteenth century, the *Bukan* format had become so familiar that in 1769 a faux *Bukan* replacing warriors and their houses with actors and their theaters was censored by the bakufu as inappropriate political satire.[42] The com-mercial appeal of published encyclopedic texts such as the *Bukan* sug-gests a readership with an active curiosity about the powerful in early modern society. In the case of the *Edo zukan kōmoku,* the rendering of such information on the map linked power to place in a cogent visual form. And within the densely populated shogunal capital, mapped in-formation in the *Edo zukan kōmoku* was not abstract or strictly "official." It was usable spatial and political knowledge, applicable to every-day life.

Everyday spatial practices found more concrete expression in Ishi-kawa Ryūsen's mapping of the sites of play and leisure. *Edo zukan kōmoku* draws the reader's attention to sightseeing venues and pilgrim-age sites in the city, including the pleasure quarters at the Yoshiwara and other "famous places," which are enlarged and prominently labeled on the map. While Ochikochi Dōin's *Shinpan Edo ō-ezu* simply listed the notable sites in the city, Ryūsen depicts them graphically, in enlarged de-tail. A popular pilgrimage site like the temple at Asakusa is illustrated prominently, as are the city's main bridges at Nihonbashi, Edobashi, and Ryōgokubashi, which served as landmarks, gathering places, markets, and staging grounds for popular entertainments. Important points along the local roads, such as the post station at Itabashi, which was the northwestern boundary of the metropolis on the Nakasendō highway and also a notorious brothel district, are also emphasized. The newly built commoner areas in Honjo, on the eastern bank of the Sumida River, are depicted in the rhombus-shaped inset detail map at center bottom; Ryūsen notes in the colophon (boxed text at top right) that the reader may want to consult his recently published large-scale maps of Honjo for a more detailed view.[43]

Despite the map's heavy use of both text and illustration, it was not meant to stand alone as a guide to Edo. To aid the reader in the use of the map, Ryūsen provided a supplementary text, bound in book format, which was meant to accompany the single-sheet map. This volume, en-titled *Edo zukan kōmoku, ken* (Outline map of Edo, part II, 1689), be-gins with several regional maps situating the Japanese archipelago in re-lation to its immediate neighbors. Following these maps are some twenty pages of text listing, by name and location, hundreds of "experts"—teachers, craftspeople, merchants, even artists and musicians—whose services a cultured Genroku Edoite might have reason to consult (fig. 2). With the help of the directory the reader could learn where to find au-thorities on a wide range of subjects: Confucian scholars, acupunctur-ists, and dentists are listed beside experts in *haikai* composition, *gō* teachers, flower arrangers, art appraisers, woodcarvers, sutra chanters, and doll makers. A separate section provides the names and locations of merchants and their specialties: swords, incense, ink, clothing (with a separate entry for those large concerns offering discounts to customers paying in cash), books, dyed goods, foreign goods, writing brushes, and

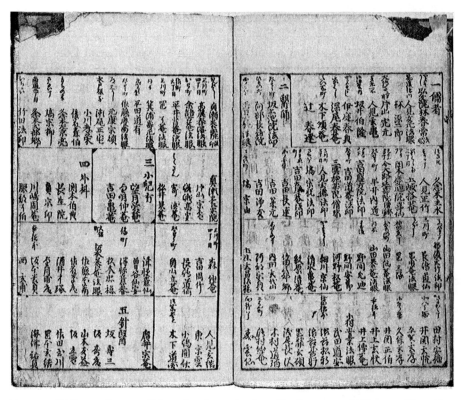

Figure 2. Ishikawa Ryūsen, *Edo zukan kōmoku, ken* (Outline map of Edo, part II), 1689. Courtesy of the East Asian Library, University of California, Berkeley.

the like. Finally, for those interested in entertainment, the last section of the text lists performers in various genres of the arts—kabuki, *nō, jōruri*—and the names and locations of their theaters. It also lists individual performers, such as flute players, drummers, and chanters of *kyōgen*. Each entry gives a specific street or neighborhood address, coordinated to the locations listed on the single-sheet map.

The content of Ishikawa Ryūsen's two-part map suggests a target audience quite different from that of Ochikochi Dōin's *Kanbun go-mai zu* and its predecessor, Hōjō Ujinaga's manuscript map. Instead of an educated or official class concerned with accurately mapping a new political and geographic order, Ryūsen's audience was the commoner elite, the literate urban merchant class whose wealth and tastes shaped the culture of the Genroku period. Unlike shogunal officials, they were in-

terested not in measuring or administering urban space, but in locating
discrete places, goods, and services. That Ishikawa Ryūsen aimed his
maps at a commoner rather than at an official audience is made clear by
Ryūsen's criticism of Ochikochi Dōin and the shogunate's mapmakers,
whom he considered overly concerned with surveying and measuring. In
the foreword to the urban directory of *Edo zukan kōmoku*, he is surprisingly frank about this matter, writing, "I say that maps that are
drawn at [a scale of] one *bu* to ten *ken* and so forth [and claim to be]
comprehensively surveyed are worthless." He goes on to state that it
is adequate simply to indicate the location of shrines and temples, and
to demarcate warrior residences from commoner ones. Depicting major roads by using thick lines, he writes, is sufficient to convey their
importance.

Ishikawa Ryūsen's *Edo zukan kōmoku* allows for multiple insights
into Edo commoner life. The goods and services listed in the directory
reflect a material culture of considerable abundance, and the existence
of the directory itself aided the reader in accessing material goods. In
short, the map helped people find their way not only in the city itself,
but also in urban life. It cracked the geographic code of Edo and laid
bare, in two-dimensional form, all the capital had to offer, including the
loci of official power and the places of commoner prosperity and pleasure. Though Ishikawa Ryūsen's motivations remain largely obscure, it
seems clear that he meant for his maps to be seen, read, and *used* to
navigate the multiple worlds—physical, political, and social—in which
Edo commoners lived.

In the evolution of Edo maps from Hōjō Ujinaga's 1658 five-page
map of Edo to Ishikawa Ryūsen's 1689 single-sheet map and its accompanying guidebook, we can see how official cartographic records were
"vernacularized" and transformed into new views of the constantly
changing urban scene. Readers wanted up-to-date information, and it
was up to the mapmaker to provide it, consistently and repeatedly.
Ishikawa Ryūsen himself seems to have realized this, for in the years
following the appearance of *Edo zukan kōmoku*, he produced neighborhood maps of the new settlements that began to appear east of the
Sumida River, as the commoner population spread from its base in the
flatlands in the east-central part of the city. Ryūsen seems to have considered each of his maps a fleeting vision of a city in constant change;
in the afterword to the directory part of *Edo zukan kōmoku*, Ryūsen
claims no authoritative knowledge. Instead, he states that he has col-

lected various types of information and "hearsay" and has offered "this assemblage of thin learning" in the hope that it might prove beneficial to the reader.

Ishikawa Ryūsen's comments should not imply that he perceived his maps to be of no consequence. The self-deprecating tone of his remarks is common in Edo-period authors' prefaces; as in book acknowledgments today, it was conventional to downplay one's own achievements and take responsibility for the faults of the work. But we also may read Ryūsen's words from a different perspective, that is, as an acknowledgment of the way maps were seen and used in the Genroku period. To say that maps were ephemeral printed goods does not mean they were meaningless. Rather, it acknowledges the key attraction of the genre: its ability to reflect, in graphic form, the changes in the political and social environment surrounding the map reader. Few other published texts were able to convey this type of change effectively. The bakufu prohibited the discussion of "current events," especially controversial political matters, and with the exception of the kind of information contained in the *Bukan,* whose content was approved by the shogunal censors, discussion of the shogunate and of the warrior houses was likewise forbidden. The government regularly posted edicts and laws to this effect on signboards throughout the major towns and cities. Certainly rumors and hearsay flowed freely through unofficial channels, both by word of mouth and in print, but there were no regularly published newspapers to speak of; such media emerged only in the Meiji period.[44] Thus, for most of the Tokugawa period, published maps filled a unique and attractive niche as providers of up-to-date information in relatively accessible graphic and verbal form.

By the late Tokugawa period, maps of the cities and of Japan had become commonplace. Ishikawa Ryūsen's maps continued to be emended and reprinted well into the eighteenth century, and newer, more detailed sectional maps *(kiriezu)* began to appear in the early nineteenth century. By the last decades of the Tokugawa period, observers of the urban scene could look back at a century and a half of published maps to evoke a sense of how the city and city life had changed. Saitō Gesshin (1824–93), the compiler of the *Bukō nenpyō,* a history of events in Edo from its founding through the mid-Meiji period, was one such observer. Gesshin was not a newcomer to Edo, but a longtime resident and third-generation city official *(machi nanushi)* in the capital's system of commoner governance. Clearly, Gesshin was not an eyewitness to the vast majority of the events that appear in his chronicle, but he combed contemporary sources, including published maps, for evidence of the various happenings he recorded. His earliest reference to maps is dated 1632, when he first notes the publication of an Edo map.[45]

Gesshin used maps not only as reference materials for changes in the city's geography, but also as indications of shifts in its daily life and customs. He uses maps in both these ways in an entry for 1632:

> Kan'ei 9 [1632]: Until the Kan'ei period [1624–44], adjoining Kanda Saeki-cho and Kiji-cho was the residence of the Lord Hori Tango no kami. To abbreviate "in front of the residence of the Lord of Tango," people would say "Tanzen." In this area there were many bathhouses, and also beautiful female bath attendants, and a lot of carousing young men and the like who were learning kabuki in [what became known as] the "Tanzen style." . . . At the end of the Kan'ei [or] around the Shōhō period the residence of the Hori moved to Shimotani. In the map of Edo from the Jōō period [1652–55] [that residence] has already been changed to the residence of the lord of Toda.[46]

Gesshin also cross-references maps with other types of geographical writings, such as illustrated famous-place guidebooks (meisho ki), paying particular attention to their changing depictions of Edo's notable sites:

> Enpō 8 [1680], eighth intercalary month: After the Meireki fire [1657], Nishi Honganji moved to Tsukiji, and the main hall was then built to the south; if one looks at the Edo meisho no ki of the second year of Kanbun [1662], it was not yet built.[47]

In the same year, 1680, Gesshin summarized the early history of Edo maps, making note of the aforementioned published maps of the city by Hōjō Ujinaga and Ochikochi Dōin:

> Enpō period [1673–81]: Regarding the moving of Eitaibashi Hachimangu to the outskirts of Edo: this area is an island reclaimed from the sea; in the far distance one can view the clustered mountains of Bōsō [peninsula], and nearby the Kanejiro Shibaura. It's said to be a place blessed with views. This should be made clear by the Enpō map of Edo. The divisions are detailed on [other] maps of Edo from this period. The additions of [the areas of] Honjo and Fukagawa[48] were begun with the Kanbun-Enpō map. (A two-volume folding map of Edo was published in Enpō 8 [1680]. It was first published by Hyōshiya Ichibee on Asakusabashi-dōri, Kawara-chō. Additionally, Edo bungen no zu [Sectional map of Edo, by Ochikochi Dōin] shows roads in detail. Kodama Jushō followed this with his Hoeki bunkenzu [Expanded sectional map].) If you render [the name] "Ochi-kochi-dō-in" into simple form it means "guide to near and far." But many people don't realize this. [In accordance with Dōin's map] from the

Kanbun era until the Kan'ei era, map scale has been set. . . . It is noted
on the map.[49]

Gesshin's careful record shows the revisions made in each map, and
the ways in which maps recorded the spatial dimensions of the city's history. But his account also suggests that, from his vantage point in the
late nineteenth century, he read maps not simply for geographical information, but also to specify the loci of significant events and cultural phenomena, and in doing so to assign particular meanings to those places.
Gesshin saw in maps of Edo historical source material to chart the evolution of Edo's local identity; this identity encompassed not only the
spatial arrangement and geographical dimensions of the city, but how
its residents lived within, and came to understand, the urban environment. By using maps in this way, however, Gesshin endowed them with
a significance that Ishikawa Ryūsen and other Edo mapmakers probably would have found curious. Maps for Ishikawa were, in his own
words, documents of "thin learning," printed matter meant to satisfy an
audience hungry for the latest news. In hindsight, of course, for Saitō
Gesshin, as for ourselves, these ephemeral documents have become historical ones.

ENVISIONING JAPAN IN PRINTED MAPS

Ishikawa Ryūsen's *Honchō zukan kōmoku*

While the administrative precursors to the commercial mapping of Edo
are quite clear, the influences are considerably less direct in the case of
printed maps of Japan that also began to appear in the late seventeenth
century. Here again, Ishikawa Ryūsen was an influential figure in the development of popular cartographic imagery. In 1687, two years before
the appearance of *Edo zukan kōmoku,* Ryūsen published what became
his best-known and most widely reproduced map, *Honchō zukan
kōmoku* (Outline map of our empire; see fig. 3).[50] Along with his other
well-known map of Japan, *Nihon kaisan chōriku zu* (Map of the seas,
mountains, and lands of Japan, 1689) (fig. 4), it ranks among the most
enduring images of Japan from the early modern period.[51] Ryūsen's
maps were copied and reproduced, usually without attribution, in atlases and on single-sheet maps in France, Holland, England, and Ger-
many throughout the eighteenth and early nineteenth centuries. In fact,
adaptations of Ryūsen's *Honchō zukan kōmoku* and *Edo zukan kōmoku*

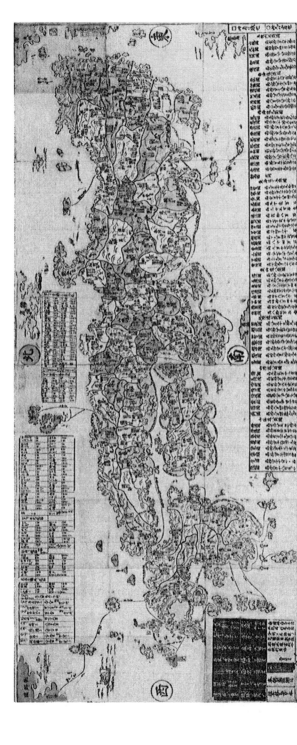

Figure 3. Ishikawa Ryūsen, *Honchō zukan kōmoku* (Outline map of our empire), 1687. Courtesy of the East Asian Library, University of California, Berkeley.

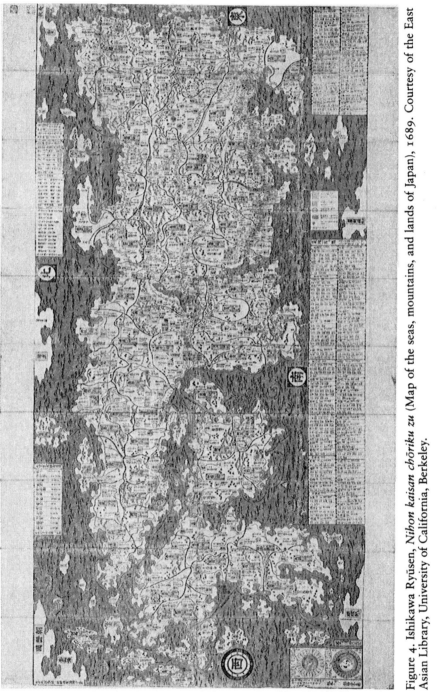

Figure 4. Ishikawa Ryūsen, *Nihon kaisan chōriku zu* (Map of the seas, mountains, and lands of Japan), 1689. Courtesy of the East Asian Library, University of California, Berkeley.

appeared in the English-language edition of Englebert Kaempfer's *History of Japan* of 1727, the first book-length study of Japan published in the West.[52]

In order to make his maps of Japan, Ishikawa Ryūsen adapted various sources, both narrative and visual. Unlike his maps of Edo, *Honchō zukan kōmoku* and *Nihon kaisan chōriku zu* were not copies of shogunal maps. Even a quick comparison of the outlines of the *Honchō zukan kōmoku* (fig. 5) and the shogunate's Keichō map of Japan (fig. 6) shows significant differences in the shape and orientation of the main islands of the archipelago. In both of Ryūsen's maps of Japan the southwest and northeast regions of the archipelago were foreshortened for printing in a rectangular format. The Ryūsen maps also show the southern tip of Ezo, the Ryūkyū Islands, the southeastern tip of the Korean peninsula, and several mythical places described in Japanese folklore, none of which appeared on shogunal maps in the seventeenth century. Finally, unlike the text on shogunal maps, which is oriented toward the map edges so that the viewer must place the map flat on the ground and walk around it, almost all the text on the Ryūsen maps, including the numerous tables and charts, is oriented to be read with north facing up.

A much more likely model for both *Honchō zukan kōmoku* and *Nihon kaisan chōriku zu* is a mid-seventeenth-century printed map of unknown authorship titled *Shinsen dai Nihon zukan* (New outline map of Great Japan).[53] The oldest extant copy of this map was published in 1678; reprints and revisions of it continued to appear until the mid-1680s under the titles *Shinsen dai Nihon koku ōezu* (New large-format map of Great Japan) and *Shinpan dai Nihon koku ōezu* (Newly published large-format map of Great Japan).[54] These maps, published some ten years before Ryūsen's, anticipate many of the distinctive characteristics of Ryūsen's maps, including their rectangular shape, inclusion of charts listing traveling distances on major roads, use of color to demarcate the provinces, and "frilled" stylization of the coastline.

It is clear that Ishikawa Ryūsen used sources in addition to the *Shinsen dai Nihon zukan* to make his maps of Japan. Indeed, both the *Honchō zukan kōmoku* and the *Nihon kaisan chōriku zu* are pastiches of the various kinds of published geographical information that would have been available in the late seventeenth century. For this reason, reading Ryūsen's maps is an exercise in epistemological excavation, as each reference or allusion is momentarily removed and examined for what it contributes to the whole. In the case of the earlier map, *Honchō zukan kōmoku,* the inquiry begins with the colophon (fig. 3, lower left). Here,

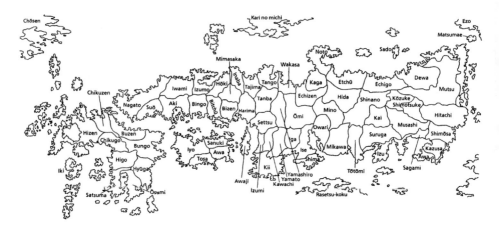

Figure 5. Outline map of Ishikawa Ryūsen's *Honchō zukan kōmoku*.

Figure 6. Outline of the Keichō map of Japan made by the Tokugawa shogunate.

Ryūsen explains the map's scheme by acknowledging his most important cartographic model, a map in the style pioneered by the aforementioned eighth-century priest Gyōki, entitled *Nansembushū dai Nihon koku shoto zu.*[55] This particular map, which shows Honshu, Kyushu, and Shikoku divided into neat bubble-shaped provinces connected by main trunk roads leading back to the imperial capital of Kyoto, appeared in a seventeenth-century reprint of the medieval encyclopedia *Shūgaishō* that would likely have been available to Ryūsen. In the text of the colophon, which appears in the colophon's bottom right-hand corner, Ryūsen writes that he has "emended" Gyōki's map by correcting its inconsistencies, then publishing it; next to this declaration is Ryūsen's name and seal.

In its general appearance Ryūsen's map does bring to mind the Gyōki-style maps' stylized geography. For example, as in the Gyōki-style maps (and early shogunate's maps of Japan), the main geographical divisions in Ryūsen maps are those of the province.[56] In many versions of *Honchō zukan kōmoku,* and in the version of *Nihon kaisan chōriku zu* reproduced in figure 4, the allusion to Gyōki's maps is intensified by the presence of two tables along the upper border of the map, both of which list the general conditions and wealth (in rice) of all the provinces during the classical era. Specifically, the table depicted in *Nihon kaisan chōriku zu* (fig. 4, upper left) emphasizes the produce of the five central provinces and seven circuits first established under the Emperor Yōmei (r. 585–87); it also acknowledges the division into sixty-six provinces, first executed under Emperor Bunmu (r. 697–707). The citation of such imperial precedents—an acknowledgment, in fact, of the origins of the province/circuit system—reinforces the idealized notion of a country unified under imperial rule, subject to a single ruler. This reference to "imperial" Japan is echoed in Ryūsen's choice of the term *honchō,* translatable as "our empire," for the title of his earlier map.

As much as they allude to times long past, however, both of Ryūsen's maps of Japan are decidedly documents of their own time. While he replicates many of the tropes of Gyōki-style maps, Ryūsen's "emendations" amount to a full-scale transformation of the Gyōki map into a Genroku map, one that attempts repeatedly to assimilate allusions to a unified polity with the reality of the divided nature of early modern politics. This can be seen most clearly in the notation, within each province, of the names of individual daimyo in rectangular labels on the face of the map. These labels served the same function—and include the same sorts of information—as the table that appears on Ryūsen's *Edo zukan kōmoku.* In Nagato (also known as Chōshū) domain in Nagato province, the map label reads "Matsudaira Nagato, 369,000 *koku.*" This indicates that the daimyo of Nagato domain, who was of the Matsudaira family, possessed lands valued at 369,000 *koku* of rice.[57] In this fashion, each label serves to mark the location of the daimyo's home domain; each also notes the productivity, in *koku* of rice, of the land under the daimyo's control. These labels were periodically altered in subsequent printings of the map to reflect changes in both personnel and landholdings.[58]

Ryūsen's maps also differ from Gyōki-style maps in that they lack a visual core. Although the Gyōki maps clearly place the province of Yamashiro, in which Kyoto was located, at the physical and symbolic center of the country, on Ryūsen's maps all roads do not lead to Kyoto, nor do they lead to Edo. Rather, his maps guide the reader's attention to the road system itself. It is this network, the fabled "five highways" (Gokaidō) and auxiliary roads, that link and integrate all parts of Japan.[59] Ryūsen not only labels post stations along major and minor roads but also provides charts on the map's borders with information relevant to travelers. In *Honchō zukan kōmoku,* the two charts at the upper border of the map list traveling distances between major destinations on the various trunk roads (fig. 3). The rightmost of the two charts lists distances between stops on two major highways linking Edo and Kyoto: the Tōkaidō and the Kisō kaidō (also known as the Nakasendō). The table to its left lists traveling distances on the Nikkō dōchū, which linked Edo to the mausoleum of Tokugawa Ieyasu in Nikkō, and distances between Ise (the Great Shrine at Ise) and other locations on the Kii peninsula. It also lists traveling distances on auxiliary roads in various parts of the country. *Nihon kaisan chōriku zu* gives similar information in the table at top right (fig. 4). All distances are expressed incrementally as the number of *ri* between successive way stations along the various roads. This type of specific information would have been essential to the many pilgrims and travelers who marked their progress by sequential progression through each town along the main roads. It also would have been of interest to idle map readers who had no plans of actually traveling but sought the information all the same. Rather than focusing on a single imperial or shogunal capital, the road network makes movement—both actual and imagined—possible. In this way Ryūsen's map "decenters" the realm and captures the growing interest in and necessity of travel and mobility in the late seventeenth century.[60] By taking the map of the solitary wandering monk and transforming it into a guide for popular travel, Ryūsen highlights the contrast between Gyōki's solitary travel and the mass phenomenon of travel and mobility in his own world.

In a significant departure from the shogunate's official maps of Japan, Ryūsen's maps depict both mythical and actual foreign countries. Like some versions of Gyōki-style maps, Ryūsen's maps depict places such as "Rasetsu koku" (fig. 3, center bottom), the land of benevolent female deities (the *rakshasas* of the Lotus Sutra), a place popularized in the late seventeenth century by Ihara Saikaku (1642–93) as the "Island of Women," or Nyōgogashima. Also present is "Kari no michi" (fig. 3, center top), literally translated as "the route of the [migrating] geese," a northern no-man's-land alluded to in the Chinese classics. Although most shogunal maps did not depict Japan's East Asian neighbors, Gyōki-style maps occasionally showed the Ryūkyū Islands, the Korean peninsula, and the tip of the northern island of Ezo. Ryūsen too depicts these countries, but whereas in Gyōki-style maps the Korean peninsula was labeled "Kōrai," in Ryūsen's maps it appears as "Chōsen" (figs. 3 and 4, upper left). The Ryūkyū islands also appear in *Nihon kaisan chōriku zu* (see fig. 4, lower left), and in some versions of *Honchō zukan kōmoku*. Ezo appears as well, although in *Honchō zukan kōmoku* the domain of Matsumae is mistakenly depicted as an island (fig. 3, upper right), a mistake the mapmaker corrected in *Nihon kaisan chōriku zu* (fig. 4, upper right). Korea, the Ryūkyūs, and Ezo, though formally characterized as "foreign" in the Tokugawa diplomatic lexicon, had longstanding trade, and in some cases diplomatic, relations with Japan.[61] Koreans and Ryūkyūans were frequent visitors to Japan in the seventeenth and eighteenth centuries, and relations with the northern island of Ezo were supervised by the daimyo of Matsumae.[62] Ryūsen depicts these "familiar foreigners" by showing their home countries to be geographically near, yet also removed from the central focus of the map. Neighboring Asian countries thus serve as a visual frame for the dominant image of Japan, their marginal status on the map mirroring their status within an idealized Japan-centric hierarchy of political relations.

As for more distant foreign countries in Europe and other parts of Asia, their presence is acknowledged in *Honchō zukan kōmoku* in another table (fig. 3, lower left, above colophon). Here, Ryūsen gives the distances, in *ri,* between Japan and a number of foreign countries: 12,500 *ri* (30,000 miles) to Holland, 1,112 *ri* (2,660 miles) to Russia, 300 *ri* (720 miles) to Nanjing, 1,700 *ri* (4,000 miles) to Tonkin, and so forth. Because international travel was forbidden, this information could not have been of any instrumental use to the average reader, but it is presented matter-of-factly, in the same format as traveling distances within Japan. By juxtaposing these foreign countries with the actual neighboring countries (such as Korea) and the mythical lands of Rasetsu koku and Kari no michi, Ryūsen presents the map reader with a playful proposition, one that, as we shall see, later eighteenth-century writers expanded upon. He visually equates the "real" with the "imagined," the "old" with the "new," and "official" foreign relations with imagined foreign countries. He does this in much the same way as writers of the same period used various settings or conventions, known as *shukō*, as framing devices for satire or parody; here, the convention is the map and geographic knowledge about places near and far. The map thus displays information about unknown or little-known places while mediating— literally "framing"—the reader's experience of them.

As different as Ishikawa Ryūsen's maps are from those produced by the Tokugawa shogunate, both share a tendency to present the viewer with an image of Japan as an orderly, legible space. In Ryūsen's maps, just as in the shogunate's maps of Japan, the multiple political jurisdictions that actually pertained on the ground and the frequent conflicts that erupted over them are completely absent in the map. Though it seems unlikely that he modeled his maps directly after those of the shogunate, Ishikawa Ryūsen did seem to inherit indirectly their placid and magisterial view of the archipelago. The dominant image is one in which boundaries are stable and the relations among domains and provinces, districts, villages, and post stations are unproblematic. The relationship between shogun and daimyo, for its part, finds no explicit representation in either map. Instead, with his references to Gyōki Ryūsen condenses in a single image the idealized imperial past and the politically fragmented present, vaguely mythic "other" lands and veritable foreign countries. His maps are analogous to earlier maps, constructed according to a vision of the unified state, but they are also, quite simply, road maps. And as road maps, they predicated their meanings on their readers' capacity for real mobility, their sense of curiosity about other places, their willingness to indulge in a certain amount of idle speculation—in short, both their knowledge-seeking and their pleasure-seeking impulses. While rendering the physicality of national boundaries clearer and more definite, Ryūsen's maps can also be read as evidence of the porousness of the more abstract boundaries separating "elite" and "popular" culture, center and periphery, private enterprise and public power. Located historically at a point of transition between the solidification of Tokugawa power and the emergence of the market economy and commoner culture, Ryūsen's maps embody no single theme or idea; rather, they represent the process of change itself.

By the late seventeenth century published maps made space comprehensible and available for possession, literally and figuratively, to anyone with the wherewithal to buy, borrow, or view them. Ishikawa Ryūsen played a significant role in advancing this "vernacularization" of space. It must be said, however, that not all commercial mapmakers shared Ryūsen's background and perspective. Other mapmakers, such as Nagakubo Sekisui, came from distinct and powerful intellectual traditions that shaped their conception of mapping in very different ways.

Nagakubo Sekisui's *Kaisei Nihon yochi rōtei zenzu*

Though they share the distinction of being the authors of the most familiar and influential map images of early modern Japan, Ishikawa Ryūsen and Nagakubo Sekisui form an odd couple; their perspectives on mapmaking and hence their maps of Japan differ in many ways. Unno Kazutaka claims that Nagakubo Sekisui's maps of Japan "marked the end of the dominance of the Ryūsen type," but this statement perhaps relies too much on a notion of mapmaking as subject to scientific progress.[63] While it is true that Sekisui developed a number of innovations in the use of cartographic technology, both Ryūsen and Gyōki-type maps continued to be produced, revised, and reprinted alongside the maps of Sekisui and others.

First commercially printed in 1774, Nagakubo Sekisui's *Kaisei Nihon yochi rōtei zenzu* (Revised complete road map of all Japan) is densely packed with information, uniformly scaled, compact, and highlighted with color (fig. 7). In many respects, it documents the technological changes made in the first half of the eighteenth century in the making and printing of maps. After the eighth shogun Tokugawa Yoshimune (1684–1751) rescinded the shogunate's ban on non-Christian Western books in 1720, European globes, atlases, and other geographical texts began to trickle into Japan. By the late 1730s, some Japanese scholars had become proficient enough in the Dutch language to begin to translate and redraw Dutch terrestrial and celestial globes. Treatises on the Copernican system were translated beginning in the 1770s, and new maps of the world soon followed. By the early decades of the nineteenth

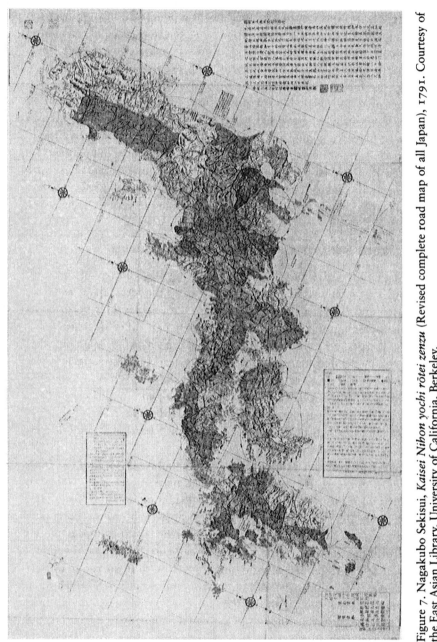

Figure 7. Nagakubo Sekisui, *Kaisei Nihon yochi rōtei zenzu* (Revised complete road map of all Japan), 1791. Courtesy of the East Asian Library, University of California, Berkeley.

century Japanese knowledge of world geography had improved considerably.[64] Nagakubo Sekisui was a product of the early part of this shift toward a new understanding of geographic and cartographic principles. Unlike Ishikawa Ryūsen, Sekisui was an official, a trained geographer from Mito domain northeast of Edo. Perhaps because he was both a scholar and an official, Nagakubo Sekisui's "comprehensive road map" owes an unmistakable debt to the shogunate's maps of Japan while also refining and elaborating upon that model.

If we compare the outlines of Sekisui's map (fig. 8) and the shogunate's Kyōhō map (see fig. 9) we can see the clear resemblance in the shape and orientation of the archipelago.[65] Although the mapmaker does not acknowledge this source, it is known that Sekisui studied with the disciples of Shibukawa Shunkai (1639–1715), an astronomer in the employ of the shogunate.[66] He learned many techniques that would influence his mapmaking from Shibukawa's students, including the use of longitude and latitude coordinates, which he employed quite accurately in all of his maps. Sekisui's respect for empirical research reveals itself clearly in his work; his were the first published maps to emphasize the need for precision in measurement and accuracy in the representation of land. Instead of working in the realm of spatial imaginary as Ishikawa Ryūsen did, Sekisui made maps that spoke to the rational intellect, explaining for the first time the way a map could, and in fact *should*, correlate directly to the observed physical world.

Sekisui articulates this principle in the legend *(hanrei)* to *Kaisei Nihon yochi rōtei zenzu* (fig. 7, center bottom). This short text is a painstakingly detailed explanation to the reader that a map operates through the use of a symbolic language:

> By our measurements [on this map], one *sun* represents ten *ri* in road distance. From one place to another several *ri* are [represented] as one [unit of measurement]. From right to left, top to bottom, all can be comprehended in a glance. However, because of the obstacles presented by steep and winding roads, in [some] places [measurements] are not the same. It would be wrong not to adjust this. Therefore in mountainous or difficult terrain ten *ri* is equal to one *fun* or perhaps seven *fun*. On the Ise Road ten *ri* may add up to one *sun* two *fun*.[67] In other words, one should be aware that in flat places distances [on the map] are longer. In steep and winding places [distances are] foreshortened.

The legend goes on to explain that the size of the map's symbols is not indicative of the actual size of the things represented. This is because "it is difficult to distinguish between the breadth of brushstrokes" that

Figure 8. Outline map of Nagakubo Sekisui's *Kaisei Nihon yochi rōtei zenzu.*

Figure 9. Outline of the Kyōhō map of Japan made by the Tokugawa shogunate.

would have to be used to differentiate between those features. Likewise, places located very near one other are not listed independently simply because the small space is restrictive, and "one cannot maneuver the brush." The dual assumption that, on the one hand, the width of the brushstroke on the map might correspond to the dimensions of an actual place or space and, on the other, that the map should be expected to represent all that exists in the physical world is remarkable and unprecedented in published maps. This type of explanatory map legend was extremely rare on European printed maps of this period, and is generally relegated to the fine print even on modern maps. While such disclaimers do not actually remedy distortion, they do convey the mapmaker's concern with precision, a concern echoed in other innovative aspects of Sekisui's maps of Japan, such as the use of longitude and latitude grids. Sekisui's commentary in the legend on the use of the grid is as follows:

> In order to adjust relative distances, calculations have been made with reference to the North Star. A distance of approximately thirty-two *ri* constitutes the difference of one degree in the cosmos *[ten no ichido]*. Therefore, if one follows the height and depth of the North Star, one will know the degrees running north to south, and one can then calculate [the degrees] east to west. . . . From the eastern sea to the western sea the span is ten degrees.

Again, in this instance Sekisui recognizes and explains the difficult and, in some respects, unnatural aspects of cartographic symbolism. This reflects a high level of awareness of the technological limits placed on the mapmaker. Also, and equally importantly, it seems to presume a high level of sophistication on the part of the map *reader,* who is expected to take all these factors into consideration, perform the arithmetic calculations, and read into the map what the map does not (and cannot) display.

Despite Sekisui's adoption of new representational techniques, and of the principles of longitude and latitude, he remains steadfast in his focus on domestic space. He does not use longitude and latitude to take the measure of the vast oceanic space surrounding Japan, nor does he use those grids to unite Japan with the rest of the world via an overarching and universally applicable technological schema. The longitude and latitude grid does not reach continental Asia, and even the presence of nearby Korea and Ezo is barely hinted at; the sketchy forms of their extreme southern coastlines float disembodied in the upper left and right corners of the map, respectively. This is not to say Sekisui was ignorant of or unconcerned with the world outside Japan. In 1785 he published a historical atlas of China, *Dai shin kōyozu* (Enlarged map of Great Qing).[68] He also made numerous world maps that, unlike his maps of Japan, relied upon the sorts of folkloric information displayed on Ishikawa's maps of Japan.[69] Despite Sekisui's knowledge of world geography, in his maps of Japan, as in Ishikawa Ryūsen's, foreign countries are pushed to the margin, and the grid within which Japan is situated serves for the most part to measure and frame the Japanese archipelago alone. Despite their seeming advances in universal standards of technological sophistication, Sekisui's maps chronicled the particularity of place rather than the universality of space.[70] The importance of individual places *within* Japan is also highlighted by the mapmaker's attempt to list as many discrete places as possible on the map. In his efforts to make the map a comprehensive replica of reality, he densely packs the mapped surface with the names of famous places, places of historical interest, old castles and battlegrounds, border checkpoints *(sekisho)*, temples, and shrines.[71] These places of significance dot a landscape connected by an equally dense network of roads. Unlike Ishikawa Ryūsen's maps, whose tables indicated traveling distances in *ri,* Sekisui's map is drawn to scale, making it incumbent upon the reader to measure and calculate distances between individual places. Rather than depending on the reader's imaginative—and therefore vague—approximation of distance it relies on the actual depiction of that distance, in relative terms, on the map itself. Sekisui's map thus depends less on the experience of travel (imagined or real) than on the careful interpretation of map language. The world for Sekisui is not "out there," but encapsulated in the text itself.

Although Nagakubo Sekisui's maps did not play to a popular audience as bluntly as Ryūsen's did, we can conclude with a fair degree of certainty that their readership was not inconsiderable in size. Sekisui's maps, like Ishikawa Ryūsen's before him, remained for generations popular and highly marketable texts. Later mapmakers borrowed freely from Sekisui's maps and published their own embellished versions of them. A copperplate print map by Matsumoto Yasuoki (also known as Gengendō, 1786–1867) published around 1835 and entitled *Dōsen Nihon yochi saizu* (Detailed copperplate map of Japan; fig. 10) shows the ways in which Sekisui's maps were adapted and rendered more accessible to a general readership in the early nineteenth century. In it, the mapmaker, who fashions himself "gen II Matsmot 'Iasqokj' " in Roman letters at the bottom edge of the map, borrows wholesale Sekisui's map of Japan and adds to it elaborate compass roses and sketches of boats

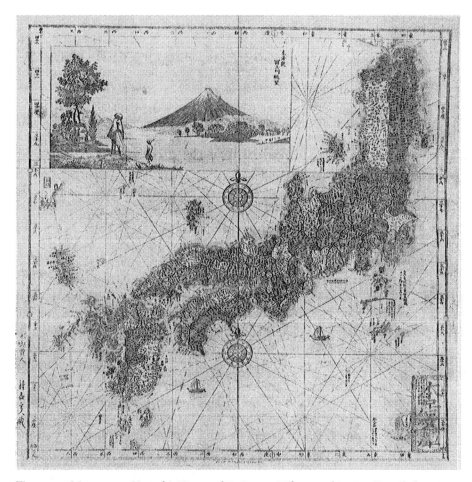

Figure 10. Matsumoto Yasuoki (Gengendō), *Dōsen Nihon yochi saizu* (Detailed copperplate map of Japan), 1835. Courtesy of the East Asian Library, University of California, Berkeley.

sailing the seas around the archipelago. More significantly, he superimposes on the top half of the map a scene of travelers appreciating a view of Mt. Fuji from the Tōkaidō. The pairing of the conventionalized depiction of Fuji with the map of the entire archipelago perhaps reflects the degree to which both the mountain and the country it represented were seen as instantly recognizable and iconic "famous places" whose meaning was obvious to any viewer.

Nagakubo Sekisui, Ishikawa Ryūsen, and mapmakers who followed in their wake expanded the notions of what a map was, and what it could do. They did so, moreover, within a broad intellectual field constrained by few preconceptions of how maps "ought" to function. To a considerable degree, commercial mapmakers worked within the parameters of a generalized spatial consciousness inherited from the classical and medieval periods. In their works we can see the echoes of many influences: shogunal maps, gazetteers, Gyōki-style maps, and mythical lands from the Buddhist tradition as seen through the lens of contemporary fiction. At the same time, however, the mapmakers discussed here took these ideas and gave them new graphic form, and in doing so created distinctly early modern map languages. Through publishing and the culture of print, these images reached unprecedented numbers of viewers. As map visions such as these became common, they established a set of assumptions about worlds near and far and began to connect maps, their makers, and their readers.

Through a combination of factors—the shogunate's mapmaking projects, the relatively free flow of "official" geographic knowledge into the public realm, the growth of literacy among the common people, and the development of the publishing industry—a set of visual and verbal conventions characterizing Japan began to take shape in the late seventeenth century. Mapmakers of artistic and scholarly inclinations such as Ishikawa Ryūsen and Nagakubo Sekisui played a significant role in creating a conventionalized view of Japan, which they parsed as *honchō* (our empire) or *zenkoku* (all the provinces). *Honchō* and *zenkoku* invoke varying levels of corporate unity, but neither translates easily as "national." In particular, the term *zenkoku,* as it was used in maps and other contemporary texts, had multiple meanings that played on the ambiguity of the term *kuni* (which can and did mean, alternately, a single domain, a province, or a country). The ambiguity of this term, as Mark Ravina has argued, embodies the contradictions inherent in the structure and governance of the early modern Japanese polity.[72]

The contradictions in both early modern mapmaking and early modern politics fostered dialectical relationships between map makers and map readers. In the Tokugawa shogunate's official mapping projects, the map mediated the spatial and political relationships between shogun, daimyo, and local communities. Published maps, for their part, were the vehicle through which a diverse cadre of mapmakers articulated and shaped popular images of Japan. At both levels, these dialectical relationships encouraged the development not only of a shared understanding of space and place, but also of a shared form of expression, a spatial vernacular. The foregoing discussion suggests that the goal of early modern mapmaking was not simply to gather, categorize, and communicate information; maps also engendered a cultural and spatial sensibility. As printed maps spread cartographic imagery to a wider audience, map reading became common sense. And once a set of stable meanings had been assigned to certain places (neighborhoods, sightseeing venues) and spaces (cities, Japan), map readers became increasingly able to transform map images in order to invest them with new meanings. As subsequent chapters will show, in the latter part of the Tokugawa period, writers and artists put map images and mapped knowledge to a wide variety of uses. In doing so they not only manipulated maps, but also altered the forms of knowledge embedded in them.

In contrast, then, to the teleological view of the map-as-science, a process-oriented analysis of early modern Japanese maps moves in the direction of understanding what Matthew Edney has called "cartography without progress."[73] From this perspective, mapping moves in a horizontal, even circular fashion rather than "improving" over time. The following chapters follow this multidirectional trajectory to trace the integration of mapping into other forms of printed discourse. Chapter 2 discusses the emergence of a new mode of travel writing in the late seventeenth century. In giving cultural definition to the landscape, travel writers added an active dimension to the map that would prove crucial to its later recreation as a form of play and creative invention.

CHAPTER 2

Annotating Japan

The Reinvention of Travel Writing
in the Late Seventeenth Century

> Order is, at one and the same time, that which is given in
> things as their inner law, the hidden network that determines
> the way they confront one another, and also that which has
> no existence except in the grid created by a glance, an exami-
> nation, a language; and it is only in the blank spaces of this
> grid that order manifests itself in depth as though already
> there, waiting in silence for the moment of its expression.
>
> Michel Foucault, *The Order of Things*

If, to paraphrase Foucault, maps create order through "a glance, an examination," then travel accounts depend on language—specifically,
upon narrative—to reveal the supposedly "hidden networks" that structure the natural world. But while maps tend to homogenize different types
of information by conveying it in a single graphic dimension, travel accounts amplify spatial and cultural difference by describing it in careful
detail. At about the same time that commercial mapmaking was flour-
ishing in the late seventeenth century, travel writers began to advocate
the firsthand exploration and observation of the human and natural
landscapes. As they did so, they began to craft a new form of mapping
in which the precise description of space—whether local, regional, or
Japanese—contributed to the understanding of the variation in culture
across space and time. Once properly "annotated" and transformed
into text, the observed landscape would serve to edify if not to enlighten
the reader. In its concern with the actual conditions of places and the
nature of the people in various parts of Japan, travel writing recalls the
connection between cartography and ethnography—both principal
tools of exploration and discovery—that was a common feature of en-

counters between peoples and cultures in many parts of the world in the early modern and modern periods.[1]

This new mode of travel writing departed significantly from the approach taken in classical and medieval travel diaries, in which the viewing and appreciation of famous places depicted in poetry was the primary aim of most travelers. Beginning with the first imperial poetry anthology, the *Kokin wakashū* (905), travel *(tabi)* was established as one of the main classificatory themes of *waka,* the thirty-one-syllable poetic form, and famous places comprised the majority of *utamakura,* literally "poem-pillows," that inspired literary composition.[2] Like famous places, travel became a stimulus for poetic composition and, indeed, for aesthetic appreciation itself. In Ki no Tsurayuki's fictionalized travel diary *Tosa nikki* (936), the author's female amanuensis notes that nature's beauty is sometimes so overwhelming that one cannot "merely look upon the splendor of this scenery" but must, as if compelled by some invisible force, record one's reactions to it in verse.[3] Travel remained a central theme in the writings of poets of the medieval period, as the journey—often trying, solitary, and intensely self-reflective—became the motivating force behind compositions by peripatetic priests and poets such as Saigyō (1118–90), Sōgi (1421–1520), and Sōchō (1448–1532).[4] Late medieval poets also had practical reasons to wander, as many fled war-ravaged Kyoto to seek patronage from Warring States daimyo and other local notables in the provinces. Even in times of war, however, for travel diarists and poets in the classical and medieval periods the natural world defined beauty and structured the organic moral order inherent in all things. The traveler's textual account of the journey, for its part, was said to activate the principle latent in the landscape and make it meaningful in the human realm.

In the early modern period, especially from the seventeenth century on, the development of a transportation infrastructure and the growth of the market economy vastly increased physical mobility in Japan. Travel by non-elites in particular grew significantly. These factors, along with the emergence of new poetic and prose genres, facilitated the development of new perspectives on travel and new forms of travel writing.

Whereas classical and medieval diarists invariably traveled from their residences in the imperial capital or provincial castle towns "out" or "down" to various renowned locales, early modern travel writers moved in different and more varied directions. Daimyo and other samurai officials were the most predictable in their routes, commuting on a regular

schedule between their secondary residences in Edo and their home domains: as Watanabe Kenji has put it, daimyo were like "migrating
birds," traveling and alighting in designated places at scheduled times.[5]
While classical travel diaries were written only by the elite, the writers
of travel accounts in the early modern period were of various classes.
And though the writers tended to be educated and male, there are
dozens of extant accounts by literate women and by commoners.[6] Unlike classical travel diaries, which described the self-styled solitary journeys engaged in by court nobles, most early modern travel accounts narrated travel taken for practical reasons such as trade, official duty, or
exploration. Many accounts describe excursions organized around a
given theme or activity in which many could participate, such as gathering plants and herbs, climbing mountains, visiting hot springs (onsen),
or viewing flowers in bloom.[7] And finally, in contrast to their classical
predecessors, travel accounts in the early modern period, whether written by scholars, officials, literati, or commoners, often were commercially published.[8]

Some titles by notable authors such as Kaibara Ekiken (1630–1714),
the focus of this chapter, and Ogyū Sorai (1666–1728) remained in
print for decades; but even accounts by non-elites, such as the merchant
who kept a diary of the variety of foods and cooking styles he encountered on a trip to Kyushu, found their way into print.[9] One scholar estimates that there are several thousand early modern travel accounts
listed in the Kokusho sōmokuroku, the most comprehensive modern
bibliography currently in use, and another has counted over eight hundred titles in the holdings of a single major archive.[10]

The spread of travel and travel writing to new and different practi-
tioners and audiences in turn engendered new sensibilities toward land,
landscape, and culture. In poetic composition Matsuo Bashō (1644–94)
pioneered what Haruo Shirane refers to as the "haikai imagination," in
which images of places, objects, and even animals that were not previously part of the classical literary canon became a source of freshness,
humor, and inventiveness in poetic compositions.[11] In the realm of prose,
writers of kanazōshi and ukiyōzōshi—moralizing or didactic tales often
circulated in chapbook-type format in the seventeenth century—also
undertook the theme of travel. In such works, ranging from Asai Ryōi's
(d. 1691) guidebooks to the Tōkaidō and the city of Edo (such as
Tōkaidō meisho no ki and Edo meisho no ki) to Ihara Saikaku's "tales
of the provinces" (Saikaku shōkoku banashi), writers spun travel stories
that were entertaining as well as informative.[12] In many kanazōshi and

ukiyōzōshi, entertainment seems to have won out over factuality, for as Jurgis Elisonas has shown, a good number of late-seventeenth-century travel guides to Edo lifted descriptive text directly out of similar guides to Kyoto with no concern for accuracy.[13] Matters of descriptive detail aside, however, in the case of both *haikai* and early modern tale literature, one can see not only an expansion of literary sensibility, but also a vernacularization of spatial concepts, as spatial and place-based references became the stuff of increasingly popular poetic and prose genres.

While travel stories were told for the entertainment of a popular audience, travel could also provide the occasion for more sober reflection. Some of the most prominent philosophers of the early to mid-Tokugawa period, including Hayashi Razan (1583–1657), Arai Hakuseki (1657–1725), and Ogyū Sorai, traveled frequently and wrote detailed accounts of their journeys.[14] Artists like Shiba Kōkan (1747–1818) and Ike no Taiga (1723–76) were restless peripatetic figures who wrote and often illustrated their own travel diaries.[15] Scholars and officials also took to the road on government business: geographers like Nagakubo Sekisui (1717–1801) and Furukawa Koshōken (1726–1807) were dispatched on official journeys by domain and shogunal governments, respectively, and both kept extensive written records that were later published. In many cases, men of letters traveled in order to seek out local notables and provincial scholars who might be transformed into followers of their own school of thought or artistic expression.[16] And not only did early modern literati travel widely and have contact with a great variety of people—from unlettered innkeepers to European traders—they also wrote with every expectation that their accounts would be read by an audience interested in such information.

By the first decades of the eighteenth century some thinkers were beginning to formulate the idea that travel was not only an opportunity to deploy finely tuned literary skills within a canonical cultural landscape, but also an opportunity to observe the physical and human worlds. Through publishing, moreover, these observations could be spread to a much wider audience. There were many reasons for the shift in perspective from passive appreciation to active observation. Most important for the present discussion are two factors: the shift toward empirical, or "practical," learning *(jitsugaku)* advocated during the Kyōhō reforms of Tokugawa Yoshimune, and the incorporation of ideals of order gleaned from the Chinese classics into the genre of travel writing.[17] Both these trends in thought emphasized the accumulation of geographic and cultural information through direct observation. In classi-

cal travel writing, the purpose of both travel and writing was to create
original and highly accomplished literary works that recreated landscapes in an interpretive mode that was quite removed from the land
itself. In the early modern period, however, travelers began to write
"glosses" on the landscapes they observed first-hand. They saw travel
writing as an opportunity to annotate the already-present narrative inherent in the natural order of things, arguing that only through the careful and direct examination of the natural and human worlds could one
comprehensively account for and analyze the organic order of things.
While early modern travel writers do not eschew references to canonical texts when describing a given place, they fundamentally reinvented
both the purpose and the practice of travel and its narration in their attention to the physicality of places and the ways life was lived in them.

The practice of travel writing as annotation was first and most force-
fully advocated by Kaibara Ekiken. Beginning in the mid-seventeenth
century, Ekiken and such figures as Kumazawa Banzan (1619–91) and
Miyazaki Antei (1623–97) undertook to critically reexamine the relationship of humankind to nature, and to determine what larger philosophical principles might be gleaned from a study of "things as they
are." [18] Were humans simply one element in an organic whole that comprised the natural world? Or did humans have a particular kind of responsibility to guide, shape, and even control nature? If they did, how
could one discern the proper, just, or moral mode of behavior? For
Ekiken, travel was one way to begin to answer such questions.[19] His accounts show us the emergence of travel writing as a distinctly early modern genre, and as a type of scholarship. Ekiken's writings also give insight into the development of a distinctive intellectual perspective on
travel and on writing, one in which the author's encounter with different types of people compels him to see himself in different ways.

KAIBARA EKIKEN'S TRAVELS AND WRITINGS

To a modern observer, Kaibara Ekiken's life seems a study in contrasts.
He was a provincial whose fame came to rival that of the best-known
scholars from either capital; he was a moral philosopher but also an
empirical scientist; and he was a member of the elite who was deeply
concerned with the common person. Rather than seeing contradiction,
however, we can see in Ekiken's life a pattern of development typical of
many eclectic and broadly learned individuals in the early modern period, whose ideas traveled the full circle of the intellectual spectrum. Far

from being an isolated figure ruminating in solitude, he lectured frequently, and his writings were published and widely read during and after his lifetime.

Kaibara Ekiken was the youngest son of a scholarly northern Kyushu family.[20] Before the Tokugawa period, Ekiken's ancestors had been Shinto priests, but by the early seventeenth century they had assumed the position of advisers to the daimyo of Kuroda domain in Chikuzen. Although he was born to a family of samurai status in service to high-ranking officials, Ekiken had significant and sustained contact with commoners. After the death of both his mother and his stepmother, he was raised by a commoner maid, and for most of his life he lived not in the castle compound, but in the residential quarters of the castle town itself.[21] Perhaps as a result of this experience, both Ekiken and his older brother Sonzai maintained a lifelong commitment to bettering society by educating the commoner population.

Because the family was not wealthy, as a child Ekiken was educated primarily by his father and brothers. Sonzai, who had studied medicine in Kyoto and come into contact with the great scholars resident there, introduced Ekiken to the study of Zhu Xi Neo-Confucian thought. Ekiken also traveled widely, accompanying his father on official journeys from his early adult years. At the age of eighteen in 1648 he traveled to Edo. The next year he went to Nagasaki, and while there he came into contact with various forms of Western science. Between 1650 and 1656, a period in which he was a *rōnin,* a samurai unattached to his home domain, he continued his study of medicine and Confucianism in Edo, at his father's behest. Upon his reemployment by Kuroda domain in 1657, he was sent by his patron Tachibana Kanzaemon to study once again in Kyoto, and for the next seven years he learned from the outstanding Confucian scholars of the early Tokugawa period, including Kinoshita Jun'an (1621–98), Yamazaki Ansai (1618–82), and Itō Jinsai (1627–1705). Ekiken also kept up his study of the practical sciences, becoming close to Nakamura Tekisai (1629–1702), a scholar of botany and astronomy who published a classification of "natural objects" in 1666. After his father's death in 1665 and his marriage in 1668 to a woman twenty years his junior, Ekiken assumed a well-paid post in Fukuoka and became an active writer, teacher, and traveler.[22] He lectured frequently at Fukuoka castle, and met with Korean ambassadors and European scholars in Nagasaki. It is said that the Dutch physician Philipp von Siebold considered him "the Aristotle of Japan."[23]

In his writings Ekiken attempted to assimilate the diverse strains of thought in his intellectual upbringing. Unlike many scholars of elite background, however, he consistently sought out the knowledge of the common people: "I followed up on what the townspeople spoke of, salvaged what I could prove out of even the most insane utterances, and made inquiries of people of the most lowly status," he once wrote. He then synthesized these random "utterances" with the ideas gained from his studies and rendered his conclusions in clear prose filled with examples from everyday life. Seeking always to make his writing useful, he spent little time tinkering with the form and structure of his prose, focusing on the message over the medium.[24]

Scholars of Ekiken's life and thought are not in agreement over the degree to which Ekiken was successful in unifying these varied perspectives. Mary Evelyn Tucker argues that Ekiken succeeded in bringing together "scholarly research and popular education," and in seeing "empirical investigation and ethico-religious practice as part of a single continuum."[25] Minamoto Ryōen, by contrast, proposes that Ekiken vacillated between the poles of empiricism and rationalism, principle and emotion.[26] What does seem clear, however, is that for Ekiken observation and experience were the critical building blocks for any understanding of human affairs. His influential texts on topics ranging from the role of women (*Onna daigaku*, 1729), to the moral instruction of children (*Wazoku dōjikun*, 1707), to natural history and botany (*Yamato honzō*, 1709), while seemingly disparate in their subject matter, were all undergirded by the strong belief that the principles guiding human behavior were to be found in the observable material and social world.[27] Ekiken asserted that there was an inherent order and value in the natural world, but the ability to manage, guide, and use natural forces was uniquely human. In his view, distinguishing between essential and superfluous things in the observed natural world meant one could distinguish between essential and superfluous matters in human affairs; this was a critical aspect of clarifying the proper "way." In the preface to *Yamato honzō* he writes that "to have inadequate information, to be overly credulous about what one has seen and heard, to make a determination in a precipitate manner—all these four modes of thinking are erroneous."[28]

The idea that knowledge inhered in "all things under the sun" was not new to Japanese thought; it reflected the commonly held belief among those educated in the Confucian tradition that order in the physical world bespoke order in society. In the *Analects* (in Chinese *Lunyu*, in Japanese *Rongo*) the Prince of Wei asks Confucius what his first priority in administering the country would be, and Confucius replies by articulating the theory that has come to be known as the "rectification of names" (Chinese *chengming*, Japanese *shōmei*):

> Tzu-lu said, "If the Lord of Wei entrusted the administration to you, what would you carry out first?" Confucius said, "It would be necessary to rectify names. . . . If names are not rectified, then what is said will not make sense, and if what is said does not make sense, then affairs cannot be successfully concluded. If affairs cannot be successfully concluded, then rituals and music will not flourish. If rituals and music do not flourish, then punishments will not fit crimes. If punishments do not fit the crimes, then people will be at a loss as to how to act. Therefore, the Noble Man applies names so that he can speak sensibly so that he can act successfully.[29]

Or, as Ekiken rephrased it, "If various phenomena are not comprehended in terms of rational principle, knowledge would lack a solid foundation." Throughout his life, he sought and found the basis for this principle immanent in the world around him.

Travel, insofar as it enabled the direct and unmediated inspection of the world, was critical to Ekiken's intellectual enterprise. His writings mark a subtle but profound shift in emphasis from the classical and medieval understanding of travel writing as self-expression, in which the world is an extension of self, toward an early modern understanding of travel writing as the literature of annotation, in which the world is other-than-self and thus must be made comprehensible through intellectual intervention. Like most changes of measurable significance it was not abrupt or complete, and vestiges of travel writing in the self-reflective "classical" mode remain pervasive even in Ekiken's writing. The difference is that these ruminations are embedded in a detailed consideration of the places, histories, and culture of the everyday as it was lived by the people in the places he visited.

This chapter examines the first of Ekiken's major travel accounts, *Jinshin kikō* (1672).[30] I chose this particular text because it best exemplifies the confrontation between the "classical" and "annotative" modes of narrating space. In doing so, it set the precedent for both the content and the style of later travel writing, by both Ekiken and other writers in the early modern period, for *Jinshin kikō*, like all of Ekiken's subsequent travel accounts, was commercially published and circulated widely. Ekiken's texts were read and cited by notable eighteenth-century writers and scholars such as Motoori Norinaga (1730–1801) and the prolific essayist and fiction writer Ōta Nanpō (1749–1823).[31] As late as 1838, the writer Yasuda Sorō took along with him on his own journey Ekiken's travel account of the Yamato area, *Washū junranki,* which he consulted and referred to constantly in his own text, *Yamato meguri nikki.*[32]

While Kaibara Ekiken's travel accounts are acknowledged as important historical texts, they have attracted little attention for their "literary qualities" (or *bungakusei,* to borrow from the lexicon of contemporary Japanese literary criticism). Itasaka Yōko, the leading Japanese scholar of early modern travel writing, has argued repeatedly that it is unfair to judge the work of Ekiken and others solely as "literature."[33] Instead, she proposes that the real art in Ekiken's writing lay in the author's ability to create "realistic" *(jitsuyōteki)* descriptions of land and landscape in prose.[34] While I do not disagree fundamentally with Itasaka's approach, I prefer the process-oriented term "annotation" to the overly declarative term "realistic" to describe the writings of Ekiken and other early modern travelers. In addition, I am less concerned with a formal analysis of Ekiken's prose style than I am with situating his travels and his travel writings in their historical context, and in the context of the development of early modern mapping.

Kaibara Ekiken was innovative and influential because he devised new ways of putting geography to work—that is, he "read" the physical environment (and its human occupants) as a text, one that articulated the essence of the natural and moral order. To capture Ekiken in the act of translating and transcribing the world as text, my analysis of *Jinshin kikō* will proceed thematically, following Ekiken's movement through three different, and equally important, intellectual and experiential dimensions: his routes through physical as well as literary space and time; his encounters "on the road" with himself and with others; and his use of the published text to consciously mediate his readers' spatial experience. Throughout, I want to examine not only what is "there" on the written page, but also what is not. As in the analysis of maps as a form of spatial vernacular in the preceding chapter, I want to try to uncover how geographical texts processed and conveyed spatial information, and how in doing so they made such information not only comprehensible, but commonsensical.

ROUTES AND READINGS: ITINERARY AS SPACE MAKING

Dwelling was understood to be the local ground
of collective life, travel a supplement; roots always
precede routes. But what would happen, I began
to ask, if travel were untethered, seen as a complex

and pervasive spectrum of human experiences?
Practices of displacement might emerge as *constitutive*
of cultural meanings rather than as their simple transfer
or extension.

> James Clifford, *Routes: Travel and*
> *Translation in the Late Twentieth Century*

In its most self-evident dimension, the travel account is a chronicle of progression along a given route, following a planned itinerary. A principal function of early modern travel literature in the annotative mode consisted of reciting this route by giving a relatively spare and sequential accounting of places visited. In Kaibara Ekiken's *Jinshin kikō,* the journey's destination was determined by official duty, in this case a trip to Edo on domain business. For Ekiken, however, the route itself—the process of "getting there"—was at least as important as the goal of arriving at the destination and accomplishing a given task. In fact, that task itself, the ostensible reason for the trip, is nowhere described in the text. Instead, the importance of the journey as the fundament of experience is written into the title of the account: *Jinshin kikō* is, in the most literal translation, "the written account of going [somewhere] in the year of Jinshin." Of all the possible ways of titling a travel account— *nikki* (diary), *yūki* ("lyric" account), and *zakki* (miscellaneous records) are some examples that will be discussed in this chapter—*kikō* alone emphasizes the process of movement across space and time, in the fashion of an itinerary.[35] The route itself is the mental and physical space in which meaning is both communicated and represented. Accordingly, Ekiken's account, like many subsequent travel accounts in the annotative mode, begins not with what Mary Louise Pratt has called the "arrival scene," in which the Western traveler (or ethnographer) first encounters the native "other,"[36] but with a *departure scene* linking the imminent journey to the ongoing intellectual process of living life: "For whatever reason, it is my true nature to be quiet and solitary, and since I was young, each year I have not ceased to venture away from home and become a traveler throughout east and west. Perhaps this is my fate."[37]

Ekiken thus evokes the familiar motif of the solitary traveler, and he implicitly invites the reader along on this otherwise lonely journey. The practical motivations of the trip are left unexplained, as is the geographical point of departure—are we leaving "home"? Or is this one interval in a more or less continuous itinerary maintained by an inveterate traveler? And why are we leaving at all? These questions are scarcely answered by Ekiken's next words: "In this fifth year of Genroku, in the Dog-Horse year, I am sixty-three years old." [38] The departure, then, is not only from a particular place, but from a particular moment in time. In the context of the life of this particular writer, the journey is an experience, momentarily shared with the reader. Unlike a map, which tends to depict space frozen in time, the travel narrative narrates space as a continuum, through time. One of the essential functions of travel writing is to convey both the discrete moments in which each described experience occurs, and the ongoing existential process of which the route itself is a part.

Of course, none of these meanings is overtly stated in Ekiken's text; they are implicit in the structure of the narrative itself. The reader, therefore, must be conditioned to such cues, and must absorb them quickly in order to move from his brief introduction directly into the itinerary. While the departure scene itself is recounted in spare, unadorned language, it does not betray a limited imagination. The informational tone in which Ekiken begins the account stresses that, for him, the observed situation is the heart of the experience of travel, and that thorough description is most useful to the reader. Some sense of Ekiken's deliberate recitation of place names, famous sites, and travel conditions can be gained by the following summary of his itinerary. Ekiken records that on the twenty-seventh day of the fourth month of the fifth year of Genroku (1672), he departed by boat from Arazu no hama in Echizen. His first destination was Imazu. From Imazu he proceeded, again by boat, to Shimonoseki and then to the Kamado border checkpoint in Suō province. He disembarked at Muro Harbor in Harima province on the first day of the fifth month. From the harbor he proceeded by palanquin to the famous mountain Shoshazan and its temple Enkyōji, all in Shokuma district. From Shokuma he went to the castle town of Himeji, passing the Zone Tenjin shrine. He then went on to Oishiko Myōjin shrine in Oishiko-mura, and from there journeyed into the mountains south of Shoshazan to visit a temple opened by Gyōki. He then proceeded to Nonaka, Osaka, and Hirano, stopping at Kuhōji in Kawachi province before heading on to Tezuka and Tachiseki. In Yamato province he visited Jianji-mura, Shiki, and Tatsuta, the latter with its river famous for autumn colors. He then went on to Tatsuno and the temple Hōshinji, and then on to the ancient capital of Nara, where he visited Ikaruga, Ikomazuka, and all the famous Nara temples and shrines. He crossed the Sahogawa into Yamashiro province, and he passed through Sagara district and through the border checkpoint at Kamo, which forms the boundary between Yamashiro and Iga provinces. From there he continued on to Suwa, and then to Ise, location of the central shrine to Amaterasu, the sun goddess. From Ise he passed through Matsuzaka and Yoshino, then through Yokkaichi, Manba, Iwazuka, Atada, Narumi, Hazama, and Goyū, all famous stops on the Tōkaidō Road linking Kyoto to Edo. He followed the Tōkaidō through Hamamatsu and made the treacherous crossing of the Oigawa, passing on through Ejiri, Kōzu, and Minobu, and pausing at Minobuzan and Minobudera. He crossed the Fujigawa, then passed through Manzawa, Kamagafuchi, Ōmiya, and Mount Fuji. He paid his respects at the Soga shrine, and then climbed the mountain pass of Hakone and visited Kamakura, the medieval shogunal capital, and its temples. From Kamakura he traveled to his final destination, the capital of Edo.

Although the modern reader immediately feels the need for a map to make sense of Ekiken's itinerary, the author, interestingly enough, included none in his text. In fact, route maps only occasionally accompanied early modern travel accounts.[39] Some recent edited editions of early modern travel writing and secondary scholarship on the subject include such maps, but they seem to be more necessary for modern readers than they might have been for Ekiken and his contemporaries. Either readers were already familiar with the places mentioned, or they consulted maps separately. In fact, in his account Ekiken specifically directs the reader to consult published maps and guidebooks for details he chooses not to include. His account, for its part, is filled with "maplike" information, focusing on famous places and notable sights, giving exact distances between places along the route (in units of *chō* and *ri*) and approximate traveling times (by boat, on foot, or by palanquin). At the same time, the reader is constantly fed information about the nature of this particular journey that would not have appeared on a map: daily road conditions, descriptions of local settlements, permissions needed to gain entrance to certain sites, and, of course, the weather. Ultimately, however, the itinerary contains within itself the logic of its own completion, for despite any hardships encountered, the journey proceeds inexorably towards its goal, its forward progress rarely interrupted.

Within the scheme of his itinerary, Ekiken reserves his lengthiest and most careful descriptions for historically and culturally significant famous places. But unlike the exclusive focus accorded these sites in classical poetry or, on the other extreme, the comparatively terse descriptions given of *meisho* (famous places) in guidebooks, within the spatio-temporal circuit of Ekiken's travel account, the network of *meisho* provides the inner structure of the ritual of travel itself. The famous place allows Ekiken the mental space in which he can describe, observe, measure, and name, but also pause, ruminate, and remember. These intellectual processes are essential to the construction of the journey as ritual, for *meisho* are sacred or culturally meaningful sites that both structure and punctuate the journey, and thus provide occasions for reflection upon the larger meanings of the travel experience. The route-as-ritual provides the frame through which Ekiken sees, and subsequently describes, the many sacred and famous places he visits, such as the temple compound at the sacred mountain of Shoshazan, encountered early in the trip. He writes:

> From the main gate to the Central Hall *[hon'in]* it is a distance of three *chō*. To the Inner Hall *[okuin]* it is about ten *chō*. First you enter what is called the Kinsenin, the monks' quarters, then you go a little farther to the Central Hall, where there is [an image of] the Nyo-i-rin kannon [in Sanskrit, *Cintamanicakra*]. That is where this mountain's main spirit is enshrined. There is a large Buddha Hall *[butsuden]*, which is seven *ken* by nine *ken*, with each ken equaling eight *shaku*. In front [of the building] is a bridge. To the right is a very large rock, which functions as a water basin. Feeding this is a robust spring where pilgrims perform ritual washing. These people are undertaking the thirty-three stop pilgrimage [of the western provinces], for [Shoshazan] is on the road to Nariai in Tango province.[40] This Kannon-dō has a tall set of stone steps leading up to it. The hall [itself] is on the south side. It is above a high bank and one can see far down below. If one gazes far out from the highest level, the views are good. The seas of Harima are right below one's eyes. This place is one of the honored *kannon* on the thirty-three stop pilgrimage of the western provinces. Anchin, disciple of Shōkū Jōnin, made the image of the *kannon*.[41] It is one *shaku*, five *sun* long; by imperial decree, it is never shown to the public. Inside the Central Hall, below the *kannon* there is a limpid pool; they call it fragrant water *[kōsui]*. You open the lid and ladle out the water. According to the *Shosha no ki*, Emperor Go-Daigo [r. 1318–39] partook of this water.[42]

Ekiken goes on to give a history and etymology of place-names in and around Shoshazan, recount the area's local folklore, comment on the productivity of the land and types of landownership, and describe the local markets and products. He notes that in spite of the area's quiet setting the local people are industrious; they cultivate and market the bamboo that flourishes on the mountainside. He compares the temple compound to others at Kōyasan (the Shingon monastery founded by Kūkai) and Hiezan (the Tendai monastery founded by Saichō), and judges it favorably. The monks, he notes, still follow the teachings of the founder

Shōkū: "They don't covet goods and they don't fawn upon men of importance. They accept the people who come on pilgrimage, and they don't seek things elsewhere. It is a most relaxed place."[43]

The description of the Shoshazan, in its blend of things seen, heard, read, and recalled, is characteristic of the treatment of sacred and famous places throughout Ekiken's account. The mix of useful knowledge with arcana, and of what we might now call "ethnographic detail" with textual research, creates a multidimensional space in which history, culture, and geography converge. The way in which Ekiken relates the minutiae of spatial arrangement and physical size (of buildings, artifacts, and land area itself) bespeaks a deep concern to accomplish several things at once. He wants to record these facts for posterity, to convey accurate information to readers, and to confirm, in his own mind as well as in the minds of his audience, his role as knowledgeable narrator and custodian of histories, both personal and place-specific.

Ekiken's description of his "memorable" visit to Ise Shrine, home to the sun goddess Amaterasu and the most revered place of worship in the Shinto tradition, fits a similar pattern. The reader is first introduced to the general area:

> Matsuzaka is flatland belonging to the daimyo of Kii. [They use] the long *chō* measurement.[44] To the south of Matsuzaka are Kaishiro, Tokuwa, Sakashita-mura, Uegawa, Ika-machi, Ihara, and other [places]. Just before this is a large river, the Kujitagawa, which you cross by ferry. If you look out over this river, [beyond] the border of Yamato, you can see that it originates in the mountains near Yoshino and flows through Awata-tani. Long ago, it is said that Yamato-hime dropped her comb here. . . . Also, to the south is Inakigawa. You cross by boat. From here you go up a hill and then you arrive at a place called the *saigū*. There is a town here. To the north of the town by the side of a large road you can see the remains of the ancient Ise saigū. Strong memories remain of [my] tour of [this place]. From east to west it is thirty *ken*, from north to south forty *ken*. The *saigū* faces south. A sign reading "This place should not be defiled. Menstruating women cannot enter," stands [in front]. Just to the west of Saigū-mura is a village called Takekawa. Because the imperial princess lived in Saigū, Taki-gun, it is called the Capital of Bamboo [Take no miyako].[45]

His descriptions of the main shrine buildings, their size and appearance, the shrine's ritual calendar, and the shrine's history and rebuilding schedule are highly detailed. In contrast to his descriptions of other temples and shrines, this one scrupulously uses honorific language when discussing the Inner Shrine at Ise, where Amaterasu is worshiped, and yet gives a frank assessment of the edifice's appearance:

With a guide following me, I approached the Inner Shrine. As we approached its entrance, we received from returning worshipers some ritual rice [o-kumayone] and sake [to use as offerings]. On the whole, at a glance the appearance of the Inner and Outer shrines is disagreeable [iyamashi nari]. The meals are unpolished rice, the thatch on the roof of the *shinden* has been left in its thick, old state, and it presents to the worshiper a modest appearance. This must be to caution against pride, and to encourage reverence for the *kami* [deities].[46]

The contrast between Ekiken's characterization of the shrine as "disagreeable" and the classical diarists' unanimous celebration of a famous site, no matter what its actual appearance happened to be, is difficult to ignore. Because it happens to be a year of rebuilding in Ise's twenty-year renewal cycle, Ekiken goes on to describe the process of constructing the main shrines anew, each in the space next to the existing shrine. He also notes the shrines' three main festivals: the most significant is the Shōsairei on the sixteenth and seventeenth days of the ninth month, when a representative of the Department of Religion (Jingikan) makes the court's yearly offering to the shrine. On this day the door to the Central Hall (Seiden) is opened. Other celebrations occur on the sixteenth and seventeenth days of the sixth month, and on the sixteenth and seventeenth days of the twelfth month. Seasonal offerings are also made.[47] Every year in the first month, an emissary from the shogunal government at Edo comes to Ise and leaves offerings of gold at both the Inner and Outer shrines.[48] To give historical weight to these ongoing official observances, Ekiken goes on to relate anecdotes of past visits to the shrine by famous historical figures. His description of Ise here functions as a reading of its durable sacredness, a characteristic not apparent in the shrine's present "disagreeably" rustic appearance. Again in contrast to classical aestheticism, in Ekiken's reading of the famous place, "real-time" function matters as much as ostensibly timeless form.

After leaving Ise and passing though towns to its north and east, Ekiken joins the famous Tōkaidō. He lists the familiar place-names and famous sites on this most-traveled part of the early modern road network. After making the treacherous crossing of the Oigawa, the often-flooded river left unbridged by the Tokugawa for security reasons, Ekiken comes upon another of the more famous sites on his journey, Minobu-san and its temples. "In olden days," he writes, "people who traveled throughout the country said that of all of Japan's mountains and their environs, one cannot find a place more majestic than Minobu-san."[49] Unlike travelers on a pilgrimage, Ekiken seems to visit Shinto

shrines and Buddhist temples in equal number, another indication that
the route, not a predetermined theme or precedent, structures the journey's itinerary. He also describes in detail other sacred places that have
become *meisho,* such as the grave of Nichiren, founder of the Lotus Sect,
and the shrine to the valiant warriors the Soga brothers, Soga Sukenari
(1172–93) and Soga Tokimune (1174–93). Together with Minobu and
Shoshazan, these sacred and famous places form the core of both the
journey itself and Ekiken's narrative because they invest the route with
meanings that acknowledge yet transcend the fact of their material existence. The famous place, as everyday space and as cultural site, endows
both the itinerary and the resulting travel account with a form of legitimacy born of history and collective memory.

As much as famous places occasion a pause *in* the route, they also
function as the main points of digression *from* the route. Especially
when he passes a site made significant due to its place in literary history,
Ekiken pulls the reader aside to compare the site as witnessed in the moment to the site as depicted in a canonical text. He does so, however,
in ways quite different from the classical uses of *meisho.* In contrast to
the journey as a *circuit* of places made famous by their depiction in a
unified, universally acknowledged set of canonical texts, Ekiken's journey is a *compilation,* wherein the route makes sense of otherwise disparate "entries" in the cultural and literary canon. Instead of playing
on a few well-known poetic conventions, Ekiken quotes from and refers
to a diverse collection of poetic, prose, and historical classics, including
the *Engishiki, Izumi Shikibu nikki, Azuma kagami,* the *Man'yōshū,* the
Nihon shoki, and collections of Chinese-style poetry. Added to this are
not infrequent allusions to other non-canonical texts, including several
travel accounts written by Ekiken himself: his description of a pilgrimage to Yamato province, *Washū junranki* (1696), and his account of travels to the eastern provinces, *Azuma ji no ki* (1685).

For example, Ekiken writes that the Murasakigawa near Ōmiya appears in a poem by Minamoto no Toshiyori (or Shunrai, ca. 1055–
1129), which was included in the fifth volume of the *Yakumo mishō,* a
poetry anthology edited by Emperor Juntoku (1197–1242). Noting that
it is an "unusual" *(meiki)* poem, he quotes it in full: "The moon glints
off the snowlike water even in summer at Fuji's Murasaki, where there
should be no frost" *(Natsu mo nao / yukige no mizu ni / tsukisaete /
koori shinubeki / Fuji no Murasaki).* In the next sentence, switching
gears, he notes that "In this river there is a lot of what is called '*Fuji nori*'
[Fuji seaweed].'" All detail, literary and mundane, falls under the cate-

gory of what is, literally, notable about this particular place, all of which, in turn, is "proof" of its status as *meisho*.

Ekiken also uses the classics as sources to confirm "doubtful" or unclear etymology. This tactic is illustrated by the case of the so-called Ishi no hōden, a shrine carved from rock in the foothills near the village of Oishiko, south of Shoshazan: "According to a *Man'yō* poem, it is called *'shizu no iwaya.'* However, because you don't really see a stone room [*iwaya*], it is not clear. . . . How strange this [place] is!"[50] Similarly, he consults the *Nihon shoki* for the correct name of a river in Sagara district, Yamashiro province, near Nara; an "old poem" refers to the river as Izumigawa, but the *Nihongi* calls it Itomigawa.[51] This debate is followed by an account of his excursion onto the river itself, famous for its moon views. Ekiken's host takes him out on a boat, and he describes the experience as follows:

> Once on board we paddled upriver a bit between towering cliffs and lush greenery interspersed with large boulders. . . . Because it was the middle of the night one couldn't see clearly, but the view afforded by the moonlight reflected off the mountain, and the water gave a sense of the intriguing shape of the land. . . . "With my loneliness, the sense of pathos increases more and more, as I must gaze at the moon, alone." So wrote Master Saigyō, perfectly expressing what was in my heart.[52]

The multiple references here, which function as serial pauses in the narrative, are indicative of the multilayered (and multiply digressive) nature of Ekiken's "accounting" of his travels. Textual research (the etymological discursus based on the classics) here combines with "fieldwork" (the excursion on the river itself), description (of the observed scene), literary allusion (to Saigyō), and expression of the emotional resonance of the entire experience. Ekiken's trip across geographical space thus emplots meanings that Ekiken constructs and then posits as part of a common cultural imaginary; he amalgamates all that his readers might know about the scenes he describes, and in doing so integrates the various ways in which they have come to know those things: by reading, seeing, and doing. He then presents these scenes back to the reader in narrative form. In this way, the travel account becomes a mosaic of space, time, and knowledge. In Ekiken's text, a *meisho* is not just another place, it is a "memoryscape," a site redolent of multiple and layered meanings.[53] In the context of the travel account, it operates as a gateway, offering a focused view extending back in time as well as a gaze outward in space.

The sites in Ekiken's itinerary also function as "sights" in a more lit-

eral sense, for his account is filled with the act of looking. Odd or unusual sights that do not quite qualify as *meisho* in the classical sense
become sites worthy of comment: a special detour is made to see the
"Zone Pine" (Zone no matsu), an ancient, enormous gnarled pine tree
that stands in front of the Zone Tenjin shrine near Kakogawa in far
western Honshu. According to the local folk the exiled poet and statesman Sugawara no Michizane (845–903) planted the tree, whose "extraordinary" character is readily visible to onlookers *(ayashiku koto
naru to miru)*.[54] Another unclassifiable yet interesting sight is the massed
tumuli *(tsuka-ana,* literally hollowed-out mounds) of Kawachi province.
Because the tombs are so numerous, the place has acquired the name
Senzuka (Thousand Hillocks). Although ancient tombs can be found
in many other places, and can be found similarly grouped in areas of
Yamato province, Ekiken asserts that "Never have I seen so many [tu-
muli] in one place."[55]

Finally, Ekiken not only views famous sites directly but compels his
readers to conjure up visions of them as well. Although, as mentioned
earlier, he does not include maps or drawings in his account, in two notable cases Ekiken refers to existing maps and to paintings, implying
that such texts complement, or even stand in for, his own narrative.
When listing the many famous places in the former shogunal capital of
Kamakura, for example, he enumerates the major sights such as the
Hachiman Shrine (whose gate is, in language reminiscent of contemporary Japanese tourist guides, "the largest [stone] *torii* in all of Japan"),
the estate of Minamoto no Yoritomo (1147–99), and that of his powerful in-laws, the Hōjō family. Ekiken then notes, however, that since
"other old places are shown in detail on maps of Kamakura *[Kamakura
no zu],* I will not elaborate upon them here."[56] Likewise, in the case of
Mount Fuji, the most sacred site in all of Japan, he repeatedly compares
views of Fuji's sacred peak *(ama ga mine)* to pictures of Fuji *(Fuji no e).*
The peak viewed from Kamagafuchi in Kawachi province is "what one
would draw in a picture" *(e ni kakeru katachi kore nari).* This observation is repeated in a description of the peak itself.[57] Such comments referencing other representations of place seem strange, given Ekiken's emphasis on the importance of direct observation of all things. But these
references, brief though they are, can also be seen to indicate that maps
can in some cases supplement narrative; pictures, on the other hand,
seem to enhance the text by activating a different aesthetic sense. Neither maps nor pictures supplant verbal narrative, but both seem to form
alternative ways of understanding a given place.

Ekiken's self-consciousness as a narrator is for the most part suppressed until the very end of his journey, when he reaches his destination, Edo. Here, he transcends his own experience to reflect on the larger meanings of travel. Once he has arrived in the capital, Ekiken does not describe the city, nor does he explain his activities there. Instead, the account ends with the journey's end, as the author draws conclusions from what he has seen along the way:

> It got dark, and we entered Edo at the Hour of the Dog. With my traveler's spirit faltering and my old body exhausted, I wondered what travel was all about. Climbing formidable mountains, crossing wide rivers, passing over dangerous bridges, navigating slippery roads—really terrifying experiences abound, it seems. But when this type of miserable experience has passed, [the journey] becomes all you can think about. Then that [experience of] travel becomes one of many interesting places seen, and is [the source of] many lingering memories. Because I want to have stories I can tell to the people back home, and because in my old age I am becoming forgetful, I am writing this all down in haste.[58]

With that, "On the tenth day of the sixth month of the fifth year of Genroku, the author from Chikuzen province Kaibara Atsunobu, in his dwelling in Kasuminoseki, took up his brush."[59] In this manner, conventional in early modern writing, the ending is the beginning; the initiation of the act of writing terminates the memory of experience, and the writer's last words return the reader to the point where the story, literally, began. Although the journey in this case is one-way, the textual itinerary of narrative and of the reading process comes full circle as the "written account of going" (kikō) comes to an end. As James Clifford suggests, the route, like the text, becomes a bounded space, constitutive as well as reflective of cultural meaning.

ENCOUNTERS: DEFINING NATURE
AND PEOPLE, SELF AND CULTURE

Routes are not meaningful apart from the experiences of the traveler who has traversed them. One defining characteristic of early modern European travelogues is the pervasive sense of otherness they construct and convey as the traveler encounters strange peoples in the far-flung places he visits. In Ekiken's Jinshin kikō, however, this tendency to "make strange" is notably absent. Certainly, the fact that Ekiken traveled only within Japan, among his own countrymen, makes his journey qualitatively different from those of European explorers. However, the nearly complete absence of negative judgments of local populations—many of them rural and illiterate or poorly educated—cannot be explained by common place of origin alone, for the mid- to late-eighteenth-century travel writers whose works will be discussed in chapter 3 display a much more judgmental and occasionally disdainful attitude toward the common people. For some of these writers, commoners were, by virtue of hereditary or acquired status, simply inferior to the educated observers themselves. Discrimination did not arise only from status discrepancy; differences in place of origin and standard of living were also important. Tokugawa Japan was not a nation in the modern sense; although the development of communications and trade networks, literacy, and travel did much to forge a common sense of belonging to a polity called "Japan," regional and local identities remained extremely strong. Educated people may well have had the ability to visualize Japan, but they almost certainly did not imagine themselves first and foremost as part of a "national" community.

Given this set of circumstances, and given that Kaibara Ekiken possessed all the qualities—samurai status, male gender, and extensive formal learning—conducive to an attitude of superiority over the common people in the places he visited, he exhibited such an attitude in his writings surprisingly rarely. Itasaka Yōko has argued that Ekiken emphasized clear description in his travel writing because it edified the reader; he shunned poetic travel diaries because they dwelled too much on the preoccupations of the author and, as a result, were not "helpful" to others.[60] Ekiken had a longstanding concern for the education and welfare of the common people; perhaps because of it, he tends to describe local people in quite favorable terms, and he often lauds them for their hospitality. In Ekiken's travels, instances of opposition or confrontation tend to occur not over matters of status or authority per se, but over issues of knowledge and interpretation. For example, in a section of *Jinshin kikō* entitled *Tatsutagawa kōshō* (An investigation of Tatsutagawa), Ekiken endeavors to provide the correct etymological designation (the philological approach implied by the term *kōshō*) for this river, celebrated in classical poetry for the beauty of its autumn maple leaves:

> To the west [of the town of Tatsuta], after going just half a *ri*, in the direction of Kokufugoshi, in a place called Tatsuno is the Tatsuta main shrine. To the west of this is a small ditch created by the Momijigawa. The people of the village [*satobito*] mistakenly call this Tatsutagawa. The eroding bank above [the river] the local people mistakenly call Mimuro no kishi, but it isn't so. The Tatsutagawa is said to originate west of Tatsuno-machi. . . .

Below Tatsutagawa is a village called Jinnan. The mountain above that
is called Kaminami-yama.[61] Below that mountain to the east flows the
Tatsutagawa. The riverbank to the east of Kaminami-yama is Mimuro no
kishi. . . . What the local people call Tatsutagawa is so small a stream it is
difficult to call it a [river]. If it is not in the foothills of Kaminami-yama, it's
not [the place to which] the old poems [koka] refer. The local people . . .
in confusion have applied the wrong name. They should not be believed.[62]

Ekiken makes similar observations in Senzuka, location of the many
tumuli. There, too, the "local customs" (seizoku) are in error: "everyone is wrong" about the history of the tumuli, he asserts.[63] In both cases,
however, the dispute is not about the people or their character; it is
about their lack of knowledge. The people may be mistaken (ayamarite),
or given to misunderstanding (higagoto nari) and "shouldn't be believed," but they are not inherently dull or wrong. Ekiken himself,
though authoritative, does not claim anywhere in the account to be right
simply by virtue of his status or his education. Rather, the information
he has gathered via his education enables him to come to conclusions
unattainable by those less learned. Instead of criticizing the ignorance
of the people, he makes note of the things they *do* know, and focuses
instead on compiling an accurate and complete record of data. He is
especially attentive to proper names, for as the *Analects* dictate, names
correspond to physical geography, which in turn reflects the guiding
principle of order itself.

In Ekiken's view, the local people were not obstacles to the proper
gathering of information; indeed, they were an integral part of it, for
they provided much of the data for his "fieldwork." He describes himself as being warmly welcomed into local communities with few exceptions, by local farmers as well as by his hosts, usually prominent villagers or headmen (aruji). In Kyūanji-mura the headman and his younger
brother welcome Ekiken into their home, and compel him to rest after
his journey. He spends an entire day there and leaves feeling completely
refreshed.[64] At an inn in Namimatsu near Horyūji in Nara, his host is a
"rich man of the village" whose warmth and hospitality is such that
Ekiken is moved to remark, "I go to a different inn every night, but rare
are such memories of the sort of heartfelt kindness [extended by] this
host. It will be hard to forget."[65] Near Ise, he meets a local notable who
is "much interested in learning, and is open-minded." The man runs a
school of sorts, lecturing daily on the classics to about half a dozen
people.[66]

One of the few negative experiences he records is of the town of

Manzawa near the border between Suruga and Kai provinces. There
Ekiken finds that, although the innkeeper is rich, the lodgings are filthy
and the food poor. Paraphrasing Sei Shōnagon's *Pillow Book,* he remarks that they were given only "'the worst scraps of vegetables and
grains.' Among other things, the straw matting was not clean, and though
[the innkeepers] apologized many times, [words alone] did not relieve
the fatigue of travel."[67] Nevertheless, he refrains from dwelling upon
these hardships; occasionally, challenges encountered during the journey even provide moments of levity, as in the case of Ekiken's description of his host in Kōfu: "My host was, like myself, hard of hearing. Neither of us could understand what the other was saying, because [both of
us] were very stubborn."[68]

Though possessed of a generous spirit toward others, Ekiken did not
hesitate to criticize himself. One statement, embedded in an otherwise
spare description of a famous stop on the Tōkaidō, stands out for its un-
forgiving tone. "Today when I climbed the Hakone road, deep emotions
welled up in me. It was because, in spite of my age, I lack virtue. Nothing had changed from the times I had passed through before. I feel
shamed. Between Mishima and Hakone is the border dividing Izu and
Sagami provinces. Tonight I will stay in Odawara."[69]

The human emotion that flowed freely in classical poetry on the
themes of travel and place, but was so noticeably restrained in Ekiken's
account, in this instance breaks through the confines of his sober narration. For this most serious of scholars, dedicated to the art of detached
observation of all things, the most emotionally significant encounter "on
the road" was the confrontation with himself.

A SPACE/TIME TEMPLATE: PRECEDENT AND EXPERIENCE
IN EARLY MODERN TRAVEL ACCOUNTS

As an educated person, Kaibara Ekiken recognized that in certain respects the literary conventions of classical travel diaries possessed a
timeless quality. He himself never hesitated to enhance his description of
a particular place with an appropriate poem from the *waka* canon. But,
at the same time, Ekiken criticized classical travel writing because its
very timelessness made it unable to fully convey the essence of travel as
a fundamentally time- and place-specific experience. Even when working off an "old poem," as in the case of his description of Tatsutagawa,
he strives to find the precise physical place to which the text referred, because for Ekiken, if a text did not locate itself in space as well as time, it

had nothing of practical or intellectual use to convey to the reader. And to Ekiken the travel account should above all be useful, comprehensible, and thus "workable" in its own particular historical context. The notion that travel writing should perform geographical and intellectual work was perhaps in hindsight Ekiken's most significant contribution to the history of mapping.

Reading Kaibara Ekiken thus gives us a sense not only of a writer's perception of the world, but of his relationship to his audience. Though Ekiken was influential he was not, and could not be, representative of the multiplicity of travel experiences in an increasingly mobile society. The very factors that endowed him with authority and a ready audience—his learning, his status, his gender, and, ultimately, his fame—were precisely the factors that made him exceptional, even in his own time. And it is this exceptionality that has played a primary role in ensuring that his writings retain their importance to this day. Because Ekiken was exceptional, his writings were not representative of all travel; for this reason, the focus here has been less on the experiential aspects of the journey, and more on its narration. My interest in tracing the vernacularization of spatial concepts requires focusing on the language used to articulate the travel experience. If maps created a particular spatio-symbolic language, travel accounts constructed a spatio-narrative language, the formal analysis of which is essential for analyzing a largely discursive process: the writing and graphing of space and place—mapping—in historical context.

In this framework, Kaibara Ekiken's *Jinshin kikō* of 1672 is not just another text. It can be said to have functioned as a template for early modern conceptions of space/time. Due in large part to his renown as a scholar and writer, Ekiken's travel accounts were published and read by learned people like himself. Elements of his style, his language, and, most of all, his intellectual reconception of what travel and its narration meant shaped subsequent travel writing in overt and implicit ways. After Ekiken, the discovery of both wisdom and practical fact by observing the landscape came to be the defining feature of travel writing: it had to be both intellectually stimulating and actually useful. These twin characteristics were of equal importance to Ekiken's audience; although Kaibara Ekiken is best known now as a moral philosopher, the publisher of many of Ekiken's travel accounts, a house called Ryūshiken, categorized them not as literature or philosophy, but as simple guidebooks.[70] In a late-seventeenth-century publishing world of growing size and sophistication, names, distances, sights, and views needed to conform rigorously to "things as they were," not for philosophical reasons, but because if they did not, they would be of little use to the reader.

In this manner, the early modern travel writer seems to belong to the same intellectual world as the eighteenth-century French Encyclopédistes, who argued that "there was no better school for life than that of voyages."[71] However, this shared concept notwithstanding, early modern Japanese and European travel accounts differed in fundamental ways. To compare the two is not to suggest that the European text is the normative model; it is to utilize the considerable critical literature on European encounters with "other" cultures in order to draw out the contrast provided by the Japanese example. The early modern European travelogue has been seen as a modern discourse of power whose main goal was to observe, describe, and thereby tame unknown and "uncivilized" places and peoples of the world. In the accounts of voyages of "discovery" and conquest, emissaries of Old World metropoles set out to systematically "normalize, codify, and rectify" their other-world subjects in the global periphery.[72] As Tzvetan Todorov has argued, European explorers assign proper names to the unknown that "serve only for denotation, but not directly for human communication . . . in the fashion of indices."[73]

In the case of early modern Japan, however, the politics of domination pitting a conquering writer against a conquered subject, or a civilized "center" over and against an uncivilized "periphery," is much less clear. This is due to several factors: first, the vast majority of travel writing produced in the early modern period chronicled domestic journeys.[74] As chapter 1 has shown, from the early Tokugawa period, maps had helped construct the notion that the "geo-body" of Japan consisted of the three main islands of the archipelago, with the borderlands of Matsumae and the Ryūkyūs inconsistently included.[75] This made early modern travel writing less about Japan and its "others" and more about defining and measuring degrees of strangeness within the homeland itself.

Secondly, the opposition between writer and subject was less firm in the Japanese case than in the European, for Japanese writers of travel accounts did not necessarily represent a single, irrefutably central place. More often than not travel writers were of provincial origin. Kaibara Ekiken himself was from Chikuzen province in Kyushu, and the travel writers to be discussed in chapter 3 were also of provincial origin: Nagakubo Sekisui was from Mito, and Furukawa Koshōken was from Hyōgo. Tachibana Nankei (1753–1805), who lived most of his life in

Kyoto, is the only writer among those discussed in the following chapters who came from a place that might justifiably be called "central," and even he was born and raised in Ise province. In addition to their varied places of origin, writers also tended to be of varying statuses and occupations. Although learned commoners or samurai of low to modest rank were among the most prolific travel writers, they continuously refashioned their own status- and place-based identities as against those of others they encountered in the course of their journeys.

Kaibara Ekiken's travel writings serve as a historical place-marker against which to assess later works in the genre. By referring back to Ekiken's texts we can chart the development of travel writing (spatially and temporally) over the course of more than a century. By the time Tachibana Nankei wrote his *Saiyūki* in the 1820s, travel writing, travelers, and readers no longer lived in the world Kaibara Ekiken so carefully described. In the early nineteenth century the shogunate was battling internal unrest and external threat from foreign countries. By that time, Japan had been mapped and charted to the point where many writers of satirical fiction saw fit to poke fun at what must have appeared to be obsessive concern with depicting, categorizing, and describing space. Unlike Ekiken, who foresaw a modest audience for his writings, later travel writers very self-consciously played to the interests and habits of a large reading audience, catered to by a publishing industry in which innovation and expertise were the keys to success. Whereas Ekiken assumed the persona of an aging storyteller on the verge of forgetfulness who counted on the tacit indulgence and interest of his readers, later writers were as conscious of the audience as they were of themselves as authors. As Tachibana Nankei wrote in the preface to his *Tōyūki*, "Of the things recorded in this [travel] account, there are many that invite reflection, but I have intentionally left them as they are. Whether to believe these assertions or not is left to the reader's instinct." [76]

Increasingly, the reader, in concert with the writer, would determine the form and function of the travel account. The meaningful encounter in travel writing in the late eighteenth and early nineteenth centuries thus became that between the writer and his audience. This fundamental relationship came to condition, in profound ways, the interaction between the writer and the objects, human and material, within his gaze.

CHAPTER 3

Narrating Japan

Travel and the Writing of Cultural
Difference in the Late Eighteenth and
Early Nineteenth Centuries

Clever people observe more things and more curiously, but
they interpret them; and to lend weight and conviction to
their interpretation, they cannot help altering history a little.
They never show you things as they are, but bend and dis-
guise them according to the way they have seen them; and to
give credence to their judgment and attract you to it, they are
prone to add something to their matter, to stretch it out and
amplify it. We need a man either very honest, or so simple
that he has not the stuff to build up false inventions and give
them plausibility; and wedded to no theory. . . . I would like
everyone to write what he knows, and as much as he knows,
not only in this, but in all other subjects.

Michel de Montaigne, "Of Cannibals"

Writers like Kaibara Ekiken reinvented the genre of travel writing in the
early modern period to emphasize the importance of direct observation
and clear description. Over the course of the eighteenth century, however, writers began to use the experience of travel to fashion themselves
as opinionated authorities on a broad range of subjects, from geography
to medicine to "foreign studies." As they ventured out to Japan's far-
thest boundaries and into the hidden rural enclaves of the country's in-
terior, travel writers increasingly saw it as their task not only to describe
but also to categorize the differences they found within their own country and place them within a larger hierarchical scheme of "civilization."
Nor were travel writers content to simply note differences in flora,
fauna, and local products. As they encountered resident foreigners like

the Dutch and the Chinese in Nagasaki, and ethnically distinct populations like the Ainu in the far northeast, they transformed themselves into
explorers of Japan and interpreters of its culture.

Each of the writers discussed in this chapter seeks to analyze culture
through the medium of travel writing. In the case of Nagakubo Sekisui,
the journey to and from Nagasaki was an opportunity to contrast "famous places" from the Japanese cultural past with unfamiliar sites and
foreign peoples in Nagasaki. For Furukawa Koshōken, travel was an
opportunity to correct the errors made by previous writers, whether
they involved judging the level of education in a remote village or mapping the coastline of northern Honshu. Tachibana Nankei, for his part,
presents the odd or arresting cultural detail and the "strange" phenomenon, all presented in highly readable and entertaining prose, but all un-
mistakably in the service of the author's concepts of a "civilized" life. In
contrast to Kaibara Ekiken's attempt to discover an underlying order
in the natural and human world, later eighteenth-century travel writers used narrative to manufacture order by establishing dichotomies
between insider and outsider, civilization and barbarity, familiar and
foreign.

AN "OFFICIAL DIARY" OF A JOURNEY TO NAGASAKI

We have previously encountered Nagakubo Sekisui as a geographer and
mapmaker, one of the first to place Japan on the longitude and latitude
grid, and creator of a number of influential woodblock-print maps of
Japan and of Asia. Sekisui also worked on the *Dai Nihon shi,* the grand
history project centered in his home domain of Mito. His study of geography, and the travels that formed part of his research, were undertaken in the context of that larger project. But in addition to his geographical and historical scholarship, Sekisui was also a prolific author
and, as many intellectuals did, he fancied himself an accomplished composer of poetry in the Chinese style *(kanshi)*. He wrote two travel accounts, *Tō-oku kikō* (Travels to the far northeast) in 1760, and *Nagasaki kōeki nikki* (Diary of official travels to Nagasaki) in 1767, both
of which blend poetry and prose.[1] In 1768 he also published a collection
of poems exchanged with Chinese residents of Nagasaki after his visit
there the previous year.

All of Sekisui's travel accounts blended poetry in Chinese with description of local scenery, routes, and roads. In this way, his writings
combine his vocation and his avocation, as long stretches of relatively

unadorned prose are punctuated by highly allusive *kanshi* verses and an occasional diagram or illustration.[2] Unlike the poems used by Ekiken to clarify etymology or to justify the status of a place as "famous," the poems in Sekisui's account are for the most part original compositions. Due to Sekisui's background as a geographer, and the attention to accurate measurement displayed in maps, one expects Sekisui's travel accounts to be rigorously empirical, but instead they reflect a notion of place that is inextricably linked to Japan's culture and history. In prose, poetic, and pictorial form, Sekisui transforms places and people into icons of historical and cultural significance, and, more often than not, he phrases his reactions to them in the self-consciously emotive language of poetry. Though it might seem that these countervailing tendencies would create some kind of conflict in the mind of a poet-geographer, Sekisui's travel account shows that the "mapping impulse" was not simply or solely concerned with land in its physical, measurable dimensions. Even committed scholars of geography were not confined by the "scientific method"; rather, they were broadly learned literati who deployed the many rhetorical tactics available to them. Of all of his travel accounts, Sekisui's "diary of official travels" best reflects the many skills of the early modern man of letters.[3]

Nagasaki kōeki nikki was written after Sekisui undertook a three-month journey to Nagasaki. On this trip he was charged with the task of meeting, interrogating, and supervising the return of a group of castaways from Mito domain whose ship had been blown off course in 1765 and who had, as a result, been stranded for several years in Annam.[4] The castaways were finally returned to Japan via Nagasaki in 1767. Sekisui, like Kaibara Ekiken, opens his account with a "departure scene" describing his embarkation for Nagasaki:

> In the eleventh month of the second year of Meiwa [1765] past, a ship from Isohara village was blown [off course] by severe winds, and drifted to a foreign country. This year in the seventh month [the crew] was brought to Nagasaki on a ship from the other country. Accordingly, as a representative of this domain [Mito], I went to Nagasaki. I took the place of the village head of Isohara, and along with the ship official Mataichi and my nephew Yūsuke, we obtained official orders, and on the twenty-eighth day of the ninth month, we left our residences and went to Suifu [in Mito]. . . . On the first day of the following ninth month, we left Suifu, and at the eighth hour of the third day, we reached the domain residence at Koishikawa in the eastern capital [Edo]. I stayed at the Daikokuya Nagayūemon in Kasuga-chō. We stayed for four days, and on the fifth day at the Hour of the Tiger, persons [by the name of] Toba Rizaemon [and] Sakabe Isuke from the

metsuke [shogunal inspector's office] made a procession at the inner precinct of the residence, and we exited the gate. [With] two palanquins, two spears, two equipment boxes, two sets of pack luggage, [and] two pack horses, [we were] altogether twenty-one people. That day we stayed at Totsuka. Following orders, we left when the stars came out, and I hadn't the opportunity to take up my brush, so the descriptions of the route were difficult to record in detail.[5]

Although details occasionally may have been "difficult to record," as one can see from the above words Sekisui's account does not suffer from a lack of specific information about the logistics of the journey. Like most travel writers, he makes daily entries describing the weather, travel conditions, and places and people encountered. But as a learned person and a connoisseur of poetry in Chinese and Japanese, he is also attuned to places of literary and cultural significance, especially those associated with travelers of times past: here he notes a carving of Saigyō, there the final resting place of Sōgi, and elsewhere the traces of Sōchō's past journeys. He is attentive as well to the details of material culture, making note of various local products and regional specialties or characteristics: a shrine in Izu is known for its calendars, the town of Kashiwahara for its fried eel, Imaizumi for its metal work, and Sakai for its palm trees. Conspicuously absent from the account, however, are the castaways from Annam, who are the ostensible reason for the journey. Like the "official business" that took Kaibara Ekiken on his journey several decades earlier, the castaways merit little attention in the text. Sekisui mentions them exactly four times, and even then only in passing: once when he takes responsibility for them in Nagasaki, another when he questions them about their stay abroad during a lull in the return journey, once again when he notes the necessity of keeping them under surveillance lest they pass on any important information, and finally when he hands them over to domain authorities at the journey's end.[6]

The two primary aspects of the *Nagasaki kōeki nikki*—its poetic and its "annotative" qualities—make it a study in the convergence of the two modes of travel writing that were dominant in the early modern period. Sekisui's blend of these two styles allows him to narrate his travels in two voices: the literary and the empirical. Once again in contrast to Kaibara Ekiken, whose pauses for literary reflection are threaded throughout his journey, Sekisui speaks in the poetic voice most clearly while on the road to and from Nagasaki, as he travels along the Tōkaidō and auxiliary roads in western Honshu and northern Kyushu. As he follows these well-traveled routes, Sekisui is given ample opportunity to reflect upon the historical, literary, and cultural significance of the many *meisho* clustered on or near them, and these inspire lengthy comment and poetic rumination. The empirical voice, for its part, takes over in Nagasaki, with its unfamiliar sights and foreign people.

On the outgoing part of the trip, Sekisui's journey often seems to center around the appreciation, in poetic form, of famous places. He writes poems inspired by the sights of Kyoto, including the imperial palace and Kiyomizudera.[7] As he climbs Sayo no Nakayama he offers his own interpretation of Saigyō's famous poem on that site.[8] At Ichi no Tani in central Honshu, the site of the famous battle depicted in the *Tale of the Heike,* Sekisui writes a poem evoking the red and white flags of the two opposing armies as they clash on the shore. His description melds with the observed scenery, for as he notes in the prose part of the text, local lore has it that the flowers on the beach bloom red and white, dividing themselves down the middle at the point where the two sides met in battle. The Heike legends also figure prominently on the return portion of the trip, when Sekisui visits the Amida temple in Shimonoseki, site of the grave of the emperor Antoku, whose tragic death in the closing chapters of the *Tale of Heike* symbolizes the Taira defeat. Giving in to the classical impulse, he states that mere prose "cannot contain [his] feelings," and writes the following:

Entering the temple above the shore
The imperial grave stands cold and alone
The headstone is all that remains of the noble family
The battle scene is like a picture gallery
Lightning flits over the open plain
There are no spirits in this sandy place
From the time the imperial sword was lost
One feels the enduring pain until now[9]

In Dazaifu in northern Kyushu, the former home of the renowned Heian courtier, poet, and scholar Sugawara no Michizane (845–903), Sekisui again pauses for poetic rumination. Michizane was a tragic hero, a prominent statesman who fell victim to factional politics within the imperial house and in 901 was made a government representative in Dazaifu, a demotion equivalent to exile.[10] Of his plight, Sekisui writes:

He rose to the level of head of state
He possessed the knowledge of a thousand years
His Japanese poems surpassed those of Kaki[nomoto and] Yama[be][11]
His Chinese poems equaled those of Gen [and] Haku[12]
His star fell to earth in Zaifu

The booming thunder can be felt at the imperial palace[13]
Today, above his shrine
Prophetic clouds gather[14]

Places associated with other heroic figures such as the emperor Go-
Daigo (1288–1339), who attempted to wrest power from the military
government and restore imperial rule in 1333, also evoke emotional responses from Sekisui. The repeated invocation of these figures creates an
"other" Japan that exists primarily in Sekisui's literary and historical
imagination.

This mode of thinking and writing, however, changes abruptly when
Sekisui arrives in Nagasaki. Unlike the familiar places depicted earlier
in the journey, Nagasaki is foreign in many ways. It has no history for
Sekisui, it is bereft of poetic meaning, and its peculiar culture is one that
he has never before observed. As a result, his description shifts away
from the classical literary tropes and instead he begins to record primarily what appears before his eyes. To borrow Clifford Geertz's terms,
the "author" becomes an "I-witness."[15] Sekisui momentarily sets aside
the persona of literatus and takes up a perspective more akin to that of
an ethnographer among the "natives." Like Kaibara Ekiken, he takes it
upon himself to describe and analyze an unfamiliar culture in ways that
are clear and comprehensible to an audience "back home."

In Nagasaki, Sekisui is particularly interested in the city's foreign residents, the Dutch and the Chinese, whose odd habits and unusual material possessions provoke extensive commentary. As Sekisui struggles to
formulate language adequate to describe these people and their culture,
pictures serve a particularly useful role in conveying what text cannot.
For this reason, although Sekisui sparsely illustrated the first half of the
Kōeki nikki, once he begins to describe Nagasaki, illustrations are numerous. Upon visiting the Dutch compound on the island of Dejima off
the coast of Nagasaki, Sekisui assesses the physical appearance of the
Dutch:

> Their eyes sparkle and their eyebrows are reddish; their facial features are
> inscrutable. . . . Their skin is extremely white. They shave their heads and
> wear black wigs. Their clothing resembles our *momohiki* [knee breeches],
> fastened at the wrist and leg with buttons. Their coats have no sleeves, and
> are closed in the front with buttons, open below the waist to resemble [the
> costume of] a *karuwaza* actor.[16] Everything is made of woven wool.[17]

The description of the Dutch here is not exceptional in its detail or its
tone; it echoes earlier accounts of foreigners in and around Nagasaki.

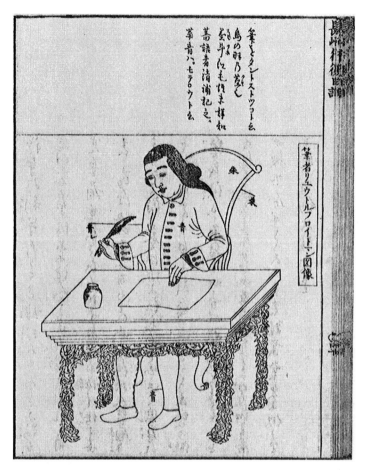

Figure 11. Drawing of the Dutchman "Froitman," from Nagakubo Sekisui, *Sekisui Chō Sensei Nagasaki kōeki nikki,* 1805. Courtesy of the East Asian Library, University of California, Berkeley.

However, the generic European in Sekisui's textual portrait is supplemented by an illustration of a Dutchman seated at his writing table, whose name is rendered phonetically in the *katakana* syllabary as "Froitman" (see fig. 11). The inscription informs the reader that the man is a secretary in the Dutch legation. Sekisui notes in the body of the text that the Dutchman's horizontal script resembled nothing so much as "sketches of clouds." [18] Pairing the pictorial and narrative depiction of a single Dutchman with a physical description of the Dutch as a people gives Sekisui's account an air of detachment that is entirely absent from the more lyrical, self-consciously dramatic first part of the travel narrative. Descriptions of unfamiliar objects possessed by the Dutch also take on a studied and deliberate tone, and illustrations are added for clarity. A thermometer becomes, in a rather ingenious turn of phrase, "a timepiece to measure the climate" *(setsuki wo hakaru tokei)* consisting of "two glass tubes containing water attached to a board and hung on the wall. On the board were written characters, but since they were in a foreign language, I couldn't make them out." [19] A billiard table becomes "a bed-like structure with tall legs . . . wrapped in wool, with holes in the four corners. When I asked the interpreter [about this] he said that it was a thing upon which the Dutch roll balls and place bets." [20]

Sekisui also depicts, primarily in pictorial form, the servants brought to Japan by the Dutch. Unlike the portrait of the "inscrutable" Dutch secretary, however, the illustrations of the dark-skinned servants, likely of Indonesian origin, evoke a different order of otherness (fig. 12). The illustration of the servant is labeled with the combined characters for "devil" *(oni)* and "slave" *(yakko),* but is glossed with the Japanese reading "*kuronbō,*" an expression meaning something like "black boy." Other captions indicate the color of clothing, indicating the red background of the shirt and headscarf worn by the servant. There is no commentary on the servants as individuals; neither are their names included in the portrait. The focus on their appearance—skin color and clothing—lends the portrait an air of objectification more akin to the descriptions of objects like the billiard table and the thermometer than to the descriptions of the Dutch. Indeed, Sekisui's only narrative description of the servants links them not with their Dutch masters, but with the domesticated animals kept in the Dutch compound: "When we went down to the kitchens, we saw pigs and cows and other [animals] penned up; it was extremely foul-smelling. In front of the oven were four or five blacks *[kuronbō].* Among them were some children. I asked them how old they were, but they didn't understand." [21]

The dehumanization of the servants stands in contrast to the generally laudatory portraits of two Chinese merchants whom Sekisui met during his visit. Unlike the "blacks," the Chinese are not generically labeled, but are depicted individually and named specifically. One portrait is of a person called Yū Ho An (fig. 13); the other is called Kyon Tei Sen (fig. 14). In addition to naming the individuals, Sekisui also labels their clothing, shoes, hats, hairstyles, and personal accessories (tobacco pipes,

Figure 12. Drawing of a servant brought to Nagasaki by the Dutch, from Nagakubo Sekisui, *Sekisui Chō Sensei Nagasaki kōeki nikki,* 1805. Courtesy of the East Asian Library, University of California, Berkeley.

folding fans). In each case, in what is perhaps Sekisui's acknowledgment of the original and therefore "proper" reading, all *kanji,* including the men's names, are glossed with the Chinese, rather than the Japanese, pronunciation.

The special treatment accorded the Chinese, who are referred to in the text as the "guests from the Qing empire" *(Shin kyaku),* indicates their importance to Sekisui. As a student and admirer of Chinese learning, and especially as an enthusiastic composer of *kanshi,* Sekisui eagerly

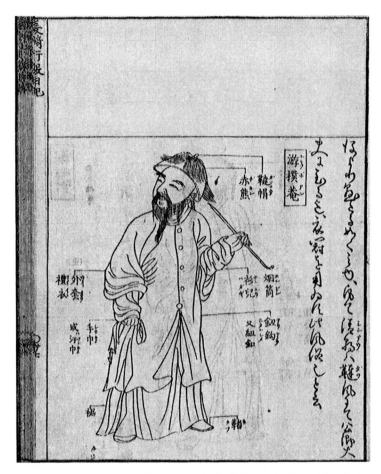

Figure 13. "Yū Ho An," Chinese resident of Nagasaki, from Nagakubo Sekisui, *Sekisui Chō Sensei Nagasaki kōeki nikki,* 1805. Courtesy of the East Asian Library, University of California, Berkeley.

anticipated the opportunity to meet Chinese people in the flesh. He recounts in the text his feverish anticipation of the rare opportunity to exchange poetry with the two men, and he and his nephew Yūsuke stay up all night preparing their verses.[22] The meeting is a success, but ultimately Sekisui laments the decline he perceives in the cultural attainments of the Chinese. In one of the very few poems in the Nagasaki section of the text, he implies how regrettable it is that the Qing merchants are not equal to "the scholars of the Han or the Tang dynasties."[23] Although he remarks that the Chinese in Nagasaki more closely resemble "our people" (*kono kata,* literally "this side") physically than do the Dutch,

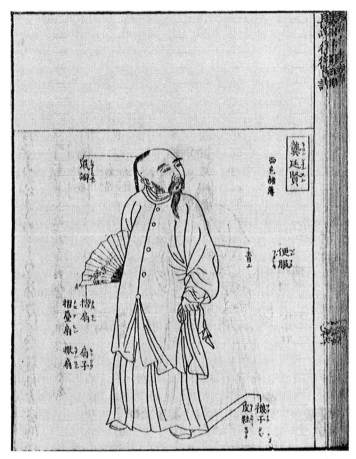

Figure 14. "Kyon Tei Sen," Chinese resident of Nagasaki, from Nagakubo Sekisui, *Sekisui Chō Sensei Nagasaki kōeki nikki*, 1805. Courtesy of the East Asian Library, University of California, Berkeley.

there is still a great deal that seems foreign about their dress and comportment—hence the many labels on their portraits indicating peculiarities in clothing and hairstyles. He also notes that their eating habits differ from those of the Japanese; at a Chinese meal all the guests sit down around a central table and partake of the food arranged upon it, rather than eating off separate trays as Japanese in a formal setting would.[24] And despite Sekisui's affinity for Chinese poetry, he cannot communicate directly with the Chinese without using an interpreter.

Sekisui's relationship to the Chinese was complex—far deeper than his connection to the Dutch, and emblematic of both the admiration and the disdain that eighteenth-century Japanese intellectuals felt toward China. In the case of a sinophile like Sekisui, the former sentiment is more in evidence than the latter, and observations about the Chinese, Chinese learning, and Chinese culture are frequent throughout the description of Nagasaki. After Sekisui visits the great Buddhist temples in the city, his observations commingle the present and past meanings of China in eighteenth-century Japan—the rich religious and intellectual heritage shared by Japan and China, but also the way that heritage played itself out in everyday life. For example, Sekisui shows himself to be quite interested in the textual traces the great Buddhist teachers left in each temple, such as inscriptions, texts, calligraphy, and paintings. But he also mentions that all of the temples—Kōfukuji, Sōfukuji, and Fukusaiji—were built by and served the various regional groupings within the Chinese community in Nagasaki.[25] He notes that classical Chinese learning also thrives in the city, and when he visits a Chinese bookseller *(tōmono-ya)*, he comes away with sets of the Four Books and the Five Classics.[26] He also visits the clearinghouse for Chinese books *(Tōhon aratame sho)*, where bakufu censors pulled aside all texts in which the government had a particular interest, leaving the remainder to be auctioned to the public.[27]

In the end, Chinese culture, as it manifests itself in Nagasaki, seems to mean many things to Sekisui. While he recognizes, if vaguely, that the Qing merchants are not the literati of the Tang, he is reluctant to surrender his idealized notions of Chinese civilization. It is clear that before his journey to Nagasaki, "China" was for the most part an imaginary space located in the classical past. Sekisui therefore reacts with some ambivalence when faced with the "Qing guests" in Nagasaki who do not, and perhaps cannot, measure up to their ancestors.

Sekisui's Japan, by contrast, seems to exist simultaneously in both the past and present realms. On the Tōkaidō, famous places evoke descriptions rich in allusions to the classical past, and Sekisui is able effortlessly to fuse these allusions to the observed landscape as it unfolds before his eyes. The multiple viewpoints adopted in the *Nagasaki kōeki nikki*—appreciation for the famous places of the literary canon, wide-eyed observation of the strangeness of the Dutch, pleasure tinged with disappointment at the encounter with the Chinese—confound modern views of authorship, which expect a consistent subjectivity. The modern rhetoric of scientific inquiry, by contrast, stresses a consistent objectivity, which Sekisui also confounds, for he employs many ways of perceiving and of representing the cultural dimensions of place. But the fact that he combines narrative strategies in ways that may seem contradictory makes his account more significant, not less, for his tactics show both a genre and an identity—"travel writing" and "travel writer"—in transition.

If there is one conspicuous silence in Sekisui's account, it is his lack of commentary on matters political. Indeed, Sekisui seems to have strictly observed the prohibitions on public discussion of political matters. By the late 1780s, however, a decade or so after Sekisui first published his account, urgent concerns in the realm of foreign relations gave travel writing a new and explicitly political set of meanings as its authors sought to position themselves in debates over Japan's foreign relations. In this context, boundaries between "this side" and the outside became critically important.

"MISCELLANEOUS RECORDS"
OF TRAVELS TO EAST AND WEST

Furukawa Koshōken was a colleague of Sekisui's, but in many ways he was a very different type of traveler from the man to whom he refers respectfully as "the Mito Confucian official Sekisui-*sensei*." Born in Bitchū province (present-day Okayama) in 1726, Koshōken came from a commoner family involved in the cultivation and sale of pharmaceutical herbs and the practice of medicine. As he states in *Tōyū zakki* (Miscellaneous records of travels to the east, 1788), he became interested in geography at an early age, and he took to the road whenever possible. This propensity for travel led him all over Japan and culminated in the writing of his two best-known works, *Tōyū zakki* and *Saiyū zakki* (Miscellaneous records of travels to the west, 1783).[28] The journey to western Japan was organized by Koshōken himself, while the journey to the northeast was undertaken when Koshōken, having gained a reputation as a talented geographer with the publication of *Saiyū zakki,* was allowed to join a party of shogunal inspectors *(junkenshi)* on an expedition to Ezo. Official recognition again came to Koshōken in 1794, when Matsudaira Sadanobu, the influential counselor to the shogun, appointed Koshōken to execute a geographical survey of Musashi province, which resulted in the production of two maps and a five-volume record entitled *Shishin chi meiroku*. In 1795, Koshōken was granted samurai status by the daimyo of Okada, his home domain; he died in 1807 at the age of eighty-two.[29]

Koshōken's career is one example of how geographic knowledge

could be parlayed into government employment and official status. Recognition came to him relatively late in life, after he had spent some years
painstakingly establishing his reputation through scholarly and political
connections, and in part through self-promotion. This latter skill derived largely from his personality; unlike comparatively staid and scholarly figures such as Nagakubo Sekisui and Kaibara Ekiken, Koshōken
has been described as an "opinionated" observer whose "biases" are revealed in his writings.[30] His texts are punctuated with sarcasm and de-
risive comments, and he exercises his powers of judgment freely, often
criticizing other scholars and geographers whose work he found sub-
standard. And unlike his predecessors Sekisui and Ekiken, Koshōken
seldom inserted poems or literary references into his accounts, instead
adopting a critical stance toward his subject matter that one modern
critic likens to that of a "human geographer."[31] In place of literary references, he seems to prefer anecdotes gleaned from interrogating the local people. He includes poetry only sparingly, making the few instances
when he does wax poetic stand out in relief.[32]

Another way in which Koshōken's accounts differ from those of
Ekiken and Sekisui is in the political valence of his opinions and judgments. Koshōken believed strongly in the necessity of direct observation
and factual accounting, and he is most harsh in his criticism when he
feels these standards have not been met. Such was the case in his infamous critique of *Sangoku tsūran zusetsu* (An illustrated examination
of three countries [Ezo, Korea, and the Ryūkyū Islands], 1786), by
Hayashi Shihei (1738–93).[33] The publication of this text had inspired
a great debate in Edo in the late 1780s over the problem of defending
Japan's northern borders against the encroaching Russians, a crisis that
became more acute with the arrival of Russian ships at Nagasaki in the
1790s. Advocates of a strong defense policy, such as Hayashi Shihei and
Honda Toshiaki (1744–1821), opposed Furukawa Koshōken and others who were of the opinion that the existing defenses were adequate. In
Tōyū zakki, Koshōken assailed Hayashi Shihei's account. He did so because he felt Shihei's descriptions of the southern part of the Tsugaru
peninsula were far off the mark. And if Shihei didn't know "his own
country," Koshōken reasoned, he couldn't be trusted to describe "far-
away foreign countries" either.[34] This particular criticism had significant effects, for Koshōken's harsh criticism is often cited as one of the
reasons Shihei eventually was punished by the shogunate for spreading
controversial information.[35] Koshōken also ridicules Hayashi Shihei's
alarm over the Russian threat. Echoing the dominant opinion within the

high ranks of the shogunate, Koshōken put great faith in the defensive capabilities of Matsumae domain in southern Ezo: "even if the Russians want Ezo, they aren't going to give it a thought because of the preparedness of the lord of Matsumae."[36] In the late-eighteenth-century debate over foreign policy, direct observation and geopolitical acumen clearly came into play for both travel writers and officials alike.

On matters of geographic and cartographic accuracy, Koshōken is slightly less critical of Nagakubo Sekisui than he is of Hayashi Shihei. Concerning Sekisui's descriptions of Matsumae in the latter's *Tō-oku kikō,* Koshōken writes, "Although Sekisui is well versed in the general characteristics of the inland [area], he doesn't know anything about Matsumae. . . . If one doesn't actually visit the place on one's own, one can't know anything about geography or customs."[37] In *Tōyū zakki* Koshōken also criticizes the bakufu scholar Arai Hakuseki's *Ezo shi* (Record of Ezo, 1720) for similar shortcomings, then offers his own map and his analysis of Ezo as a more accurate representation of the geographical and cultural characteristics of the area.[38] In the *Saiyū zakki,* he is less specific in his criticism of previous travelers, instead lambasting published travel accounts and guidebooks that, in his opinion, grossly misrepresent geographical as well as political reality much, he feels, to Japan's detriment. He writes:

> While traveling about the country I took along a recently published [guidebook] entitled "Detailed Account of Routes and Roads" [Dōchū gyōtei saikenki], and I found that there were many significant errors. In these foolish writings they say that Japan is a [small] island country, but it is a large country, the most superior land in the world. Because they fear offending China, they intentionally make [Japan] out to be a small country, and shrink its size. They'd record [a distance of] a hundred *ri* as fifty. It is absurd.[39]

Perhaps to make up for the deficiencies he perceives in previous texts, the original *Saiyū zakki* apparently was full of hand-drawn maps and landscape drawings of the regions and places Koshōken visited. Unfortunately, all but fourteen of these illustrations were lost when Koshōken's house flooded, destroying most of the manuscript. The *Tōyū zakki,* by contrast, contains few maps; because this was a government-sponsored journey, Koshōken could not explore as freely as he did on his previous trip to western Japan. Perhaps because of this constraint and because shogunal officials themselves had made maps of the lands visited, Koshōken had fewer opportunities and less incentive to draw his own maps.

Furukawa Koshōken clearly placed great value on accuracy, both in graphic depiction and in narrative description. However, his attention to the physical features of the land cannot be divorced from his interest in, and judgments of, the culture that animated it. For Koshōken, observing and judging are inseparable activities. Indeed, the portrait of the author that emerges from *Saiyū zakki* and *Tōyū zakki* is that of an active observer and critic who gains his information by training his astute and somewhat skeptical eye on the various communities he passes through. For even though Koshōken's "miscellaneous records" sometimes retain the air of casual random jottings, he employs methods and standards of investigation that he does not attempt to conceal. One of his most-often-used standards for assessing local cultures is the people's ability to speak Japanese that is intelligible to him. The phrase "the people and their language are extremely poor [in quality]" *(jinbutsu-gengo hanahada iyashii)* is his most frequently exercised opinion. That the local vernacular might be entirely comprehensible to someone other than himself seems of little consequence. In fact, throughout his writings Koshōken makes it clear that his judgments are based on his own experience. He explicitly states that his standards derive from comparisons to his native region, west-central Japan, as well as to other regions of Japan that he has seen. But unlike other travelers, he also tends to abstract what is familiar to him into a concept of "normalcy" *(heizei),* a standard against which he assesses the conditions—material and human—that he observes during his travels. The labeling of people as "poor" in quality or not "normal" marks an important shift in perspective from observer to critic, from one who describes to one who defines culture. It is a short step from this type of judging to the discourses on "civilization" that begin to appear in the travel writings of Tachibana Nankei and others published around the turn of the nineteenth century.

The links between place and culture are made clear in Koshōken's sharp observations of regional economic conditions and local industry. General living conditions indicate to Koshōken not only material prosperity or poverty, but also the overall wealth or impoverishment of the spirit. Thus he is especially attentive to the material culture of everyday life, depicting in detail the useful or unusual objects he finds in the communities he visited. During his travels to western Japan, for example, he sketched a variety of farming tools used in rural inland communities, such as scythes, plows, and ox-drawn carts. Unusual dwellings caught his eye as well, such as the distinctive woven-bamboo doors and walls of houses in the southern Kyushu province of Satsuma, which to Koshōken resemble the "huts of the poor beggars" in the more developed areas of central Japan.[40]

As was the case for Nagakubo Sekisui, defining and classifying culture becomes more challenging when Koshōken is faced with foreign and unfamiliar places and peoples. Foreigners and outsiders fall under Koshōken's critical eye in borderlands like Ezo and Nagasaki; in these places, he assesses the foreigners' civility by simultaneously describing and judging their language, behavior, customs, dress, and standard of living. In contrast to the decisiveness of his views of his fellow countrymen, however, Koshōken directs a more ambivalent gaze toward the Dutch, Chinese, Ryūkyūan, Korean, and Ainu populations he encounters in the course of his travels. In *Saiyū zakki,* for example, Koshōken describes the Chinese in Nagasaki as follows:

> Because there are a great number of Chinese, inside the Chinese residence *[Tōjin yashiki]* it is quite loud. To Japanese, their way of speaking, "chin-pun-kan," is funny. From the gate, several lower-class Chinese come out to look. They stop passing Japanese and say ridiculous things to them, and when they see a woman, they squirm and gesticulate in their excitement, and they say things among themselves and laugh.[41]

Upon entering the Chinese residence, he observes the arrival of a group of courtesans. Nagasaki officials assigned the Dutch and the Chinese their own groups of courtesans, whose dealings with the foreigners were regulated by the government. The courtesans were not, for example, allowed to stay overnight in the Chinese residence, but were allowed to stay on Dejima, and were one of the main connections between the Dutch and the Nagasaki community at large. Koshōken describes the scene, writing "A half-dozen courtesans came in, and the lower-class Chinese rushed out from the rooms left and right in great numbers, calling out in loud voices, appraising [the women]. Their laughter and [voices] sound like 'chin-pun-chin-pun.' Later, I heard that lower-class Chinese don't have any money and can't buy courtesans."[42]

It is important to note the characteristics Koshōken attributes to the Chinese: verbosity, unintelligibility, and an unrestrained and somewhat adolescent interest in women. "Chin-pun-kan" was a generic mimicry of foreign languages as nonsensical babble, and it underscores the way in which language, for Koshōken and perhaps universally, has been a prime distinguishing feature of cultural difference. The gesticulations, the "inside" talk that Koshōken can't understand, and the perceived absurdity of it all seem initially to be hallmarks of Koshōken's ostracizing of the "other." But in the next sentence he admits that the Chinese "are not bad as people, and however you look at them, they are still thought to be of better quality than [some] Japanese."[43] The undercutting of the distancing description with a familiarizing one is a tactic Koshōken uses with the Dutch as well and reflects his divided opinions of the foreigners and their culture.

While in Nagasaki, Koshōken is not able to enter Dejima to observe the Dutch directly, but he stations himself outside the gates of the compound and watches the proceedings from a distance. His description of the physical appearance of the Dutch is fairly standard for the time and is not much changed from the description given by Sekisui and others: "The Dutch are white, and their eyes and noses are very different from those of Japanese and Chinese. Their eyebrows are light red, and when you look at them, their facial features are disagreeable."[44] Like Sekisui, he notes their shaved heads and wigs. He also observes that the servants to the Dutch are "short in height, black in color, their noses flat."[45] But instead of providing illustrations as Sekisui did, Koshōken defers to the visual aid of available woodblock prints, writing that "since [the servants'] characteristics are depicted in detail in the prints, I will abbreviate my comments here."[46]

As in the Chinese residence, the women of the pleasure quarters are in attendance at Dejima, though apparently under duress. Koshōken reports that about thirty-five women served the Dutch residents, and an equal number served the Chinese. However, "the courtesans hate going to the Dutch residence, and it is badly regarded [by others]. But because the government has ordered them, they have no choice but to go."[47] Koshōken also reports that although the favored courtesans of the Dutch can earn a good deal of money, so great was the humiliation of having to serve the "red hairs" that some preferred to pay off other courtesans to go to Dejima in their place.[48] The Dutch themselves may not have been the kindest of patrons, for Koshōken relates an anecdote describing how some courtesans who behaved improperly while at the Dutch residence were stripped of all their belongings and chased out of the compound. One such woman, according to local lore, had ink hurled at her by her Dutch patron and had to flee to a neighboring house, waiting until dark to return to the pleasure quarters wearing borrowed clothing.[49]

Despite such hearsay, the Dutch, like the Chinese, are not uniformly bad in Koshōken's view. He tells of his visit to the home of Yoshio Kōsaku (1724–1800), one of the principal Dutch translators. Since the

Yoshio family hereditarily held this post, as Koshōken notes, their house had become a museumlike repository for foreign goods. They also had established especially close relations with the Dutch over the years. He writes:

> According to Kōsaku, the Dutch are very emotional, and when they think of their imminent departure, and the fact that they may never return to Japan again, the sorrow of parting causes them to weep for thirty, sometimes fifty, days. Upon leaving, they give their most precious possessions [to Kōsaku]. Since Kōsaku's family has for generations been associated with the Dutch, a great number of interesting objects have been given to them, and [the Yoshio residence] has come to be called the *Kōmō zashiki* [the Dutch residence]; it's something for travelers to see.[50]

A similar ambiguity characterizes Koshōken's descriptions of the indigenous Ainu people, at Japan's opposite geographical pole, the far northeast.[51] He describes the Ainu language as laughably unintelligible ("chin-pun-kan"), just as he does the Chinese language, and he designates Ainu habits as "inferior." Yet his attitudes toward the Ainu go beyond dismissive derision. He seems to find in them an unsullied state of nature, and he comments often on the purity of Ezo's isolated society, as compared to his own: "They know nothing of things like gambling, thievery, and patronizing prostitutes, such as in Japan."[52] The distinction between Ezo and the rest of Japan is made extremely clear here: the Ezo people are unalterably, even laughably, different, and yet Koshōken uses their difference in order to make them into examples of a kind of noble savage. Consider, for instance, his description of marriage patterns and male-female relations among the Ezo inhabitants. Because there are more women than men, he explains, most men have more than one wife, and the wealthier among them have three to five spouses who live in separate residences, where they bear and raise their husband's children. This practice, far from being seen as improper, is commonly accepted.[53] If, on the other hand, a woman does something deemed improper, the male, "without a word of reproach, takes a spear and runs her through, and tosses her [body] into the ocean."[54] This, Koshōken explains, is the "Ezo way." Moreover, he continues, "In Japanese custom, even if a woman commits an improper deed, because she is not punished, little by little customs change and are broken down, such that today, among rich and poor, shameless impropriety is tolerated by a great number of people. Even if it is pointed out, it is passed along as hearsay without a thought. Isn't this vastly inferior to the customs of Ezo?"[55] The example of the "Ezo way" brings to light the ways in which

Koshōken makes rhetorical use of Ainu society by positing it as lacking civilization—but in both favorable and unfavorable ways. Like Montaigne writing about the "cannibals" of the New World, Koshōken extracts morality from barbarism to point out the shortcomings of his own society.

While Koshōken's praise of the Ainu idealizes their "indigenous" customs, it also objectifies the Ainu themselves. This tendency is evident in the illustrations that accompany the Ezo section of *Tōyū zakki*, in which Koshōken sketches the clothing, jewelry, and tattoos worn by Ezo men and women. His illustrations, however, never show entire human figures, for the body only appears in fragmentary representations, for example a hand sketched in order to depict a tattoo. In this manner the Ainu are representationally reduced to the material coverings and markings they bear on their bodies, which in turn come to function largely as vehicles for visible indicators of difference.[56] Koshōken was not alone in this practice, for European travelers to the New World in the eighteenth century also evinced a preference for describing things rather than people. Mary Louise Pratt argues that the systematic and detailed focus on objects drew attention away from people and offered up a landscape unencumbered by culture and amenable to European possession.[57] While the dynamics of power differ considerably in Japanese travel accounts written by Japanese travelers, I would argue that the desire for possession was common to travel writers in both contexts; in the Japanese case, however, it was not material goods but knowledge that travelers sought. Travel writers themselves did not seek to control or dominate local territory and local populations, although by the late eighteenth century the shogunal government very much did want to control Ezo, with its strategic location and rich fishing industry.[58] It is perhaps no coincidence that Koshōken's characterization of the Ainu as uncivilized is expressed during his travels to the northeast as an adjunct to a shogunal inspection party. By defining the Ainu in this way, he lent credibility to his opinion that the local daimyo could easily control the Ainu and police the border, while at the same time justifying Japanese control over the area.

Koshōken's semiofficial role on this trip may have influenced his perspective in other ways as well. The reception accorded him as an official in the places he visited was no doubt much more elaborate and formal than the reception he gained as a private traveler, alone or with a small retinue. And most likely he was more limited in his freedom to wander and to talk to local residents. Sugae Masumi (1754–1827), who traveled in the northeast at the same time as Koshōken, attested to this fact when he made note in his own travel account of a group of workers hastily repairing a road in Iwate over which Koshōken and his party were soon to pass. Sugae preceded the group again in Aomori, where he saw boats being prepared and inns being cleaned in anticipation of the group's arrival.[59] Another account written by a local official in a small village in the northeast in the early nineteenth century gives an idea of the kind of preparation and commotion caused by the arrival of official inspectors. It describes how the villagers anxiously awaited the anticipated hour of the inspection party's arrival, having set up a sentry system to keep on the lookout for them. It goes on to recount in detail the arrival of the party, the interactions between the two sides, the clothing of the village representatives, the food prepared for the officials, and the preparation of their lodgings.[60] Such accounts suggest that members of an official delegation had virtually no chance of visiting a village unnoticed.

As a quasi-official observer at a time when defense of the northern boundaries was becoming a serious political issue, Furukawa Koshōken had everything to gain from his display of knowledge and erudition. For him, the uses of cultural difference were clear: by expressing the opinion in his writings that the Ainu were distinct from the Japanese, he could establish a clear boundary between this peripheral group and the core population. And in the "logic of difference" that governed Tokugawa political, social, and spatial relations, designating the Ainu as different meant relegating them to a separate and inherently inferior place in the status hierarchy. In Koshōken's case travel writing had two uses: it was a way for Koshōken to establish his "expert" status as a writer, and it provided a rationale for shogunal authority in the northern borderlands. Indeed, travel writing garnered significant rewards for Koshōken. His expertise and experience would eventually gain him samurai status and official appointments as well as a significant readership for his writings. In the context of the diplomatic crises over the northern territories in the 1780s, his skills in mapping, used here in the broadest sense, were highly valued by bakufu officials. By contrast, Koshōken's ambivalence about the Chinese and Dutch in Nagasaki perhaps reflects the relatively stable nature of Japanese trade and diplomatic relations with those countries. Since there was less at stake in Japanese-Chinese or Japanese-Dutch relations than there was in Japanese-Ainu relations in the late eighteenth century, for scholars like Koshōken there was comparatively less to gain from cultivating new knowledge and expertise about China and Holland.

Official approbation was not the only route to success for travel writers, however. Like Furukawa Koshōken, Tachibana Nankei embarked on long journeys throughout eastern and western Japan. Unlike Koshōken, however, Nankei gained notoriety not through his insights into contemporary politics, but through the accessibility of his writings on the strange and fascinating things he discovered about Japanese and foreign cultures. In Nankei's case, travel writing led not so much to political gain, but to popular acclaim.

"LYRICAL" JOURNEYS TO EAST AND WEST

Nagakubo Sekisui's construction of "famous" and "foreign" places in a descriptive yet literary mode and Furukawa Koshōken's self-proclaimed expert perspective on local cultures form compelling contrasts to the physician Tachibana Nankei's sometimes ethereal musings on the meanings of place and experience. Nankei wrote two long travel accounts, Saiyūki (Lyrical record of a journey to the west) and Tōyūki (Lyrical record of a journey to the east), both of which were published to great acclaim in 1795.[61] Born in 1753 in Ise province, Nankei, unlike either Sekisui or Koshōken, was of the samurai class.[62] At age nineteen he went to Kyoto to study medicine, and he eventually settled there. At the age of thirty, accompanied by one of his students, he left on a long journey to the western provinces. He departed in the fourth month of 1782, and he returned in the summer of the next year. His trip to the east began two years later, in the ninth month of 1785; he returned once more to Kyoto in the summer of the following year. His travel accounts were both published in 1795, the Saiyūki in the third month followed by the Tōyūki in the eighth month. The latter contained illustrations by a number of well-known artists, most prominent among them Maruyama Ōzui, disciple of Maruyama Ōkyo and head of the Maruyama school at that time.[63] Both texts sold well after their publication and continued to be reprinted into the early nineteenth century. In 1786, Nankei was appointed to the corps of imperial physicians, and he was invited to the investiture ceremony of Emperor Kōkaku in 1787. He was called to official service in 1796, and thereafter took priestly vows. He continued his study of medicine and wrote sequels to the Tōyūki and Saiyūki, which he published in 1796 and 1797, respectively.[64]

In the preface to *Saiyūki,* Nankei offers the following reason for undertaking his lengthy journeys:

> The main reason for my traveling about in the four directions is to observe the topography and climate of all the provinces, and then to chronicle this as accurately as possible in medical texts, so as to benefit sick people everywhere. Also, in traveling about, I want to become aware of strange illnesses, and to learn interesting remedies, and [in this way] my travels will be of not inconsiderable medical benefit. Therefore, more than [being concerned with] literary matters or military-political matters, I am interested in looking at people as my textbook from which to learn; meeting the common people myself will form the core of my thought and consideration.[65]

In drawing a distinction between himself and others—such as Sekisui and Koshōken—who are concerned with "literary" or "military-political matters," he creates a niche for his own style of observation and writing. Individual inclination led him to eschew structuring his narrative according to the succession of places on his travel itinerary, as most other writers did. Instead he organizes his accounts in a thematic way. As he claims in this preface, Nankei offers his readers a primer of folk beliefs and "interesting" stories. And although he does not state it in so many words, he also writes with a tone of quizzical surprise, and he celebrates, sometimes to the detriment of fact, the "odd" *(mezurashii)* phenomenon and the "unbelievable" *(shinjigatai)* tale.[66] If Nankei did in fact write with the intent to publish, this intention perhaps explains the embellished language of his account and its tendency to focus on the arresting detail.

Nankei's inclination to exoticize is evident in his entries on the northeast and the southwest; in these cases his writings can be compared to those of Furukawa Koshōken, who visited and commented upon many of the same places. Both writers, for example, make note of the Ezo *kosabue,* a type of flute made out of rolled tree bark. Whereas Koshōken simply sketches the flute, notes its dimensions and the materials from which it is made, and then quotes "an old poem" by Saigyō referring to the *kosabue,*[67] Nankei devotes a long passage to it. He explains that the poem (which he mistakenly attributes to Fujiwara no Tameie) was inspired by the belief that "Ezo people possess a variety of magical skills. Among these is [the ability] to exhale from the mouth a sort of mist, such that when they meet with an enemy, or encounter some wild beast, they can conceal themselves, and [thus] escape harm. This is called '*kosabuki.*'"[68] He goes on to give "another explanation" of the *kosabue,* which is more or less the same as Koshōken's, but leaves it off abruptly to move on to the "strange" and interesting phenomenon of sandstorms in the windy northeast.[69]

Nankei's impressions of Nagasaki also illustrate his tendency to take unusual objects or phenomena and use them as the basis for expansive ruminations or elaborate theories. In one of his entries, entitled "Curious Goods" (kiki), he offers a list of objects of Dutch provenance that he finds worthy of comment. The list includes the erekiteru (an electricity-generating box), a mushimegane (an early microscope), a zongurasu (from the Dutch zonneglas, a type of telescope for celestial observation), a tonarimegane (a type of periscope), and other types of glasses for seeing into the distance and for seeing at night. Nankei is quite taken with these various types of glasses; in fact, the very idea of being able to observe previously unknown and invisible worlds leads him to remark:

> This mushimegane is like the eye of the Buddha [hotoke no tengan]. No one would believe that a variety of living things can exist in one drop of water, but now that one can see it, there is no doubt. Furthermore, we can't know what types of tiny things live in the minuscule world this looking glass cannot penetrate. If one were able [to see that far], there would be so many infinitely minute things. If you push this reasoning further, there should also be limitlessly larger things. So this world inhabited by man would be like one drop of water; other worlds would be several million times larger, and from those worlds who is to say there isn't someone with a mushimegane looking [at us]? But with the instruments the foreigners have made, we can gain knowledge from the heavens. It must be said that this is truly interesting.[70]

In contrast to Furukawa Koshōken's tendency to equate material culture with economic well-being, for Nankei the foreigners' unusual objects do not simply indicate the wealth and power of the Europeans. Rather, the objects are keys to unlocking a different and previously unknown intellectual universe. The power of these "curious goods" is also evident in Nankei's reactions upon viewing a map of the world (bankoku no zu) brought by the Dutch. Although he later claims (in Tōyūki) to be well versed in the art of surveying, and in the calculation of latitude and longitude, he notes in this earlier entry in Saiyūki that "[this map] has much more detail about the world than maps published here. Its depictions of Japan and other places are extremely detailed. How they make such maps is unclear."[71] Given that world maps had been published for more than a century by the time Nankei wrote, and that new and more sophisticated world maps were being made by his time, this remark seems somewhat disingenuous, and calculated again to emphasize the extraordinary and the exotic.

In Nagasaki, Nankei also encounters the foreign residents themselves, including members of the Dutch legation and its head, Isaac
Titsingh, as well as Chinese merchants. He notes that the Dutch are the
most accomplished of world travelers, and that their contact with all the
world's people leads them to be unafraid of the Japanese. Of the Chinese, he notes, "of all the foreign people I've encountered, the Chinese
[Tōjin] differ from people here only in dress and language. Their character and habits differ only slightly from those of Japanese. If you
dressed them in our style, corrected their language, and sent them out
into our country, no one would know [they were not Japanese]." [72]

His statement stands in some contrast to Koshōken's description,
which emphasized the observable differences between the Chinese and
the Japanese, and Sekisui's depiction, which emphasized cultural connections while stressing practical differences in dress and custom.
Nankei's attitude toward the Chinese is perhaps due less to direct observation than to a theory—a sort of climatic determinism—he professes in his writings that relates cultural characteristics to climate. By
this logic, since the Chinese inhabit a neighboring *geographical* area,
they occupy the same *cultural* category as the Japanese. Since climate de-
termines the variety of plant and animal life, Nankei reasons, people
from similar climates (within, he notes, the same latitude ranges) have
similar personalities, while those from vastly different environments differ greatly in character. He explains:

> Although there are several million *ri* in distance separating east and west,
> if there is not a difference in cold and warmth, many and varied things will
> grow similarly. Between north and south, if over four or five hundred *ri,*
> or a thousand *ri,* separate [places] the climate is vastly different, the sun
> and shadow, the level of humidity, all will be different, and many and var-
> ied things will, in this way, be different; one can see that people's character
> also, according to this, will differ. Within Japan, which encompasses one
> or two hundred *ri* in difference, the northern and southern provinces have
> different vegetation, and people are also different in temperament. [73]

He goes on to explain that the Dutch live in a cold, northern country;
thus they tend to be distant and reserved in personality: "they are seen
by Japanese to be rather lukewarm." [74] Nankei also applies this reason-
ing to the Ryūkyūans, whom he encounters in Kyushu, noting that they
are "too warm" in personality to pass for natives, although they resemble the Japanese physically. [75]

In theory, Nankei's ideas about cultural difference acknowledge that
even within a relatively small country like Japan, the climatic (and hence

cultural) differences are substantial. But, more often than not, Nankei's observations about his fellow Japanese diverge from his climate-based methodology, and he utilizes more conventional indicators of culture to judge his countrymen. For instance, like Furukawa Koshōken, Nankei judges the degree of culture and civility of a given place by the speech and literacy of the local people, and he finds that these differ substantially by region. He praises the spread of learning in western Japan, describing how schools have proliferated as the various domains established their own schools and academies. The appreciation of the value of learning has also spread, according to Nankei, for wealthy local families are vying to outdo each other in funding the construction of school buildings. The philosophical foundation of these new schools was, of course, Confucian (he notes the role of Kumazawa Banzan in establishing a school in Bizen), but Nankei states that the teaching of practical knowledge is also important: "for the first time, things that are useful in the world are being [taught]." [76] He later adds,

> As I have traveled through the various provinces, people not only have a fondness for learning, but wherever I go [the inhabitants], from lords and officials to poor fishermen and woodcutters, treat me politely, and I have been able to wander with ease. This is the result of a transformation toward learned culture *[bun-un no ka]*, and this virtue is extended even to the likes of myself. Isn't this truly something to be thankful for? [77]

The situation is quite different, however, in the northeast. While he claims to eschew explicitly political statements, Nankei not only stresses the alterity and thus the inferiority of the Ainu, but also strongly suggests the desirability of incorporating Ezo more fully into the Japanese cultural sphere. He writes, "The island of Ezo is not yet endowed with learning. [People here] do things only simply, as in the China and Japan of ancient times." [78] He reports that Ezo people have no precious metals, no money economy, no elaborate clothing, and no organized religion. [79] The few cultural or economic attainments Ezo people have shown, according to Nankei, are due to trade and exchange with the core population of Japan. [80] About the relations between the two sides and the level of "civilization" attained by various populations in the far northeastern part of Honshu, he writes:

> Even now, in the area around Uteshi, the customs are quite like Ezo in type, and Tsugaru people, too, are contemptibly referred to as "seeds of Ezo." [81] To my way of thinking, it's not only the area around Uteshi, but in the southern area, and in the villages around Tsugaru, too, that the majority of the people should be "seeds of Ezo." In areas that were more quickly

incorporated into the realm [further inland], customs and language were reformed, and from the time of their ancestors, people thought to make themselves into the likes of Japanese. Therefore, [those] people long ago learned polite behavior and civilization [reigi bun-ka].[82]

The unambiguous distinction between the "seeds of Ezo" and the more thoroughly assimilated northeasterners is striking, and far more forceful than the "noble savage" characterization put forth by the otherwise opinionated Furukawa Koshōken. Nankei elaborates upon the theme of cultural transmission from Japan to Ezo when he presents examples of two extraordinary texts, the "Illiterate's Calendar" and the "Illiterate's Sutra." These fascinating texts, known generically as mōreki (literally, "blind calendars"), have a long history in northeastern Honshu. Both utilize a symbol language of pictographs in place of characters, and both were originally written to pass on local folklore and customs among people living in the harsh climate of the snowbound far northeast.[83] As Nankei explains, "[there are] places that do not yet know kana syllabary . . . [such as] extremely remote mountain regions around Tayama; they make signs out of clay as in ancient times. At present in Ezo they do not use characters [moji], but have learned to carve signs in wood." [84] These calendars, Nankei claims, were used up to and through the late eighteenth century in some isolated regions of the northeast.

While learning seems to be the standard by which Nankei judges the level of a civilization, there are instances in which he does not consider learned culture the only defining characteristic of an exemplary society. Nankei reports on isolated populations in the province of Satsuma in southern Kyushu, where he finds people extremely "simple" (shippoku, or soshitsu), their habits and lifestyles uncorrupted by the ways of their more urbane contemporaries. Much in the way that Ezo symbolizes an idealized state of nature for Koshōken, so Satsuma is for Nankei an example of a pure and unsullied community, whose upright character (or "giretsu," the title of the chapter describing this area) is not to be found elsewhere in Japan. Because Satsuma is "way out on the frontier" (goku henkyō naru yue ni), and since the domain guards its borders and its independence strictly, travelers and merchants are few. Here, more than anywhere else in his travels, Nankei describes himself as a "foreigner in these parts" (marōdo), and a "person from the capital" to whom the simple, unadorned life of the provinces seems governed by basic codes of morality, whose tenets have been much diluted in the rest of the country.[85] In other chapters, he links the simple lifestyle of the people in the country to the health and longevity he perceives to be more widespread among rural populations. Unrefined foods and uncomplicated lives, he reasons, lead to greater health and spiritual well-being.[86] As a person from Kyoto, Nankei is in many ways engaging in self-criticism when praising "simple" things. At the same time, the security of his own status, a status linked to sophistication and erudition, and of his perspective as a person from the capital allows him to make rhetorical use of the "unrefined" periphery.

Nankei's commentary suggests that the divide between civilization and barbarity lay not only in literacy but in some ineffable quality linked to comportment, demeanor, and morality; both conditions, however, seem to be intimately linked to place. The people of western Japan are blessed with culture even when they are illiterate, whereas the people of Ezo are illiterate and therefore uncivilized. This logic exemplifies what Nankei describes as "the extraordinary difference in civilization [bun-ka] between the western part of the country and the eastern part." [87] He concludes by stating that, "at any rate, one can see that Japan expanded from the west [to the east]." [88] Aside from reflecting long-standing cultural and regional biases not uncommon in educated people from Kyoto and its environs, these statements have clear political implications. For while Nankei seems to prefer that the "simple" people of Satsuma remain in their curio-like state, a reminder of the goodness of the past in the decadent present, the people of Ezo are prime prospects for the civilizing process. They are not "yet" as acculturated as some of their provincial brethren, but it seems only a matter of time until the Ezo natives, like the Ryūkyūans, become subjects of the Japanese state. From his theories linking climate and personality to his discourse on the microscope's relativizing power, Nankei is interested in the effects of the physical and social environment on culture, but he is also, in practice, constructing and disseminating cultural ideals of his own. Far out on the periphery though Satsuma may be, it remains unambiguously part of Japan. Its rural residents thus can be accommodated as a curiosity, but truly marginal people such as those in Ezo, at least in the crisis period of the late eighteenth century, are in need of thoroughgoing reform before they can be admitted to the "inside." From this perspective, Nankei's texts, despite their whimsical tone and supposed lack of interest in "military and political matters," cannot be separated from the cultural and political worlds of which they were a part; indeed, they are a sharp commentary on their own times. Although Tachibana Nankei did not aspire to official advisory roles in the way that Furukawa Koshōken did, his writings articulate ideals of civilization that were politically relevant and culturally defining. They do so, moreover, in a style that was attractive to the reading public and, as a result, their impact on the general climate of opinion may have been greater in the long run. The *Tōyūki* and *Saiyūki* exemplify how even a "lyrical" account of a journey can become a process of structuring political and social relations and, ultimately, of encouraging the practices of domination.

GEOGRAPHIC KNOWLEDGE AND CULTURAL DIFFERENCE

The travel writers discussed in this chapter observed a great deal of the world around them, a world in which change was real, immediate, and challenging. For individuals such as these, expertise in matters geographical and cultural could be put to good use, in both the public and private realms. Certainly gathering, synthesizing, and publishing information about Japan, its people, and its topography contributed to the general process of acquisition and systematization of knowledge. But for men like Nagakubo Sekisui, Furukawa Koshōken, and Tachibana Nankei, the boundary between public good and personal gain became very faint, for by the late eighteenth century, travel writing offered the opportunity for these educated, innovative, and curious individuals to fashion themselves as writers for a public audience, attracting renown and patronage. As published travel accounts proliferated in number, in order for any single account to stand out it had to have some distinguishing characteristic, some selling point that its publisher could highlight as uniquely important or interesting. When Nagakubo Sekisui's 1767 diary of his journey to Nagasaki, *Nagasaki kōeki nikki*, was republished in 1804, in the preface his publisher made a point of emphasizing that Sekisui's diary was an up-close, "realistic" chronicle of direct encounters with the strange customs of foreigners. While other travel writers needlessly embellished their texts with exaggeratedly dramatic detail, the publisher declares, "[Sekisui] unites travel and history. He states things as they are and refrains from adornment." [89] Tachibana Nankei's accounts of his travels throughout Japan became tremendously popular after their publication in 1795, not so much because they accurately described the local topography, but because they played up the unusual aspects of local culture and folklore and provided readers a window onto heretofore undiscovered places and peoples. The reception of Nankei's account suggests that travel writing had evolved into both a literary and scholarly genre and a diversified marketing niche.

Working within the structures of travel writing, Sekisui, Koshōken, and Nankei employed their erudition to give meaning to the unfamiliar landscapes through which they passed. And though none of them went quite so far as Ogyū Sorai, who refashioned his observations after the fact to better fit his intellectual outlook, neither could they avoid the inevitable editing process that occurs as a function of representing the observed world.[90] For them, the observed world itself was the whetstone against which notions of "culture," "civilization," and Japaneseness were sharpened. As Hayden White has put it, "if we do not know what we think 'civilization' *is*, we can always find an example of what it is not."[91] Indeed, in these writers' shared vocabulary, distance from the "center" was gauged in terms that were rooted in the geographical and the material, but slid steadily toward the cultural. The language of judgment inherent in expressions connoting rusticity and cultivation, inside and outside, poverty and wealth, was woven into standards of normality, strangeness, and intelligibility.[92] Although the "others" observed by travel writers on journeys within Japan were "real" people with distinct characteristics, they took on vastly different symbolic meanings and uses when represented in (and as) text, for as the object of scholarly attention and expert analysis and reportage, local—indeed Japanese culture as a whole—became objectified in travel writing. The publication of travel accounts exacerbated this process, as texts describing Japan's "others within" competed with one other for prominence in the publishing marketplace of the late eighteenth century. More critically, travel writing itself diffused the power to define the "other" in many directions. As it did so it simultaneously expanded and diluted the "civilizing process."[93] In this manner, the increase in travel writing chronicled the process by which Japan's actual and metaphorical boundaries were contested and reconstituted, but *not* firmly and unambiguously established, in the mid- to late Edo period. These texts document the negotiation, if not the determination, of external, political boundaries that divided Japan from the rest of the world, as well as the amorphous internal, cultural boundaries that structured the relationship between status and power, self and identity, description and representation.

Early modern travel writers also negotiated new forms of subjectivity. Literary critics have addressed this issue at length, and they universally place the emergence of modern subjectivity in the Meiji period. Karatani Kōjin has argued that the late nineteenth-century "discovery of landscape" *(fūkei no hakken)* was an integral part of the "discovery of interiority" *(naimen no hakken)*, both of which in turn were necessary for the emergence of modern consciousness and thus for the development of "modern literature" *(kindai bungaku)* itself.[94] In positing the discovery of landscape as a natural extension of the modern self, Karatani differentiates between the uses of landscape in Edo-period literature on the one hand, and in modern (late Meiji) literature on the other. In the former, he argues, a "transcendental" concept of place held sway, one in which a painter depicting a pine grove "meant to depict the concept (that which is signified by) 'pine grove,' not an existing pine grove." In the latter case, the modern writer, by contrast, overturns the transcendental vision of landscape and comes to see the pine grove as part of a (preexisting) natural world, of which he himself is a conscious part.[95] Nature is thus subsumed by culture in the totalizing manner characteristic of modernity.

This chapter suggests some revisions to this view of the relationship between subjectivity and landscape. First, because he focuses his discussion on "literature," Karatani refers primarily to the canonical works of fiction from the Tokugawa and Meiji periods. Although he is interested in the practices of ethnology and ethnography as they developed in the modern period, particularly as they were defined by the renowned early-twentieth-century anthropologist Yanagita Kunio, he touches only very briefly on the subject (and not the texts) of travel writing.[96] What we have seen in the foregoing discussion of early modern travel writing, however, are representations of place that are neither solely "transcendental" nor wholly acculturated. They are not solely literary nor are they merely descriptive. They evince their authors' ambivalence about whether human perception shapes the landscape, or vice versa. They also document differing notions of cultural difference and similitude, thus confounding any linear narratives about the origins of Japaneseness.[97] In this way, the landscapes discovered in eighteenth-century travel writing are not, strictly speaking, modern or classical; neither can they be described as purely ethnographic or literary. They are distinctly early modern "process geographies," wherein the shifting subjectivity of the writer provides the lens through which the reader views and assesses familiar and foreign terrain.

By the end of the eighteenth century, even as travel had become increasingly common, the travel account continued to emphasize discovery, strangeness, and difference. The publication of travel accounts familiarized readers with the genre itself as well as with the characteristics of the foreign and the culturally different places and people described therein. The following two chapters discuss the development of popular parodies of the archetypal travel account in mid- to late-eighteenth-century fiction, for fiction writers took on the increasingly familiar theme of the journey and the structure of the travel account and radically exploited both. Relieved of the burden of factuality, mid-eighteenth- to early nineteenth-century fiction writers deployed satire and parody to create in their written works fantastic "other" worlds whose most "outlandish" characteristics ended up being remarkably similar to those of the Japanese.

CHAPTER 4

Imagining Japan, Inventing the World

Foreign Knowledge and Fictional Journeys in the Eighteenth Century

As the works and lives of Kaibara Ekiken, Furukawa Koshōken, Tachibana Nankei, and others have shown, early modern travelers mapped Japanese culture as well as its topography in their desire to witness, analyze, and catalog difference. Despite their different intellectual inclinations and narrative strategies, they took their study of Japan, its land, and its culture, and most of all their own roles as its interpreters, seriously. But not all early modern accounts of journeys were similarly sober; in fact, many were fundamentally playful. Funny, ribald, and decidedly frivolous, tall tales of journeys both domestic and foreign became frequently used conventions in comic fiction of the mid-eighteenth to early nineteenth centuries. The present chapter discusses how fiction writers built on the foundation of published information about foreign lands and people in order to journey abroad using the vehicle of the imagination. In doing so, they ventured quite far afield from the orderly worlds laid out in maps and travel writing.

The fictionalization of the travel account appealed greatly to both writers and readers. From its inception comic fiction, referred to then as now by the omnibus term *gesaku,* was written for an audience consisting primarily of educated urban commoners.[1] Although its earliest authors tended to be educated men of the samurai class, by the late eighteenth century, many writers were themselves commoners. By this time, many commoners had traveled themselves, and the wealthier among them had access to the printed maps, travel guides, and travel accounts that proliferated due to the growth of the publishing industry, familiarizing them with the various forms of mapping and their narrative or representational tropes. The topics and the vernacular language of *gesaku* both enshrined and parodied the lifestyles of those who, regardless of class, aspired to be up-to-date in their knowledge and stylish in their comportment. For the *gesaku* writer whose stock-in-trade was the recasting of a well-known story or scene in a new way, with elaborate plot twists and clever puns and double entendres, the journey provided an ideal setting for the reinvention and the critique of reigning geographic, cultural and, ultimately, political conventions.

As common as the experience of travel within Japan had become by the eighteenth century, however, there was one type of trip very few early modern Japanese could claim to have taken. This, of course, was the journey abroad, to foreign countries well beyond the boundaries of the archipelago. Because international travel was forbidden by government decree beginning in the early seventeenth century, the only way that Japanese could experience foreign travel was by means of the imagination. Fiction thus became one of the main conduits for the experience of other worlds, as authors composed fantastic tales of far-flung lands and foreign peoples. Based in part on information gleaned from contemporary encyclopedias, maps, and other descriptive sources, these fictive foreign journeys had a loose basis in fact. But over and above any informative function they may have possessed, these texts were read as entertainment and, in their satirical dimension, as social commentary.

This chapter will focus on one of the earliest works of fiction that extensively engaged the theme of the foreign journey: Hiraga Gennai's *Fūryū Shidōken den* (The tale of dashing Shidōken), published in 1763. Gennai's text reconstructed and reshaped its source materials in novel ways, and it inspired a spate of imitations and sequels over the next half century. It ingeniously uses "foreignness"—in the form of alien landscapes and unknown peoples—as a foil to comment on and obliquely criticize Japanese social and political norms. In this roundabout manner, imaginary foreign journeys became a way to uncover the hidden character—the illicit, exotic, and sometimes unpleasant characteristics—of the homeland itself. Unlike travel writers who chronicled actual journeys taken within Japan, fiction writers did not see the travel account as a way to make sense of the observed world. Instead they saw in the imaginary foreign journey an opportunity to make the familiar strange—and in so doing to render it open for exploration and imaginative remappings.

ENCYCLOPEDIAS AND THE CRAFTING
OF THE GEOGRAPHIC IMAGINARY

Although fiction writers had a very different agenda from nonfiction writers, understanding the world outside Japan was never a simple matter in the Tokugawa period. Like the mapping and cataloging of the Japanese archipelago, foreign relations and knowledge of foreign countries were serious matters for both the government and the people. Authors of comic fiction lived in an intellectual world in which certain tacit and longstanding assumptions about Japan's relations with other countries were widely held. In creating their fictions, writers worked both with and against the grain of received knowledge about the rest of the world.

Thanks to a generation of scholarship in Japanese and in Western languages, it is now widely understood that early modern Japan was not a "closed" country; the system set up by the Tokugawa sought not to eradicate contact with foreign countries, but to regulate and routinize it. The so-called expulsion edicts banning contact with Spain and Portugal and their proselytizing Catholic missionaries in the 1630s were only a partial solution to the foreign relations problem. Trade with Holland, China, Korea, the Ryūkyūs, and, through China, with various countries in southeast Asia was of great importance in maintaining economic and political stability, and was consistently pursued and cultivated throughout the Tokugawa period. Knowledge about Asia, Europe, and the Americas trickled in through these select trading partners. This knowledge was, in turn, disseminated through intellectual networks within Japan to the extent that by the early eighteenth century, managing, defining, and describing the foreign in its various manifestations had become a serious preoccupation for a growing circle of scholars and writers.

The most pressing political and intellectual dilemma facing both the Tokugawa government and those interested in foreign studies was how to devise a new hierarchy of relationships between Japan and other countries in the region, particularly China. In late medieval times, under the rule of the Ashikaga shoguns, Japan had assumed for a time the status of a satellite state within the "Chinese world order." By the Tokugawa period, however, this situation had become wholly unpalatable. The attempt to establish a new diplomatic order in the eighteenth century was spurred on in great part by the shogunate's efforts to make Japan, rather than the "Middle Kingdom," the central power in Asia.

Growing out of the ideas of official shogunal advisers such as Hayashi
Razan (1583–1657) in the early seventeenth century and Arai Hakuseki
a hundred years later, political philosophy and diplomatic practice
slowly converged in a new Japan-centered worldview.[2] Centrality, as
Tokugawa rulers and their counselors reformulated it, was no longer
solely geopolitical (China being the largest and historically most powerful state in the East Asian region), nor strictly philosophical (China
alone possessed the mandate of heaven); instead, centrality operated on
a more abstract level. After the fall of the Ming and the establishment of
the Qing empire in 1644, Japanese thinkers began to develop the idea
that "barbarians"—the Manchus from the northeast—had overrun
China. The comments of Nagakubo Sekisui upon meeting the "Qing
guests" in Nagasaki confirm these sentiments—the Han Chinese, the
inheritors of the great traditions of empire, had ceded control to the
Manchu Qing dynasts; surely the mandate sanctifying Chinese civiliza-
tional centrality had been decisively lost. Japanese intellectuals argued
that since Japan, unlike China, had never succumbed to foreign invaders
and continued to receive tribute from states such as Korea and the
Ryūkyūs, it was only logical that Japan should assume the mandate of
heaven so clearly abdicated by China.[3]

The "demotion" of China to the lower rungs of the diplomatic hierarchy was articulated decisively in 1715, when Arai Hakuseki, acting on
Tokugawa Yoshimune's approval, issued new regulations for trading
with the Chinese at Nagasaki.[4] The revised rules required the Chinese to
obey Japanese law when trading in Japan, to acquire licenses similar to
the tallies required by China itself during the heyday of the Ming trading empire, and to communicate only with low-ranking administrators
rather than with shogunal officials.[5] Moreover, rather than referring to
China in diplomatic parlance as the "Great Qing" (Dai Shin) empire, the
Japanese began to use the term for the Tang dynasty (Tō) in generic fashion to refer to all Chinese, and sometimes to all foreigners, in written
discourse.[6] This terminology rapidly entered into popular usage and
indicated that, however subconsciously, the dominant conception of
China was one rooted in the distant past. The Tokugawa leaders thus
not only denied the Qing its political centrality and legitimacy, but implied that China was static, unchanging, and irrelevant to the contemporary world.

Despite the changes in trade policy with China, however, the "demotion" of the Qing and the concurrent "promotion" of Japan occurred for
the most part at the rhetorical level. In practice, China remained a val-

ued trading partner and ally, and eighteenth-century Japanese intellectuals remained deeply influenced by Chinese classical philosophy. In this
period, however, those interested in foreign matters were also influenced
by texts in a more descriptive vein, such as encyclopedias and gazetteers.
The latter were collections of geographical and political information on
the various regions and localities in China. The former included compendia such as the *San cai tu hui* (Illustrated encyclopedia of the three
elements, 1607), a comprehensive treatise on the "three elements" constituted by heaven, earth, and man. Assembled in its multiple volumes
was information on physical geography, astronomy, astrology, political
structure, folklore, and culture.[7] Equally influential was the *Shanhai jing*
(Classic of the mountains and seas, ca. early second century B.C.E.), an
early geographical and cosmographical encyclopedia that articulated
the principle of the "nine divisions," into which the heavens, earth, and
land of China were all divided.

Encyclopedic treatises on geography and cosmology such as these
were representative of the Chinese classificatory system of knowledge,
and they influenced both the form and the content of early modern
Japanese texts on these subjects. In 1720 the eighth Tokugawa shogun,
Yoshimune, surveyed the bakufu archival holdings in natural history for
the first time and found the collection lacking in Chinese gazetteers and
geographical writings. Within two decades, focused collecting increased
their number significantly.[8] These gazetteers constituted important models and sources for subsequent Japanese writings on foreign culture and
geography. At the same time, Yoshimune began to relax the strict regulations governing the importation of Western books. In a famous direc-
tive of 1720, he allowed non-Christian Western texts to be brought into
the country, and in the subsequent decades texts on medicine, botany,
geography, and other sciences entered Japan freely. From treatises on
anatomy to Johann Blau's atlases, these texts added to the fund of geographic and cultural knowledge about the outside world, and, under the
rubric of *rangaku* (Dutch, or Western studies), led to new ways of con-
ceiving of and representing the world at home and abroad.[9]

As influential as the Western texts were on the concepts and practices of science, especially medicine, Chinese-style encyclopedias, on the
whole, perhaps more directly affected the representation of foreigners
and the foreign in the eighteenth century. Texts like the *San cai tu hui*
and *Shanhai jing* were models for eighteenth-century Japanese encyclopedic texts such as Nishikawa Jōken's *Ka'i tsūshō kō* (Thoughts on trade
and communication with the civilized and the barbaric, 1695, revised

1709), and Terajima Ryōan's *Wakan sansai zue* (The illustrated Japanese-Chinese encyclopedia of the three elements, 1712).[10] Both were compilations of text and illustrations describing the location, customs, and products of various foreign countries, and both attempted to arrange this knowledge within one overarching epistemological system inherited from the Chinese. Both fundamentally shaped the work of later Japanese writers and illustrators—including authors of satirical fiction—who depicted foreign countries and peoples.

In *Ka'i tsūshō kō,* first published in two volumes in 1695, then revised and reissued in five volumes in 1709, Nishikawa groups countries by their degree of "foreignness" vis-à-vis Japan, a status directly linked to trade relations. First and most extensively covered is China. Illustrations accompany short gazetteer-like descriptions of local conditions in each of the "fifteen provinces."[11] These include information on population and local products, and details about shipbuilding and the staffing of ships. This section also contains maps of the world and of China, drawings of Ming and Qing Chinese nobles, and diagrams of Chinese ships. Next come similar descriptions of the *gaikoku,* or "outside countries," which, as Nishikawa explained, are outside the boundaries of China proper, but within the sphere of Chinese influence. The *gaikoku* are subjects of the Chinese empire, use Chinese language, and practice the "three teachings" of Buddhism, Confucianism, and Taoism. This category consists of Korea, the Ryūkyūs, Taiwan, Tonkin,[12] and Cochin.[13] After the *gaikoku* come the *gai'i,* or "outside foreigners," countries that for the most part engaged in trade with China but were outside the Chinese imperial system and did not speak the Chinese language. These include Champa,[14] Cambodia, Tani,[15] Rokkon,[16] Siam, Malacca,[17] Jakarta, Java, Bantan,[18] Mogul,[19] and Holland. After Holland follows a list of thirty-one countries, trading partners of Holland, also classified as *gai'i.* These include, in no discernible order, countries such as Norway, Bengal, Ceylon, Spain, Turkey, and Persia. This in turn is followed by a catalog of sea animals, and finally an additional list of thirty-six more *gai'i* countries. The latter puts Mongolia, Arabia, Ireland, and Egypt in the same category as Amazonia ("the country of warrior women," as the text informs its readers) and the Land of Dwarves.[20]

Some of these lands were what we would now label "fantastic" or "imaginary," while others were actual countries, albeit ones that had never been seen by any Japanese. Still others were countries with which Japanese had occasional or regular contact. In the organizational scheme of *Kai'i tsūshō kō,* foreign countries form a series of concentric circles radiating out from China, and by extension Japan.[21] As a resident of Nagasaki, Nishikawa Jōken had ample opportunity to observe foreigners, their customs, and the volume and nature of international trade. When he revised *Ka'i tsūshō kō* in 1790, he explained in the preface that the emendation came at "the behest of the publisher," adding that the revised edition was a vast improvement on its predecessor.[22] The demand for a revision seems to indicate that the work met with some interest upon its first appearance; Nishikawa also notes in the same preface that he has added illustrations of foreign ships and of the foreigners who come frequently to Nagasaki, and that all readings for place names have been rendered in Japanese phonetic pronunciation of the Chinese, to make them more accessible to the reader.[23]

After the appearance of *Ka'i tsūshō kō* other encyclopedic texts soon followed. Among them was the *Wakan sansai zue,* whose editor and compiler, Terajima Ryōan, began to publish the compendious work in 1712. Over a period of thirty years it reached more than eighty volumes. Like its model, the Ming encyclopedia *San cai tu hui, Wakan sansai zue* was divided into three principal sections, each dedicated to one of the "three elements" of heaven, man, and earth. The discussion of the heavens comprised the first seven volumes of the encyclopedia. In accordance with the ninefold division inherited from the Chinese classics, it contained diagrams *(zu)* of the "nine layers" of heaven, and the "nine [orbital] routes" of the moon, as well as detailed information on astronomical and climatological phenomena, and explanations of the Chinese calendar.[24] The seventh through the thirty-sixth volumes comprise the section on "humanity" *(jinrin),* under which was grouped a vast amount of information on subjects ranging from social classes and gender relations to customs, folklore, technology, economy, foreign relations and foreign peoples, art, religion, military matters, clothing, toys, and shipbuilding. Within this section, the "foreign peoples" *(gai'i jinbutsu)* section was a particularly important source of information about other cultures.

Like Nishikawa Jōken's text, Terajima's discussion of "foreign peoples" made no categorical distinction between the sort of foreigner who might occasionally have visited Japan in the eighteenth century, and people whose existence was known largely through folklore or hearsay. In this manner, Russia and France, at least in formal terms, occupied the same category as people from the "Land of the Long Legs" or the "Land of the Giants." Unlike *Ka'i tsūshō kō, Wakan sansai zue,* as indicated in its title, modifies a Chinese text to fit Japan. This is evident in its concluding section, a lengthy examination of "the land" *(chi)* that comprises the last fifty volumes. This section contains detailed information on China (divided into fifteen provinces) and Japan (divided into eight circuits, consisting of the Kinai, Tōkaidō, Tōsandō, Hokurikudō, San'indō, Sanyōdō, Nankaidō, and Saikaidō), with additional information on the Ryūkyūs, Ezo, and the far northeast (the regions of Michinoku and Dewa). Also in this section are maps and descriptions of more familiar foreign places such as India and countries in southeast Asia. This section of the *Wakan sansai zue,* instead of discussing foreign countries in terms of their relation to Chinese language, culture, and history, depicts the various countries as connected by the common religious heritage of Buddhism, which ties them to Japan culturally as well as geographically.[25]

The compilers of information-laden encyclopedias like *Ka'i tsūshō kō* and *Wakan sansai zue* sought consistently to make these texts comprehensible to the interested general reader. As we have seen, Nishikawa Jōken tried to edit *Ka'i tsūshō kō* to make it more accessible. And a rare source providing insight into the reading habits of the rural educated class, a diary kept by one Mori Nagaemon, headman of the village Kusaka in the foothills of Mount Ikoma between Osaka and Nara, shows that in the late 1720s Mori purchased an eighty-volume version of *Wakan sansai zue* from a traveling representative of an Osaka bookseller. He then sequestered himself in his house for a fortnight in order to scrutinize it. Mori also makes note of lending books to fellow villagers, and borrowing books from them as well, indicating that despite the fact that they cost significantly more than single-volume texts, encyclopedias like *Wakan sansai zue* may have circulated even in rural areas.[26] If this was in fact the case, such broad familiarity with foreign places and peoples could only have contributed to the considerable interest in fictional works about foreign adventures.

IMAGINARY FOREIGN JOURNEYS
AS ENCYCLOPEDIC FICTIONS

Encyclopedic texts such as the *Ka'i tsūshō kō* and the *Wakan sansai zue* were not only treasure troves of information for interested readers, but also gold mines for writers and artists searching for new ideas they could spin off into fictive tales. Collections of medieval tales *(otogizōshi)* published in the early eighteenth century also fed the imaginations of writers and readers.[27] Together, these texts informed and educated the reading audience by familiarizing them with things foreign. By the mid-eighteenth century the ground was prepared for fiction writers to exploit the geographic imaginations of their readers by using the concept of the foreign to explore the metaphorical boundary between "self" and "other." In doing so, fiction writers in this period created a distinct form of satire. Satire as a literary technique involves juxtaposing characters or settings that stand in direct contrast to one another, and often it involves reversing or inverting their roles. In early modern Japanese satires of foreign lands, writers "deconstructed" the foreign in order to reveal within it the familiar characteristics of "home." The repeated unmasking of the hidden characteristics of a foreign people, language, or topography thus reveals in the foreign a recognizably "Japanese" world, which itself takes on anew an air of exoticism. Fiction writers like Hiraga Gennai and others took the neat geo-cultural categories of the foreign in encyclopedias and travel accounts and turned them every which way, as their protagonists travel through foreign lands and have experiences that profoundly relativize their perspectives on themselves and on Japan.

Satire as a genre also assumes the existence and persistent execution of multiple readings; working through a text's complexity in order to get the joke is the reader's reward. Instead of offering a single definition or description of the "foreign," fiction writers opened up new worlds into which they invited their readers to wander, imagine, explore, and, possibly, to "poach"—to actively gather, rather than passively absorb, meanings and messages.[28] Fictional travel accounts invite such "poaching." They evince a preoccupation with false appearances and hypocrisy; they use mock etymologies and verbal puns; they borrow descriptive conventions from other genres of literature (travel accounts, guidebooks, and encyclopedias). To grasp the humor in such texts, readers cannot be passive; they must make connections, and through those connections, construct meanings. Armed with a certain amount of basic geographical knowledge and with satire as a rhetorical tool, writers like Hiraga Gennai *and* their readers made the "foreign journey" theme a common convention in later Edo fiction.

SATIRE AS SPATIAL DISCOURSE

Celebrated as a polymath in his own time as well as in ours, Hiraga Gennai has been the subject of a fairly constant stream of critical interest since a decade after his controversial death in 1779.[29] Born Shiraishi Kunimune, the son of a low-ranking samurai in Takamatsu domain of

Sanuki province in northern Shikoku, Gennai at the age of twenty-one changed his name to Hiraga in order to suggest he had a more distinguished lineage. [30] Educated in botanical studies, or *honzōgaku,* from the age of twelve, Gennai earned a year's study in Nagasaki in 1752, where he also began to study Western science and oil painting; his interest in art would continue throughout his life. Two years after his stay in Nagasaki, Gennai realized that his scholarly ambitions were too great for him to stay in the provinces, and he formally freed himself from family and domain responsibilities. He handed the family headship over to an adopted cousin, and he requested exemption from the post of supervisor of rice warehouses that he had inherited from his father. Shortly thereafter he left Takamatsu for Edo, where he embarked on various scholarly endeavors, including Confucian studies at the Tokugawa Confucian academy and nativist thought at Kamo Mabuchi's private academy.[31] Never married, and prevented by his domain from accepting official appointment by another domain, Gennai became a true *rōnin,* a samurai with no master and few formal responsibilities.

Despite his many scholarly achievements, or perhaps because of their disparate nature, Gennai appears to have had difficulty finding a role in which he could utilize and benefit from his talents. In addition to his formal studies, he also pursued a remarkably wide variety of projects and experiments, including the manufacture of embossed paper, asbestos, and pottery; the construction of electricity-generating machines (*erekiteru,* which later were commented upon by the travel writer Tachibana Nankei); the raising of sheep for wool; and the mining of ore. His written oeuvre is similarly diverse; in addition to his fiction, most of it written under the pen names Fūrai Sanjin and Tenjiku Rōnin, his works include scholarly tracts on Japanese botany, descriptive travel accounts of journeys within Japan, and essays on various topics. He also made several maps of Japan and the world, which he chose to reproduce on ceramic plates. One map depicts the Japanese archipelago in a form very similar to that in Nagakubo Sekisui's maps of Japan.[32] The wide circle of Gennai's friends, colleagues, and acquaintances constitutes a network of the dominant schools and strains of thought during this period. His largely Edo-based cohort included the Western-studies scholar Sugita Genpaku (1733–1817), the astronomer and official Katsurakawa Hoshū (1751–1809), the writer and Western-studies scholar Morishima Chūryo (1754–1808),[33] the poet and writer Ōta Nanpo (1749–1823), the artist and printmaker Shiba Kōkan (1738–1818), the Chinese-style painter Sō Shiseki (1715–86), and the artist Koikawa Harumachi

(1744–89). Though Gennai preferred an unfettered life, his lack of formal ties to the official bureaucracy invited a considerable sense of insecurity, and perhaps contributed to the fervor with which he engaged in intellectual pursuits that had remunerative potential. For him, writing popular fiction fell uncomfortably between the categories of literary activity and profit making. Nevertheless, he pursued themes in which he thought readers would have an interest, and travel was chief among them.

Understanding how Hiraga Gennai mapped Japan through his narratives of fantastic foreign journeys must rely on close readings of his digressive, pun- and reference-laden tales. *The Tale of Dashing Shidōken* and, indeed, all of Gennai's fictional works have been discussed fairly extensively in the Japanese-language scholarship and are familiar to specialists in Japanese literature and cultural history, but neither *Shidōken* nor Gennai's other works have been widely read in English.[34] For a number of reasons, concision not least among them, I have chosen not to translate the text in its entirety here; instead I will give a brief narrative summary of the tale's plot, followed by a more detailed analysis. The summary functions as a verbal map that gives the "big picture" as well as selected, framed "views" of a text that was, I will argue, a satirical cultural geography of the world and Japan.

HIRAGA GENNAI'S *FŪRYŪ SHIDŌKEN DEN*

The Tale of Dashing Shidōken was published in the eleventh month of 1763 by two Edo booksellers turned publishers, Okamoto Rihei and Honya Matashichi, both of whose establishments were located near Hiraga Gennai's residence in Kanda's Shirakabe-chō. Okamoto Rihei also published Gennai's first work of fiction, *Rootless Grass (Nenashigusa)*, in 1763.[35]

Gennai mined available textual sources like *Wakan sansai zue* and *Ka'i tsūshō kō* for information about foreign places and peoples, and he derived the plot of *Shidōken* in part from previously published works.[36] Nevertheless, the originality of Gennai's story lies in its sharp satirical twist on the nature of foreignness, for in *Shidōken,* as in all good satire, appearances lie. The story opens with the introduction of the protagonist, Shidōken (also known as Fukai Asanoshin), a storyteller *(kōshaku shi)* who recited "bawdy and comic" tales for a public audience.[37] Shidōken, whose actual existence is testified to in a number of accounts of Edo cultural life in the eighteenth century, was a Buddhist priest who

performed near the compound of Asakusa Temple in Edo in the early
eighteenth century. He was quite aged when Gennai wrote about him,
perhaps in his mid-eighties. An account of unusual happenings in Edo
entitled *Tōdai kōtō hyaku bakemono* (One hundred mysterious things
in the capital [of Edo] today) describes him as a "corrupt priest" *(kuse
bōzu)* who chanted tales so fantastic they transported the listener to
other worlds.[38] In Ōta Nanpo's miscellaneous writings, compiled between 1774 and 1822, Shidōken is also described as a storyteller whose
performances were so profane that priests and women fled from them in
horror.[39] Beating out a rhythm with a mushroom-shaped wooden mallet, an instrument of undeniably phallic dimensions that is woven into
Shidōken's fictionalized life story as told by Gennai, he attracts great
crowds for his recitations.

In the beginning of *Shidōken den,* after being introduced to the protagonist in the narrative present, the reader is taken back to the time
of his miraculous birth. Shidōken's father, a samurai of respectable rank,
was still childless at the age of forty. Desirous of an heir, he sequesters
himself and his wife in a temple to pray for a son. The couple are re-
warded by a dream in which a giant golden mushroom (bearing a close
resemblance to Shidōken's phallic mallet) enters the wife's body through
her navel and impregnates her. When the young Shidōken (then known
by the name Asanoshin) is born, the parents dote on him and provide
him with a proper education and schooling in the arts. It is decided that
Asanoshin should enter the priesthood, which he dutifully does.

One spring day while Asanoshin is daydreaming in his study, a
swallow flies into his window and lays an egg on his desk, from which
springs a figure of a woman. The woman is surpassingly beautiful, and
she beckons Asanoshin toward the garden. He follows her to a cave, enters it, and emerges into an idyllic hidden world populated by beautiful
women. Forgetting his Buddhist teachings, which focus on eliminating
desire for people and things, he accepts in quantity the food and drink
offered by the women and soon passes out cold. When he wakes he finds
himself in a forest, and before he can clear his head, a strange figure
dressed in a suit of leaves and a Chinese-style hood appears before him.
This is Fūrai Senjin, an immortal who claims to have been born during
the Genpei War in the late twelfth century.[40] Senjin is in many ways
Hiraga Gennai's alter ego, voicing the author's concerns in digressive,
ranting monologues at the beginning and end of the story. After dis-
coursing at length on the ills of society, Senjin exhorts Asanoshin to
learn the ways of "the common people" *(zokunin)* in order to lead them

to better themselves. But Asanoshin objects that he knows nothing of the ways of the people, having led a sheltered life of religious austerity.[41] To remedy this, Senjin produces a magical feather fan, which gives its bearer the power to change the climate, view the tiniest of objects, and fly unhindered anywhere he wishes. The magic fan will be Asanoshin's passport to other worlds, where he will gain his true education. Senjin further instructs Asanoshin that since human passion is the essence of humanity itself, the common denominator binding all people in all places, he must first acquaint himself with passion and desire. Senjin then disappears, leaving Asanoshin to awaken back in his study, but with the fan on his desk as a souvenir of his strange visit to another world.

While puzzling over the difference between illusion and reality, Asanoshin soon finds that the dream has left him with a new way to view the "real" world—through the feather fan's magical powers. Using the fan, he embarks on a narrative "tour" of famous places in Edo. The fan allows Asanoshin a panoramic spatial and temporal view of the city. Through it, he can see all of the capital's famous sites at once, and he can also observe "the happenings of one year in an instant."[42] Awed by the fan's magical powers, and with his curiosity whetted by Edo's sights, Asanoshin resolves to take Senjin's advice to heart and explore not only Japan, but also China, India, and "all the foreign countries." His goal, as proposed by Senjin, is to make a survey of human desire in all parts of the world.

Asanoshin begins his journey of discovery in Edo, where he ventures out into the real world of pleasure and finds that passion, more than anything else, is the motivating force behind most human activity. Asanoshin is initiated into the arts of desire in the Yoshiwara, the Edo licensed pleasure quarters, where he quickly and enthusiastically embraces a life of indulgence with the women there. Having acquainted himself with the merits of female love in the Yoshiwara, Asanoshin moves on to sample male love *(nanshoku)* in the theater district of Sakai, renowned for its male prostitutes who catered to fans of the all-male kabuki theater.[43] He then proceeds to inhale the "aroma of the foreign" in the Korean tenements,[44] to dally in the cheap, "grimy" pleasure quarters at Ishibashi and Kekurobashi, and to have a look at the *maruta,* lower-class prostitutes whose specialty was dressing up as Buddhist nuns. When he has exhausted Edo's possibilities, Asanoshin heads off down the Tōkaidō, stopping at various inns served by *ojare,* or maid-prostitutes. Gennai cleverly describes these women as "blotchily made up with cheap white face powder, their cheeks rouged with circles so round that if they were presented to [the celebrated archer] Nasu no Yōichi, he would have mistaken them for a target and taken aim."[45] Asanoshin visits in turn the pleasure districts of all the stops along the Tōkaidō, giving special attention to the licensed quarters in Kyoto and Osaka. He then proceeds west toward Kyushu, through Nagasaki and up the Japan Sea coast to the northeast, and finally he arrives on the northernmost island of Ezo.

Asanoshin utilizes this borderland region of Ezo as a point of departure for his travels abroad. The many difficulties of actual overseas travel—navigation and potential shipwreck chief among them—are dispensed with here as Asanoshin simply seats himself on the feather fan and rides aimlessly until he alights in the Land of the Giants (Daijin koku).[46] Here he finds people twenty feet tall, carrying babies who are "bigger than the average Japanese."[47] Translating his words into the Giants' language with the help of the handy feather fan, Asanoshin is warmly welcomed by the local people. But after a few days he finds that his hosts plan to put him on exhibit as a freak in a sideshow (a *mise-mono*, a type of popular entertainment frequently seen in eighteenth-century Edo), and he escapes in haste to the neighboring Land of the Dwarves (Kojin koku).[48] The dwarves range in height from fifteen inches to "the size of a bean," and they seem to have a very orderly society, ruled from a tiny castle town. When Asanoshin by his curiosity inadvertently causes the suicide of a loyal retainer to the dwarf princess, he flees that country in grief.

After departing the Land of the Dwarves, Asanoshin meanders without direction until he comes to a land whose vegetation and topography appear quite different from anything he has seen. This, he soon finds, is the Land of the Long-Legs (Chōkyaku koku),[49] whose inhabitants have average-sized torsos but legs that are four times their body length. The neighboring country is the Land of the Long-Arms (Chōbi koku), with whom the Long-Legs eventually conspire, unsuccessfully, to steal away Asanoshin's magic fan.[50] After foiling the attempted theft, Asanoshin again escapes to a country much farther away, called the Land of the Chest-Holes (Senkyō koku).[51] The rough-mannered inhabitants of this country all have gaping holes in the chest; the poor carry the wealthy on their shoulders, palanquin-style, by means of a bamboo pole threaded through their chest hole. The Chest-Holes are much taken by Asanoshin's refined manners, and it is decided that he should be married to the king's daughter. However, when it is discovered he has the irremediable defect of a holeless chest, it is seen as a shocking deformity and he is banished from the country.[52]

Shamed by his rejection by the Chest-Holes, Asanoshin proceeds without pause to other foreign lands, all of them countries known, if not visited, by the Japanese. His experiences in these "actual" places, however, are not accounted for in any detail. Names of destinations— Mogul, Champa, Sumatra,[53] Borneo,[54] Persia,[55] Moscow,[56] Pegu,[57] Arakan,[58] Armenia,[59] India,[60] and Holland[61]—many of them lifted directly from the *Wakan sansai zue,* are simply reeled off without comment.

Next on Asanoshin's itinerary are countries that were of Gennai's own invention; these receive more detailed commentary in the text. The invented countries all represent types of people prevalent on the eighteenth-century Japanese urban scene with whom Gennai was familiar, but for whom he had little patience. The countries include the Land of Hedonists (Utentsu-koku), the Island of Blusterers (Kyan-jima), the Land of Quack Doctors (Gui-koku), and the Land of Boors (Buza-koku). The portraits Gennai paints of these countries' inhabitants is distinctly unfavorable, and his protagonist Asanoshin exhausts himself in his efforts to engage these obtuse people in meaningful exchange. Frustrated, Asanoshin ventures to Korea to reinvigorate himself on ginseng porridge, and to the Land of the Night (Yakoku), a polar land mass often represented on early modern Japanese maps of the world, where he can sleep through a six-month night.

Asanoshin's final stop on his journey is the one that is, literally and figuratively, closest to home: Qing China during the reign of the emperor Qianlong (r. 1736–95).[62] He finds much to admire in the capital of Beijing, especially the women of the imperial court, upon whom he spies secretly with the help of the powers of invisibility bestowed upon him by the feather fan. He is soon, however, caught intruding by palace officials and is hauled before the emperor himself, who instead of meting out punishment finds Asanoshin's travel tales unexpectedly intriguing. The court is particularly interested in his descriptions of the glory of Mount Fuji. Surely, they argue, Fuji cannot rival their own sacred mountains. This gives Asanoshin the chance to extricate himself from his difficult situation by proposing to construct a papier-mâché Mount Fuji in China, so the court can see for itself how majestic the Japanese mountain is. Claiming he needs to go back to Japan to measure the original Fuji in order to make a proper copy, he coaxes the emperor into preparing 300,000 ships to sail for Japan. Each of these is loaded with paper, paste, craftspeople, and laborers to execute a papier-mâché model of Mount Fuji. The project runs aground, however, when the gods of Fuji, enraged by the thought of a copy being made, send a typhoon to wreck the ships. All the ships except the one bearing Asanoshin are destroyed in a single blow.

Asanoshin's boat drifts on the seas until it reaches the Island of Women (in Japanese called Onna no shima or Nyōgogashima, the island was frequently represented on Japanese maps, including those of Ishikawa Ryūsen discussed in chapter 1). There are no male inhabitants of this place; when women wish to reproduce, they stand facing in the direction of Japan and loosen the sashes of their robes. Subsequently, they conceive and bear female children. The women appear to be overjoyed at having a boatload of men arrive on their shores, and they set up a brothel system on the Yoshiwara model to regulate access to these precious human commodities. The pleasure quarter they build is an exact replica, down to the arrangement of streets and brothels, of Edo's Yoshiwara. The men are installed as courtesans and called *nanrō* or *yūnan*, in imitation of the terms for female courtesans, *jorō* and *yūjo*. All the *yūnan* adopt the mannerisms of female courtesans of the Yoshiwara district, and their female patrons likewise adopt the sometimes coldhearted ways of the male brothel patrons.[63] After a time, however, the strain of such work begins to take its toll on the male courtesans, and soon all the Chinese collapse and die from exhaustion. Only Asanoshin, the lone Japanese, seems blessed with the strength to carry on. But he becomes despondent, at which point the Senjin reappears to counsel him. The Senjin chastises Asanoshin for thinking only of himself and, at the end of a long diatribe produces a mirror that shows Asanoshin that while he has been out cavorting, he has aged into a wrinkled, toothless old man. Shocked, Asanoshin sees a vision of an obscure object descending from the heavens. This turns out to be the mushroom-shaped mallet, which the Senjin tells him is a manifestation of the Asakusa *kannon*, the goddess of mercy who sacrificed herself for him. The Senjin declares that in order to return the *kannon*'s kindness, Asanoshin must return to the Asakusa *kannon* temple in Edo and teach the people, "[leaving] nothing unsaid in giving the people full warning of the miseries of this ephemeral world." [64] The story ends, as most travel accounts do, with the return home, as the reader is returned to the scene of the aged Shidōken, seated outside the temple in Asakusa, beginning to chant a tale to an enraptured audience.

READING *SHIDŌKEN*

There are many ways to read *Fūryū Shidōken den;* one could see it as a parody of encyclopedias, as an early modern *otogizōshi,* or simply as a tall tale. I read it as a convoluted map of the many worlds of Tokugawa Japan. In this looking-glass view, familiar places and people, as well as familiar discursive tropes—the *meisho,* the travel account—are refracted in distorted form. The genius of Gennai's satire is that the distortion is not so great as to render the original forms unrecognizable; they are clearly there, but the reader is forced to look at them from a new perspective.

Finding the Foreign in Familiar Places: Inverting the *Meisho*

For the protagonist of *Shidōken,* the encounter with the foreign begins and ends at home. Asanoshin is reintroduced to Edo after a journey to another world inhabited by the swallow's-egg princess and the Senjin. But to Asanoshin, with his sheltered sensibilities, the Edo he encounters at the outset of his journey is at least as enchanted as the otherworldly realm. In this way, his initiation into the mysteries of the foreign begins with his tour of the capital. With the aid of the feather fan's magical powers, Asanoshin is able to experience all of Edo's famous places in an instant. He uses the fan to "see the tiniest of objects," and he watches in fascination as the events of an entire year unfold before him in an unbroken stream of sights and events. Spring days turn slowly to winter, the rituals of the New Year unfold, and the months roll by, from the airing of winter clothing in the fourth month, to the rains of the fifth month, the fireworks of summer, moon viewing in the ninth month, and so on. Asanoshin can focus in on the places in which these events occur, for they are all within the scope of the fan's magic viewfinder: "when he took out the fan and looked [through it], to the south was Shinagawa, to the north Itabashi, to the west Yotsuya, to the east Senju and beyond; all of it was as if he held it all in the palm of his hand." [65] His words upon viewing Edo in this way, through a magic lens, recall the surprised and delighted reaction of Tachibana Nankei upon looking through a microscope, except in this case the other world is Edo itself. [66]

More important for Asanoshin's education in the ways of the world, however, is his tour of the seamier side of the capital. Instead of visiting the places depicted in published guidebooks and maps of Edo, which

take the reader from Nihonbashi at the city's center to famous sites like
the Asakusa *kannon* temple and the shops of Suruga-chō, Asanoshin
makes a circuit of the city's *infamous* places: its brothels, theaters, teahouses, and other popular entertainment venues. Among the places he
visits, only the licensed quarter of the Yoshiwara could be considered a
"legitimate" *meisho.* The others, by contrast, are *okabasho,* literally the
illicit "other" places forming the hedonistic underside of Edo culture.
Together these places constitute an inverted cultural geography of the
capital.[67] Gennai's description, like guides to the conventional *meisho,*
moves sequentially from neighborhood to neighborhood around the
city, as Asanoshin, according to Senjin's instructions, receives his initiation into the carnal pleasures of the capital.

The tour begins in Edo's most famous site of pleasure: the licensed
quarters of the Yoshiwara. The Yoshiwara is only a stone's throw from
Asanoshin's home, but it is a world away from his experiences. He takes
in the sights, sounds, and customs of the quarters. He strolls Edo-chō,
along which courtesans promenade, and surveys the other streets, lined
with brothels, that make up the Yoshiwara: Sakai-chō, Kyō-machi,
Sumi-chō, Shin-chō. He marvels at what seems to be a world unto itself:

> As he gazed about, paper lanterns waved above the clatter of *geta.* Inside
> the fences (of the brothels), the lanterns burned brighter than daylight, illu-
> minating the sumptuously bedecked courtesans as they sat before tobacco
> trays coolly smoking, or writing letters.[68] Wayward strands of black hair
> lay quaintly against their white collars. . . . Women such as this could not
> be of this world, he thought.[69]

The description of Yoshiwara women as belonging to another world
echoes the description of his brief excursion with the princess born from
the swallow's egg at the beginning of chapter 1 of *Shidōken.* The Yoshiwara (a "real-world" place in Edo) shares mythical and mystical characteristics with the fantasy world to which Asanoshin is led by the
princess. Within the boundaries of Edo, Asanoshin gains his initiation
into this netherworld, as he delves into the life of pleasure with a number of courtesans, "keeping the god of Izumo very busy entering the
running tally of his night's relations into the [temple] register."[70] The
narrator remarks that the manners and procedures of the bedchamber
itself need not be elaborated upon, since these have been gone over in
detail long ago. Here he is perhaps referring to the great seventeenth-
century encyclopedia of pleasure, *Great Mirror of Love (Shikidō ōkagami),* or any one of its many successors.[71] The reference to such texts

lends credence to the Senjin's declaration that pleasure was the main preoccupation of the "common people" Asanoshin is supposed to learn how to lead.

This circuit of Edo's *okabasho* serves a threefold purpose: it allows Gennai to set the scene against which the rest of the world will be compared in coming chapters; it advances the plot, presenting Asanoshin, who knows so little of the "common" world, with knowledge of the capital city as an initiation to the world at large; and it also serves to orient the reader, who may or may not have been familiar with the Edo setting. By placing Edo at the beginning of the narrative in this manner, Gennai suggests that Edo is the center of the map of pleasure and is the standard against which the rest of the world is measured.

Finding the Familiar in Foreign Places: Inverting the Travel Account

As the foreign is found at home, so is the self revealed most clearly in the presence of others. The first thing Asanoshin must do in foreign lands is identify himself in some way to his hosts. This introduction is made to sound quite commonplace: "I am a Japanese person" *(Ware wa Nihon no mono nari),* declares Asanoshin to the Giants. By contrast, in descriptive travel accounts, as we have seen, writers rarely identified themselves so explicitly as "Japanese," utilizing instead relative expressions such as "this side" and the "other side" or, more often, resorting to a kind of sliding scale of difference, according to which distinct markers of culture put a given population closer to or farther from a norm of "civilized" behavior defined by the writer on the basis of his native place. In travel accounts, more often than not physical distance from the writer's place of origin corresponded to cultural distance from the norm of civilization; the farther one was from home, the stranger things and people became.

In the case of the fictional journey, however, foreignness and familiarity take on an inverse relationship. In the fantastically odd world in which Asanoshin finds himself, extreme difference is taken for granted: one expects to find strange people abroad. The satirical inversion in this case makes these outlandish characteristics strangely familiar. Take, for example, the ways in which the various "foreigners" respond to Asanoshin's introduction. Instead of greeting him with suspicion and fear, the foreigners welcome him with great interest. The Giants seem to know all

about Japan and immediately put on a great celebratory feast for Asanoshin. Unlike the writer of descriptive travel accounts, the protagonist
is not the mysterious stranger gaining unprecedented access to a distant
place; he is not, as Tachibana Nankei put it, a *marōdo*, a stranger in a
strange land. Instead, all the foreigners seem to know who the traveler
is and where he came from. And what the protagonist and the reader simultaneously discover is that the far-flung foreign places into which the
traveler has stumbled are familiar: the incongruities and failings of the
foreigners are mirror images of the faults at home.

The Giants, for example, after welcoming Asanoshin propose a trip
to the countryside, but this turns out to be a ruse to exhibit the Japanese
man as a sideshow attraction. They take him to an open shack around
which people have gathered and, beating a rhythm on drums, they begin to call out: "See here a live Japanese! An exquisite tiny man! Put him
in your hand and watch him crawl! No fakery, no tricks, see him live!"[72]
The parallel to the rage for *misemono*, or popular carnival-like exhib-
its, in mid-eighteenth-century Edo is quite clear here. Often a feature at
kaichō, or temple fairs, *misemono* usually catered to onlookers' fascination with the strange or the exotic.[73] Gennai himself, in one of his
more eccentric moneymaking pursuits, set up a *misemono* in 1778 that
consisted of a black calf with a gold *nenbutsu*, or prayer to Amida,
painted on its side. Gennai and his co-exhibitor, Utei Enba, claimed this
to be a divine revelation, and they charged spectators to view it.[74] The
satirical point here, of course, is that Asanoshin, an average Japanese
person, is just as rare as a blessed calf in the Land of the Giants, and the
Giants are quick to take advantage of his exotic qualities for moneymaking purposes. The strangeness of Asanoshin is meant to profoundly
relativize the notion of foreignness for the Japanese reader, but in ways
quite different from that of the domestic travel account. In Asanoshin's
case, the anthropological gaze is turned back on the observer himself.

A similar situation arises from Asanoshin's experiences in the Land
of the Dwarves. Fascinated by the dwarves' tiny castle town, Asanoshin
watches as a procession approaches. When he spies what appears to be
a tiny, bean-sized princess riding in a tiny palanquin, Asanoshin plucks
her from the procession and puts her in his medicine case *(inrō)* as a
keepsake. Most of the retainers scatter in fear, but one of the princess's
attendants remains, running about in great agitation, so Asanoshin
takes him, too, and puts him in a different compartment of the case.
Later that day, when it comes time to view his "specimens," Asanoshin
is much aggrieved to find that the tiny attendant, probably distressed at

having failed to protect the princess, has sat himself down on a cough drop in the medicine case and slit his stomach with his sword. Finding the little corpse face down, Asanoshin bursts into tears at the thought that "people so small could have such a great sense of duty." This tragicomic observation was clearly an implicit criticism of the warrior's lot in the mid-eighteenth century; as the life experience of Hiraga Gennai himself showed, samurai were not nearly so valorous in Japan.[75]

The discovery of all-too-familiar faults and human failings in foreign places occurs repeatedly in *Shidōken*. The expulsion of Asanoshin from the Land of the Chest-Holes is due to his innate inability to conform to the standards of elite status in that country. His fine manners and comportment would make him fit as a consort for the king's daughter, were it not for the hereditary "deformity" beyond his control—that his chest has no hole. The fact that heredity replaced merit as a determination of status within the warrior class was a common complaint among low-ranking samurai. This fictionalized incident implies that the Tokugawa class system was as deformed as the one in the Land of the Chest-Holes, for practical accomplishments could rarely overcome inherited status.[76]

The denizens of Gennai's invented countries also resemble characters who subsequently became familiar stereotypes in Edo culture, and hence in Edo fiction. There are the Hedonists, who resemble newly rich Edoites, and the Boors and Blusterers stand in for the much-maligned "backwoods samurai" *(inaka bushi)*, who offended Edo's wealthy and stylish commoners with their unrefined ways. The Quacks are a parody of doctors who strut about in their scholarly robes but only vaguely understand outdated Chinese medical principles. Each of these types was the object of Hiraga Gennai's invective in his other writings. In *Shidōken*, they are roundly criticized by Gennai's mouthpiece, Fūrai Senjin.

The height of the tension between the foreign and the familiar is reached, however, in China, which was, as we have seen, a particularly problematic foreign country. Asanoshin's fictional adventures in China served to highlight the contrasts between the two cultures, usually to Japan's advantage. The influence of nativism on Gennai's thought is particularly noticeable here, if in caricatured fashion.[77] Yet Asanoshin finds much to be admired in Chinese culture. Beijing, the capital, is "expansive beyond compare, its prosperity beyond description," and the court women, whom he observes surreptitiously, again via the magic fan's powers, are indescribably beautiful: "three thousand court ladies rouged and powdered, hair like clouds, eyebrows like mist, beautiful as a string of jewels." [78] With the help of the magic fan Asanoshin is able to sneak into the court women's quarters, but palace officials soon find him out, and he is brought before the emperor himself for judgment. "You do not appear to be a lowly person," muses Qianlong. "Why did you steal into our palace with these hidden powers?" Asanoshin explains:

> I am from Edo in Japan. My name is Fukai Asanoshin. In accordance with the instructions of my teacher Fūrai Senjin, I am traveling from country to country to learn more about human passions in various lands. I sneaked into the inner apartments of this palace, and before I knew it my heart was so stirred by the beauty of all the court women that I quite forgot my true purpose. . . . A moment ago I was in paradise. Now I stand before you naked [79] and laughed at as an idiot. Now there's nothing left but to abandon myself to embarrassment in a foreign country. You should punish me immediately. [80]

Despite Asanoshin's admission of guilt, the emperor and his officials are fascinated by Asanoshin's story, and they offer him clothing and food so that he might tell of his travels in greater detail. Here the inverted satirical plot is turned right side up again, as the reader is treated to the ironic sight of a man from one of the more isolated countries in the early modern world telling the leader of an empire that had historically maintained much more extensive contact with Europe and Asia what he has learned in his travels. Gennai, of course, was not unaware of this. In the story, the emperor is made to realize that Asanoshin's tale is not the "sleep talk of some Japanese" *(Nihonjin no negoto),* as he might be inclined to think, but information of real interest. [81] Ministers of the court, the emperor, the empress, and the crown prince are all assembled to hear Asanoshin's travel stories. He begins by describing in categorical, encyclopedic fashion the people, animal life, and geography and topography of various countries. At this point, the traveler's tale takes an absurd twist. After hearing Asanoshin's account, Qianlong declares, "while the world is certainly vast, there cannot be a mountain comparable to the Five Sacred Mountains of our China." [82] Asanoshin quickly replies that, although the Five Sacred Mountains are indeed peerless, "in my home country of Japan, there is a famous mountain called Fuji. Its size is far greater than that of the Five Sacred Mountains, and on its eight-pronged peak there is snow the year round; from whichever province one looks at it, the view seems 'like a white fan hanging upside down.'" [83] Qianlong is struck by this information, and he recalls a beautiful painting of Fuji by Sesshū he had once seen but had assumed was "an artistic conceit" *(ezoragoto)* and not a realistic representation of the glory of Fuji. The notion that observed reality cannot match artistic representation recalls travel writers' declarations that certain famous places were in effect too beautiful for words. Asanoshin, however, manages to convince the emperor of Fuji's true beauty. Flustered by the thought of his glorious and vast China losing out to Japan in this regard, the emperor agrees to allow Asanoshin to build a replica of Fuji to compare to China's sacred mountains.

There are several points worth noting in this contest. First, the contest for superiority between Japan and China is determined by the preeminent symbols of the natural landscape itself, each country's sacred mountains. The Five Sacred Mountains and Fuji come to embody the greatness of the Chinese and Japanese civilizations. The absurdity of separating the mountain from its natural setting becomes evident in the ensuing debate over building a Chinese Fuji. When Asanoshin proposes returning to Japan to make a giant papier-mâché cast of the original Fuji, one of the ministers, sensing a plot to escape, objects. "Long ago, in the time of the first emperor of the Qin, there was a great swindler [dai yamashi][84] named Hsu Fu who went to Mount Hōrai in search of the elixir of immortality called Fuji[85] [and never returned]. If you try to put that one over on us, we won't fall for it."[86] Moreover, the minister insists, the cost of the paper would be prohibitive. Asanoshin assures him that he will return to Japan with a Chinese retinue guarding him, and, as for the paper cost, he suggests that if the emperor were simply to make the rendering of paper and paste an imperial edict to all the provinces, the problem would cease to be an issue. This suggestion is certainly a jab at the demands for labor and goods the Tokugawa frequently made of its subordinate daimyo in order to reduce its own expenditures.

The sad fate of the Chinese ships, destroyed by the divine typhoon winds, and of the Chinese men who are worked to death as male courtesans on the Island of Women, leave little doubt as to the "natural" superiority of the Japanese. Yet if the effect of Gennai's story, in the end, is to celebrate the image of Japan as a whole, he nonetheless criticizes its parts. The symbol of the mighty Fuji seems to be just that—a meaning in search of a reality; or perhaps, to use the story's own papier-mâché metaphor, it is a seemingly impressive entity when viewed from afar, but upon closer inspection proves to be an empty paper shell. Rather than uncovering precious knowledge in the course of his journey, Asanoshin uncovers the futility of knowledge seeking itself.

The juxtaposition and interpolation of foreign and familiar in the fictional travel account chipped away at the epistemological foundations of the travel-as-knowledge paradigm. Whereas the "real" writer of travel accounts, even if he embellished details now and again, emphasized describing things as they actually were, fiction writers like Hiraga Gennai made their names by creating improbable other worlds explored by less-than-authoritative protagonists. Far from an expert, Asanoshin is a bumbling *naïf* who must be guided on his travels by the all-knowing Senjin and aided at every turn by the powers of the magic fan. Instead of following the established route to well-known sites where he can confidently summon up poetic references dating back to ancient times, he is deposited by his magic fan in utterly alien places where his ignorance gets him embroiled in dilemmas from which he barely escapes. But perhaps the most incisive observation made by Hiraga Gennai in *The Tale of Dashing Shidōken* is doubly, if unintentionally, ironic. Gennai suggests that if the traveler discovers familiar problems in foreign lands, it is perhaps to be expected, for "real" travel writers did the same thing; in their drive to be learned, objective, and original, they always ended up revealing what they already knew best—themselves and their own concepts of culture.

SATIRE, SPATIALITY, AND THE SPREAD OF THE GEOGRAPHIC IMAGINARY

Hiraga Gennai's fictions of the foreign turn the assumptions of the descriptive travel account inside out. In doing so, however, Gennai reveals assumptions of his own, specifically, assumptions about the type and degree of cultural and geographic knowledge his readers possess. His satires, in their topsy-turvy way, show how narratives of space and place had become widely, perhaps instinctively understood. The reader, it seems, always knew which way was up, for the seriocomic mode of satire allowed for the participation of the reader as part of the text's narrative strategy. Like writers of satire in the classical and early modern European contexts, Gennai adopts an attitude of complicity with the reader. He assumes the reader is aware of—and likely shares—his critical perspectives on society and politics. Satire allows Gennai to paint with broad strokes; through Asanoshin's adventures he invites the reader to share his appraisals of civilization and culture at home and abroad. As we have seen, he does this by making the bizarre aspects of foreign lands and people recognizably similar to the accepted social and political practices of Tokugawa Japan: the foreigners have a rigid class system, they disregard merit in favor of inherited power, and they are greedy, opportunistic, and hedonistic. True valor and loyalty are everywhere lacking. By crafting such a portrait, with its thinly veiled double meanings, Gennai points out that truly "civilized" behavior is rare, within as well as outside of Japan.

To make his broad critique work, that is, to make it clever, funny, or meaningful at all, Gennai had to play off common knowledge. Satire can never be successful if the audience does not understand its references; the in-joke degenerates into absurd nonsense. The obvious referents in *Shidōken* are, as mentioned above, what Gennai perceived to be warped characteristics of Tokugawa society and politics. But there are less obvious referents embedded in the structure of Gennai's tale; these have to do with the understanding and representation of space and place, which were the fundamental dynamics of mapping in both its cognitive and narrative forms. First and most obviously, Gennai is playing with the timeworn tropes of the travel account: an omniscient observer makes his rounds of the famous places, pausing to comment on the (intriguing, surprising, odd) local culture. These conventions are skewered in *Shidōken,* for the protagonist, his itinerary, and his experiences are all the opposite of what Gennai's readers would have expected. Second, and less obviously, Gennai plays with the notion—so sacred to Kaibara Ekiken and others—that travel is a form of education. In contrast to the old Japanese adage that one should "send a treasured child on a journey" so that he might learn the ways of the world, in the course of his travels Asanoshin seems to have learned the *wrong* ways. Always the voice of conscience, Fūrai Senjin informs the protagonist of his failings in a vituperative outburst at the end of the story:

> My instructions to you were that once you had learned about human passions all over the world, you were to escape through the medium of humor. But you were so taken with material things and your own emotions that time and again you have found yourself in trouble. . . . Men of this world lose their sense of judgment over material things and ruin themselves and their homes. Overindulging in pleasure with courtesans is not the only source of this loss of judgment. Becoming attached to anything has its costs. You of all people should know this well, having toured all the countries and islands of the world.[87]

As a result of his inability to learn from his travel experience, Asanoshin grows up to be not a respected sage, but a petty entertainer, a wrinkled old man chanting bawdy tales to which no respectable person should listen.

At the same time that he is poking fun at the high-minded seriousness of travel accounts, however, Gennai counts on his audience's familiarity with that genre. Lacking that familiarity, the audience could not fully appreciate the humor. If, for example, a reader were not familiar with Edo's many *meisho,* he would be unlikely to find it amusing that Asanoshin ignores the canonical famous places in favor of lesser, tawdry attractions. Likewise, if the reader were unaware of the travel writer's propensity for "discovering" the unusual in out-of-the-way places, he might find it less ironic that Asanoshin finds in far-flung exotic lands only variations on the same wearisome "Japanese" traits. The same argument could apply to the readers' familiarity with information in encyclopedias. If the reader had previously encountered the *Wakan sansai zue's* terse and dry descriptions of the various people encountered by Asanoshin—the Long-Legs, the Long-Arms, the Chest-Holes, the Giants, and the Dwarves—he might find Gennai's version of their personalities and predicaments vastly more entertaining. Reading satire on the theme of the foreign journey was not rewarding if the reader did not possess a well-developed spatio-cultural consciousness. This consciousness could be acquired in many ways, and it did not need to be comprehensive; Gennai as author counts far less on the reader's knowledge of actual geographical or cultural facts gleaned from encyclopedias or travel accounts than he does on the reader's familiarity with each genre's discursive characteristics. But while the forms of mapping previously discussed make sense of space by subjecting it to a systematizing, rational gaze, satire is fundamentally irrational; its doubled and inverted meanings demand the reader's knowledge and attention while at the same time poking fun at the very notion of received knowledge.

It may seem questionable to suggest that an audience in the mid-Tokugawa period had mastered reading strategies of such complexity, and indeed it is always difficult to make assured statements about what readers knew and what they did with that knowledge. The contention here and in the next chapter, however, expands upon the argument presented in previous chapters: by the late eighteenth century, for a significant number of readers, spatial knowledge was common sense. Whether the knowledge was gleaned through maps, travel accounts, fiction, or actual travel itself, many readers likely possessed more than a modicum of such knowledge. It is clear that later writers borrowed and elaborated upon the foreign journey theme in the late eighteenth century and, in doing so, they both testified to the genre's popularity and gave the spatial vernacular a distinctly irreverent comic inflection.

One of the more notable works to build on the theme of the foreign journey so inventively elaborated by Hiraga Gennai was *Wasōbyōe's*

Intriguing Foreign Journey ([Ikoku kidan] Wasōbyōe), published in 1774.[88] It describes the adventures of a shipwrecked Nagasaki merchant who drifts (first on a boat, later on the back of a giant bird) to many of the same fantastic lands visited by Asanoshin. Instead of emulating Gennai's sharp satirical approach, however, the author of *Wasōbyōe,* Yū Koku Shi, inserts into his story didactic "morals" *(yōjō),* each conveying a pithy teaching to the reader. Over the years the Wasōbyōe story, like *The Tale of Dashing Shidōken,* gained a sequel and many imitators.[89] For example, in *[Kyōkun kidan] Morokoshi saiken banashi* ([Didactic curiosities] Detailed discussions of China), published in 1783, a foreign-goods proprietor from Kurumae in Kyushu is lofted on an east wind to China, where he is given a feather coat by a mountain spirit *(tengu).* This coat allows him to travel to various realms, each of which is illustrated in the fashion of *Shidōken* and other works of its genre.[90] In *Jōsendama hitokuchi gendan,* a 1785 work by Kiku Kyūga Sanjin Kō Bunba (a.k.a. Ōe Bunba), a Kyoto man falls in love with an angel and is abducted by lightning. He too travels by the power of a magical feather coat and lands in South Africa, where he meets up with none other than Wasōbyōe himself. After they exchange many tales of travels, a Taoist sage, or *sennin,* descends and begins to lecture them both. The lectures of the *sennin,* heavy on Buddhist teachings, take up a good part of the remainder of the text.

The foreign journey theme continued to influence plots through the turn of the century, with the appearance of *[Arayuru sekai] Mitekite banashi* (Tales seen and heard here and there in the world) in 1799, in which a rich Kyotoite named Sōemon journeys to foreign countries on the back of a camel in order to sample the pleasures of love in the Land of the Giants, and the pleasure quarters of paradise, hell, and the underwater Dragon Palace.[91] In the sequel, he encounters a *sennin* and travels on the back of a phoenix to a land of women, where he, like Asanoshin in *Shidōken,* sets up a male brothel. Exhausted by his work, he seeks the powers of the Buddha of healing (Yakushi nyōrai) in the end and returns to Japan.

Finally, in 1800 a work attributed to Yaku Tai entitled *[Zusan man-shin] Doro bawaki* tells the story of a beautiful young man named Seitarō whose conceit knows no bounds. Seeking otherworldly powers, he manages through various contrivances to be ordained a priest in a magical realm.[92] Through his special powers he visits famous places in China as well as the Land of Great Shame, where he receives the teachings of a great master named Meitoku ("Bright Virtue") and gives up his dissolute ways.[93] In book four of this work, one character complains that although booksellers seem to seize upon the theme of the foreign journey, "all of [the books] end in dreams or ridiculous fairy tales," instead of with serious teachings.[94] These stories testify to the prevalence of the foreign journey theme, and to its influence on later satirical fiction. It was not only the subject matter, but also the style of exposition, that made satirical literature on the foreign journey theme appealing to both writers and readers.

By the end of the eighteenth century and the beginning of the nineteenth, writers and readers seem to have tired of the foreign journey. In light of the restrictions being placed on even vaguely political writings under Matsudaira Sadanobu's Kansei reforms, writers turned their attention to new variations on *sharebon,* books of manners and style. *Sharebon* were intensely inward looking; their subject was not the outside world, but the latest fads and happenings in the entertainment districts of Japan's cities. From the inception of the genre in the early eighteenth century, *sharebon* were designed for the connoisseur, the *tsūjin.* At the same time, however, they poked fun at those who exaggerated their style and savvy, or who mindlessly aped whatever trends were in fashion at the moment. *Sharebon* might seem a less-than-promising genre in which to study the mapping impulse, but this, it turns out, is hardly the case. The following chapter will examine how writers of turn-of-the-century *sharebon* turned their satirical gazes not to narratives of travel or the suggestive experiences of the journey, but to the presumptive certainties of the map, whose image they co-opted to both display and parody urban culture in ingenious ways. In the context of the profoundly self-referential urban culture of the fin-de-siècle, the map was once again domesticated. Reduced to their most conventionalized semiotic form, maps were made to symbolize the most insular of subcultures, that of Edo's premier pleasure quarter, the Yoshiwara. No longer metaphors for the acquisition and display of foreign knowledge, maps became, literally and figuratively, the vehicles of pleasure at home.

CHAPTER 5

Remapping Japan

Satire, Pleasure, and Place
in Late Tokugawa Fiction

By disrupting the familiar order of famous and foreign places, fiction writers called into question the seemingly stable and natural connection between place and identity. In doing so, they not only parodied world geography, they also relativized familiar notions of spatial and cultural order. In works of satirical fiction dating from the late eighteenth and early nineteenth centuries, we can see the emergence of new themes that connect geography and satire more explicitly and more self-referentially than did the texts of Hiraga Gennai and his contemporaries. This was most evident in the use of geographic and cartographic conventions to dissect the "way of love" *(shikidō)* that governed the pleasure quarters of Edo and other cities. The writers and texts discussed in this chapter remapped the small, self-contained world of the pleasure quarters as a separate country, one that, like the foreign countries of earlier satirical fiction, often bore an uncanny resemblance to Japan itself. Inverting the conventions of maps and travel writing also destabilized familiar epistemological and spatial relationships, for the map, whose primary function was to lay out the objective features of the physical environment, becomes in these texts the vehicle for revealing the hidden world of Edo's fabled pleasure quarter, the Yoshiwara.

Unlike tales of fictional foreign journeys, these geographies of pleasure were not fantastic. They were utterly mundane in that they depicted, named, and mapped familiar places and real people. In their focus on local places and on the pleasure quarters, they reveal a shift in the fictive discourse of mapping toward the everyday practices of production and consumption. As Peter Stallybrass and Allon White have put it, "discursive space is never completely independent of social place and the formation of new kinds of speech can be traced through the emergence of new public sites of discourse and the transformation of old ones."[1] The pleasure quarters—in reality and in print—were such discursive spaces. The ingenious parodic rewriting of these spaces through the deployment of almost every form of mapping we have discussed so far marks a key moment in the integration of space, place, and culture.

LOCATING PLEASURE

Ample textual evidence documents the exchange of money or other material reward for entertainment and sexual services dating at least to the Heian period.[2] The great diarists and writers of the classical era, male and female alike, attest to the existence of common prostitutes, whose main job was to provide sex for payment, as well as highly trained entertainers, or courtesans, valued for their skills in the literary and performing arts.[3] By the early modern period thriving brothel districts had been established in many cities. Although many of the brothels were privately run, in the early seventeenth century the Tokugawa shogunate began to attempt to regulate and control prostitution by licensing pleasure quarters in Kyoto, Osaka, and Edo. These quarters were to cater to the overwhelmingly male samurai population that tended to concentrate in urban areas. In 1617 the Yoshiwara in Edo was the first of these official districts to be built; over the next two decades the shogunate authorized similar areas in Osaka's Shinmachi and Kyoto's Shimabara districts.

The government's treatment of prostitution reflected prevailing political and ethical concerns about sexuality and sexual activity. In general, official attitudes were shaped by several currents of thought. On the ethico-religious front, Shinto teachings, although not condemnatory of sexual activity itself, cautioned against the polluting nature of male-female intercourse. The Buddhist clergy in theory opposed both same-sex and heterosexual relations as forms of attachment to worldly pleasure, but there are countless literary and historical references to priests who broke vows of celibacy with women and with men. In the realm of political thought, Chinese classical philosophy dictated that it was not sex itself but the exercise of moderation and modesty that was of greatest concern. In this broad context it was entirely rational for the shogunate, as a matter of governance, to authorize licensed pleasure quarters in order to control and regulate, if not to condone, sexuality by providing its samurai retainers access to certain sexual services.

Beginning in 1617 the shogunate issued laws regulating the conduct of both courtesans and clients in Edo's official pleasure quarters. The government set down strict guidelines confining the pleasure industry to the designated area of the Yoshiwara, restricting the length of clients' stays, and even regulating the fabrics used in courtesans' clothing.[4] The laws were characteristic of shogunal legislation in that they were moralistic and ambitious in scope, and thus difficult to enforce. Ultimately, like many of the shogunate's declarations, the laws were ineffective. For although the government attempted to contain pleasure and the profits made from it to certain narrowly prescribed places and persons, contemporary literature shows that both brothel owners and courtesans flouted these rules consistently. In fact, the Yoshiwara tended to operate according to its own set of rules governing etiquette, ritual, and even language.[5] Many contemporary writers enhanced the Yoshiwara's exoticism, noting that entering the Yoshiwara was like entering another country, if not another world.

The original Yoshiwara was a square parcel of land of slightly less than twelve acres, located near Kyōbashi southeast of Edo castle. In the early decades of its existence, the Yoshiwara brothel owners and courtesans, like other government stipendiaries, were charged with official duties. These included the requirement that courtesans of the highest rank *(tayū)* serve the shogun and other important officials, and that the licensed quarter pay taxes on its land. Much changed, however, when the original quarter, along with much of Edo, burned down in the Meireki fire of 1657. In rebuilding the city after the fire, the shogunate took the opportunity to move the Yoshiwara toward the margins of the city. Ultimately it was rebuilt to the northeast of Edo castle, near the temple at Asakusa.

The new Yoshiwara (Shin-Yoshiwara) was considerably larger than its predecessor (which became known as Moto-Yoshiwara), occupying an area of about seventeen and a half acres. In terms of its basic layout, it resembled the former quarter in that it was a perfect square, bounded by moats on all sides, bisected by a wide boulevard called Naka-no-chō, and accessible only through a single gate. Also like the old Yoshiwara, Shin-Yoshiwara had three main brothel districts, Edo-chō, Kyōmachi, and Naka-no-chō; the new quarter also had four smaller districts, called Ageya-chō, Sakai-chō, Sumi-chō, and Fushimi-chō. In terms of population, Shin-Yoshiwara was more than double the size of Moto-Yoshiwara.

According to the *Azuma monogatari* (Tale of the east), a guidebook to Edo published in 1642, there were 987 courtesans in some 117 brothels and several dozen houses of assignation *(ageya)* in Moto-Yoshiwara. More than a hundred of these women were of the two highest ranks, *tayū* and *kōshi*. By the mid-eighteenth century, there were more than two thousand courtesans in Shin-Yoshiwara. However, the vast majority of them were not *tayū* or *kōshi*, but courtesans of the lower ranks. A published guide to the Yoshiwara dating from 1761 lists only one *tayū* among some eighty brothels then in operation.[6] These figures are the measure of the Yoshiwara's shift from a small enclave serving the elite in the seventeenth century to a place catering to a broader commoner clientele in the eighteenth century.

The decline of the high-ranking courtesan had everything to do with larger socioeconomic shifts occurring in the mid-Tokugawa period. By the turn of the eighteenth century, constraints on shogunal and daimyo finances, decreasing opportunities for official appointment, and the growth of the market economy, in which samurai theoretically could not participate, conspired to considerably reduce the financial means of the samurai class, while favoring the growth of merchant wealth. This shift was felt in the pleasure quarters, where merchants and other commoners came to comprise the core of Yoshiwara patrons. To serve this population, new classes of courtesan appeared, notably the *sancha*, who tended to be less skilled at the fine arts of music and dance so prized in higher-ranking courtesans, and more inclined to provide sexual services. And while the Yoshiwara continued to be associated with elegance and uniqueness, increasingly its courtesans found themselves in competition with privately run brothels. As discussed in the previous chapter, Hiraga Gennai adeptly described the diversity of the eighteenth-century pleasure districts in the early chapters of *Fūryū Shidōken den*. In Gennai's view, the market for sex was like the market for goods, in which every seller had a specialty. Neither was the spread of prostitution limited to the major urban areas; as the research of Watanabe Kenji has shown, pleasure quarters in the early modern period existed in almost all regions of Japan, and there was considerable variation in practices from place to place.[7] This was a far cry from the regulated system the bakufu had legislated in 1617.

But even as brothel and entertainment districts sprang up in Edo outside the licensed quarters and in other cities and towns, the Yoshiwara still set the standard. As the first formally established pleasure quarter it developed a unique subculture that early on became romanticized, so much so that a certain aura clung to the Yoshiwara even after its material fortunes began to decline. It remained one of Edo's most famous places, the subject of constant description, cataloging, and mapping throughout the eighteenth century. Likewise, the high-ranking courtesan continued to represent the peak of attainment in the arts of pleasure, even though her numbers had been severely depleted by the late eighteenth century. The bulk of this chapter focuses on the form and function of this nostalgia by examining the mapping of the Yoshiwara in two different types of text: the so-called "detailed views" *(saiken)* of the Yoshiwara, and map-illustrated satirical "books of style" *(sharebon)*. By utilizing every form of expression in the early modern mapping vocabulary, the authors of these texts made the Yoshiwara the symbol of a prideful yearning for the past and an assertion of an Edo-centered self-referential cultural identity. Yoshiwara *saiken* and satirical maps played off other spatializing genres and their conventional forms of expression in order to redefine political and cultural space in the late Edo period.

THE MEANING OF STYLE IN *SAIKEN* AND *SHAREBON*

Residents of Japan's large cities in the late eighteenth century did not pursue pleasure carelessly. Like most forms of social interaction, pleasure-for-pay was governed by status, class, gender, and politics. The shogunate, as we have seen, did its best to restrict access to the pleasure quarters from above. But equally forceful in governing public attitudes toward pleasure and play were the standards of refinement *(tsū)* and elegance *(sui)* that were fashioned by and for the patrons of the pleasure districts themselves. The Yoshiwara was one of the principal sites for defining and practicing these arts of comportment.

Both the "detailed views" of *saiken* and the skewed perspectives of satire operated as literal and figurative maps of the Yoshiwara. They represented the pleasure quarters as an actual place and a discursive site, where the rules of taste were continually made and remade. For the Yoshiwara was, in actuality as in discourse, an invented place, an ideal given substance and form materially as well as textually. At the same time, it came to function as a relatively independent society whose rules both coincided with and contradicted those of the "real" world. The Yoshiwara can thus be seen as part of "an exchange network, an economy of signs, in which individuals, writers and authors are sometimes but perplexed agencies."[8]

Knowing the Yoshiwara (or any brothel district) was not a simple matter of mastering geography. Those aspiring to become *tsū*, or connoisseurs of the pleasure-seeking life, required extensive place-specific cultural knowledge. Although published guides to the arts of love had long been available in many forms, in the late eighteenth century illustrated guides to specific pleasure quarters began to appear in considerable number. Most relevant to the present study are the *saiken* and the *sharebon*. Both genres focused on Edo and integrated text and image in very different ways to provide extremely place- and time-specific information and commentary on the city's cultural life.

Yoshiwara *Saiken:* The Detailed View

Yoshiwara *saiken* began to appear as a distinct genre in the last decade of the seventeenth century, and they became standardized in format and style in the mid-eighteenth century. In many respects, *saiken* resembled the *yūjo hyōbanki* (ratings of courtesans) that were published between the mid-seventeenth and mid-eighteenth centuries.[9] Due in great part to the nature of their readership—samurai patrons of the early Yoshiwara—*yūjo hyōbanki* focused on the high-ranking courtesans, the *tayū* and *kōshi*. But as the pleasure quarters began to cater more to the needs of their commoner clients, both the structure and the representation of life in the Yoshiwara began to change. First, as the demand for the low-ranking *sancha* increased, the need for detailed ratings of the artistic merits of high-ranking and high-priced courtesans declined. Second, in the Genroku period the shogunate began to crack down on writers and publishers of *hyōbanki* for their explicit descriptions of various courtesans' charms; in 1697 the publisher of one *yūjo hyōbanki* was punished under new and more restrictive censorship laws.[10]

For these reasons, writers of *hyōbanki* began to shift toward a less embellished, more factual way of describing the Yoshiwara, a way that would be widely comprehensible to common readers and that would attract less attention from official censors. The result was the Yoshiwara *saiken.* These documents combined the visual and verbal schema of two types of records: maps and population registers *(ninbetsu aratame chō).* Quite similar to the detailed records kept by local governments in Japan today, *saiken* listed the names of individual residents, house by house, on schematic maps of the pleasure quarters. Each brothel's courtesans are listed, in descending order of rank, within the mapped space allocated to the brothel itself. In later *saiken* the fee charged by each courtesan was noted below her name. This format, like the text-laden printed maps of Ishikawa Ryūsen and others, succeeded in conveying a great deal of information in economical visual form. Deciphering a *saiken,* in fact, required certain map-reading skills, without which the text would have made little sense.

Saiken were first published as appendices to *yūjo hyōbanki,* but they began appearing in single-sheet form in about 1689. In 1728, the first *saiken* published in what became a distinctive horizontally bound book format *(yokobon)* appeared, and shortly thereafter many variations on this style were published. Among these book-length versions were small-format *(kaichū)* editions, some as tiny as thirteen by fifteen centimeters. These compact books were intended to be carried on the reader's person so he could consult them quickly and easily. The afterword to a Yoshiwara *saiken* published by Iseya in 1727 states, "Although Yoshiwara *saiken* maps are widely used by the public, this time we offer a revised *small-format book.* Because in previous times the reader *could not easily consult [these books] discreetly,* [we] have made them in horizontal format."[11] Perhaps discretion was a selling point, but ease of use was equally important for publishers of *saiken:* "[our] new revised editions are now in *easy-to-use compact format,* in two volumes," declared another publisher.[12]

Saiken were further standardized and gained wider circulation in the 1770s, when the publisher Tsutaya Jūsaburō began to dominate their production. By 1782, Tsutaya had secured a monopoly on the publication of Yoshiwara *saiken.*[13] With prefaces and texts written by popular writers such as Hiraga Gennai and Hōseidō Kisanji, Tsutaya made numerous innovations in the style and format of *saiken,* all of which had a lasting impact on the genre. In a move not unknown to modern publishers, Tsutaya printed advertisements for his other publications on the back pages of his Yoshiwara *saiken* in hopes of again reaching the audience the first texts had attracted.[14] More importantly, Tsutaya did a great deal to standardize the various formats of *saiken.* He made common the use of *aijirushi,* or symbols denoting the ranks of courtesans. Once familiarized with these triangular icons, readers could easily ascertain the rank of any courtesan at a glance. Tsutaya also made it common to publish courtesans' fees *(agedaikin).* The decline of the high-ranking courtesan, however, caused the publisher to eliminate personal names in later *saiken* and replace them with generic descriptions of the courtesan's rank and the number of her attendants, if any.[15]

The standardization and simplification of the *saiken* format made the genre accessible to a wider audience, and this contributed to their popularity. *Saiken* were generally updated twice a year, in spring and fall, and the publication of a revised *saiken* was apparently something of a public event. According to *Kokkei Yūjirō* (Comic Yūjirō), a *sharebon* written in 1802, peddlers would take to the streets to hawk the newest updated *saiken,* calling out "revised *saiken* of the Yoshiwara's five districts, a treasure-trove [of information]!"[16] Simplified and standardized, *saiken* became, as their publishers were wont to declare, more user-friendly. No longer to be read only in the privacy of one's home, the small-format *saiken* were meant to be taken along on a journey to the Yoshiwara, where, slipped into the folds of one's jacket, they could be perused easily and discreetly.

Sharebon: Fictions of Taste

The many styles and forms of *saiken* and the self-promoting cries of publishers and peddlers alike reveal the competitive nature of publishing in the late eighteenth century. No doubt it was in the interests of *saiken* publishers as well as readers to be stylish, and this required not only money, skills, and knowledge, but also certain social sensibilities, namely a sense of timing, impeccable taste, and a keen awareness of place. Building on the information and the readership cultivated by Yoshiwara *saiken,* writers of *sharebon* in the late eighteenth century invented and elaborated upon the pursuit of pleasure in ways that expanded the boundaries of the *saiken* format. For like printed maps, *saiken* were essentially informational in nature, and could only get a reader so far in the three-dimensional world of the actual pleasure quarters. *Sharebon,* however, were different. They fleshed out and gave voices and faces to their fictive personalities. To the extent that any type of text could convey the Yoshiwara experience in an animated form, *sharebon* did.

As a genre, *sharebon* were a variation on the tradition of comic fiction of which Hiraga Gennai's writings were earlier examples. At the peak of their popularity, roughly between the 1770s and 1820s, *sharebon* entertained and instructed their readers in the fine arts of pleasure: where and how to procure it, and how to behave as a person of refinement.

Since good manners were situationally specific, *sharebon,* like *saiken,* were intensely place-conscious. What worked in Edo's Yoshiwara might be deemed ridiculous in Kyoto's Shimabara or Osaka's Shinmachi, and vice versa. Should a patron violate the codes of conduct in any of these places, he risked being labeled a "half-baked *tsū*" *(hanka tsū)* or, worse yet, a *yabō* (boor), both stock characters who appear in *sharebon* as glaring examples of how *not* to behave.

The *tsū,* the *hanka tsū,* and the *yabō* are on full display in one of the earliest *sharebon, Yūshi hōgen* (Words of a playboy, 1770), written by a publisher-turned-writer whose pseudonym was Inaka Rōjin Tada Okina (literally "just an old man from the countryside").[17] The story follows the exploits of a man who takes his twenty-year-old son to a teahouse in the Yoshiwara's Naka-no-chō to initiate him into the life of pleasure. Though he pretends to be in the know, the father immediately shows himself to be a laughably half-baked *tsū* and earns the ridicule of the teahouse women. While the father makes a fool of himself, the reader is introduced to two other patrons of the same establishment. One, a rural magistrate, is the archetypal *yabō,* loud, boorish, and with no sense of refined city manners. The other patron is a consummate *tsū,* tasteful and cultivated in every way. A spirited dialogue among these three characters ensues, and from this, as well as from the interaction of the three types of patron, the reader gains a clear and very detailed picture of what should and should not be done on a visit to the Yoshiwara.

Later texts in the *sharebon* style followed a format similar to that of *Yūshi hōgen,* both in their embedding of "how-to" information in fictional narrative, and in their emphasis on colloquial language and dialogue. The stereotypes of the *tsū* and the *yabō* are reinforced in two of the genre's defining texts, Santō Kyōden's *Edo umare uwaki no kabayaki* (Connoisseur, grilled Edo-style, 1785) and its sequel of sorts, *Tsūgen sōmagaki* (Words of the connoisseur, all wound up, 1787).[18] The two texts follow the exploits of the hapless half-baked *tsū* Enjirō, for whom true refinement is ever elusive (his failings earn him the "grilling" of the title). A wealthy Edo commoner, Enjirō spends huge sums to acquire what he thinks are the hallmarks of style. He pays a prostitute to act like a spurned and jealous lover, so as to enhance his reputation as a man-about-town; he hires people to gossip loudly about him in public; and he contrives a public beating for himself at the hands of a band of thugs, who act as if they are bent on revenge for a past offense at the hands of the daring Enjirō. Finally, and most dramatically, he stages a

double suicide for himself and his imaginary lover. In the course of telling Enjirō's story, Santō Kyōden conveys a great deal of information
about the Yoshiwara and about the lives of the wealthy Edo commoners
who were its primary patrons in the late eighteenth century. And like
many writers of *sharebon* and other subgenres of *gesaku*, Kyōden frequently wrote sequels to his own works and updated previously published stories, thereby keeping his readers abreast of the latest trends. In
Tsūgen sōmagaki, for instance, Enjirō's saga continues two years later
when, having achieved the status he coveted for so long, he becomes
connoisseur-in-residence at the most prestigious and expensive brothel
in the Yoshiwara.

The didactic functions of *sharebon* were enhanced by their heavy use
of illustration. Indeed, in them there is little division between text and
image. Dialogue, asides, and narrative all encircle illustrations of the
people and places being depicted. Getting the joke thus required both
mental and visual acuity, and knowledge of both visual and verbal conventions. The resulting effect is a distinct form of immersion in both narrative and its discursive space. The microgeography of *sharebon* captures, as much as is possible in two dimensions, a real-time experience
in the Yoshiwara.

SHAREBON AS GEOGRAPHIES OF PLEASURE

As a genre, *sharebon* manipulated visual, linguistic, and narrative tropes
to create a densely self-referential form of humor. Though the allusions
were most often to literary works, in numerous cases encyclopedic and
geographical texts functioned as the stepping-off point for excursions
into the realm of parody. We will examine here a number of *sharebon*
that explicitly make maps and geographies their *shukō,* the convention
or setting within which the play of satire occurs.[19]

Guidebooks to the "Way of the *Tsū*"

Some of the earliest parodies of geography took as their subjects
the illustrated geographical text or guidebook. These works began a
process of bringing together the conventions of maps, encyclopedias,
guidebooks, and satires. Road guides, or *dōchūki,* were transformed
into "guides to the way of the *tsū*," or *dōtsūki.* In 1782, Tenjiku Rōnin
(1754–1808) wrote a faux guidebook entitled *Tōsei dōtsūki* (Current
guide to the way of the *tsū*).[20] Landscape drawings done in a style rem-

iniscent of both picture scrolls *(emaki)* and Edo-period road maps illustrate the metaphorical journey of a young man toward his ultimate "destination" as a *tsūjin*. In his preface, the author writes:

> The difficulties of travel are not [in crossing] mountains and rivers, but rather in the changeability of human nature. . . . They say to "send a treasured child on a journey" *[kawai ko ni tabi wo saseyō]*. [But since] it is the love of another that overcomes difficulty, they should say instead "make your way on [the strength of] human emotion" *[ninjō ni watarraseyō]*.[21] This story takes that sentiment as its general setting *[shukō]*. . . . Not to start the lesson from the beginning is the root of bad taste.[22]

Tenjiku Rōnin thus begins to transform the conventions of the road map into a guidebook of taste. This tactic was taken up by later writers who replaced the guidebook metaphor with the model of encyclopedias such as Nishikawa Jōken's aforementioned *Ka'i tsūshō kō*. Two texts by Ishijima Masatane parodied Jōken's text as well as maps of Japan and the pleasure quarters; both were entitled *Ka-ri tsūshō kō* (Thoughts on the pleasure quarters and the peddling of refinement).[23] Whereas Nishikawa's encyclopedia divided the world's countries into "the civilized and the barbaric," *Ka-ri tsūshō kō* instead takes as its subject the various pleasure and entertainment quarters of Edo and the types of people that patronize them. Ishijima substitutes these places and people for the "myriad countries" depicted in Jōken's world maps. In a narrative style similar to that of the *Ka'i tsūshō kō*, it assesses how each place or type of person measures up to ideals of civilization and cultivation; but this time the standards are those of refinement and elegance that identified the *tsū*.

The two extant versions of Ishijima's text both contain maps. In the earlier version of *Ka-ri tsūshō kō*, published in 1748 under Ishijima's pseudonym Sanjin, the "country of Yoshiwara" is depicted as the largest island in what seems to be an archipelago; a smaller map shows it in detail.[24] In this map, rendered in the Gyōki style, Yoshiwara-koku has a river originating from the "spring" of Naka-no-chō that runs up its center and bisects the "provinces," which represent the five districts of the actual pleasure quarters. In the text, all the "countries" depicted are given Chinese-style character readings *(on-yomi)*; thus, Yoshiwara becomes Kitsugen, Shinagawa becomes Honsen, Otowa becomes On-u, and so on. An additional country called Senkun (or Funagimi, literally "boat princess") also appears.[25] This is the land of prostitutes who worked on the boats plying Edo's rivers. Like the streetwalkers, called "nighthawks" *(yotaka)*, they are described in the text in pejorative terms. The boat princesses are "old ladies" who "powder up their faces in hopes of covering up wrinkles. In the summer they use fans to direct poison vapors at people. When they sing, it is like a flock of crows. This is a land of many toxins, of which one should be afraid."[26]

In the later version of *Ka-ri tsūshō kō,* published in 1754, Edo's pleasure districts are mapped as neighboring countries on an unidentified continental mass.[27] "Central Civilization" (Chūka) is the largest country and occupies the middle of the map. While Chūka was a term used to refer to China in the early modern period, given the "Edo-centricity" of Ishijima's text, it is unlikely that it denotes the Middle Kingdom. Judging from the structure of the map, Chūka seems instead to represent the center of Edo, at the core of which lay Edo castle and its surrounding daimyo residences. Located to the north of Chūka (in approximate relationship to its actual location within the city) is the "country" of Yoshiwara. In good guidebook fashion, the text describes the geography, customs, and "famous products" of "Yoshiwara-koku."[28] Other Edo places such as Shinagawa, Azabu, Otowa, and Susaki also are shown on the map in their proper locations relative to Edo castle (i.e., to the south, southwest, northwest, and east of Chūka, respectively); most of these places were known as brothel districts. Still other "countries" do not represent actual places, but the types of courtesans, prostitutes, or other entertainers to be found there. There is, for example, Land of the Dancing Girls (Odoriko-kuni), described as a beautiful country where the women entertain their guests with court music, and Land of the Buddhist Nuns (Bikuni-kuni), whose residents are bald, study "old-world customs" *(Tenjiku no fūzoku),* and believe in the Buddhist law.[29] Land of the Streetwalkers (Yahotsu-kuni) is peopled by the lowest class of prostitute.[30] None of these "countries" seems to be located in any particular geographic location in the city, though it is worth noting that Yahotsu-kuni occupies an island in the middle of a body of water in the northeast corner of the map, and is thus at a considerable remove from "civilization."

The innovation made in both of these texts is the mapping of Edo's pleasure quarters and pleasure purveyors as worlds unto themselves. In the earlier version of *Ka-ri tsūshō kō* there was a "central civilization" that connoted Edo castle, but despite its seeming geographic importance, Chūka is never mentioned in the text. Like the blank space that marked the shogun's castle on most printed maps of the capital, Chūka is just "there." In this way, the text uses both visual and narrative metaphors to mark the central place but does not dare to describe it. By contrast, the marginal places—the pleasure quarters and brothel districts—become the central focus.

The guidebook metaphor is played out to its logical end in a text entitled *Rokuchō ichiri* (Six *chō* to one *ri*), which was written sometime in the Meiwa era (1764–72).[31] Its title juxtaposes two units of distance measurement in China and Japan (six Chinese *chō* equaled one Japanese *ri*) and refers to the Japanese translation of Chinese measurements into indigenous terms. The metaphorical meanings of this title become clearer when one reads the preface to the work, which reads in part, "People nowadays are like frogs in a well, ignorant of the deep sea. Believing [only] Chinese and Indian hearsay leads to deception."[32] The author indicates here and in the body of the text that the Japanese should not follow classical teachings blindly; they should instead observe the world around them, investigate all possibilities, and devise an appropriate response or solution.

Following this logic, the text is a guide to various "countries" that, it soon becomes apparent, stand in for different types of people. These people are not necessarily exclusive to Edo, but represent more generalized stereotypes of those who succumb to the herd mentality criticized by the author in the preface. One meets, for example, the residents of the Land of Literature who study constantly and prefer to live the life of the mind in poverty. Their "famous products" *(meibutsu)* include dictionaries and medicines, but they trade only with certain select communities, namely Printer's Island (Insatsu-jima), the State of Students (Shosei-shū), the District of Taoists (Rō-Sō fū), and the Land of Booksellers. The Land of Doctors (Ian-koku) is populated with the same sorts of self-important quacks lampooned by Hiraga Gennai, while the Land of Buddha-Worshipers has its own provinces of heaven and hell. Market Price Island (Sōba-jima) has three districts, but, depending on the island's economic prosperity, sometimes this number dwindles to one. Sōba-jima is noisy, and its people are highly mobile; they can go around the world in one night, go to bed poor, and wake up rich. Much more reserved are the people of the Land of Tea Connoisseurs (Chajin-koku), who are prideful, obsessed with ritual, and extremely polite. In the Land of Physiognomists the residents are busy telling fortunes, while in the Land of Youth (Shōnen-koku) they pursue countless fads like sumo wrestling, *haikai* poetry, theater, kabuki, and music. Rounding out the accounts of these various countries are descriptions of the Island of Male Love (Nanshoku-jima) and the State of Kabuki, neither of which, of course, has any female residents.

Both *Ka-ri tsūshō kō* and *Rokuchō ichiri* play on well-rehearsed stereotypes of the "foreigner," some of which appear in the works discussed in the previous chapters. Like previous works of satire and parody, they also rely heavily on familiar geographical and cultural references at the same time that they poke fun at the insularity of the world connoted by those terms. Because they contain little that could be termed innovative in literary terms, they occupy a minor place in the canon of Edo fiction. However, it is precisely the ways in which these works are conventional—how they utilize and play upon stereotypes—that makes them important for the present study. For although the characterizations of places and people described by texts like these were not new, the use of the convention itself—parodying the travel account, the map, and the encyclopedia—was significant. The fact that minor writers such as Ishijima picked up on the satirical possibilities of maps and geographical writings suggests that such texts were familiar to most readers. As in the case of satires of foreign journeys, satires on the theme of maps of the pleasure quarters would not have worked had there not been an audience knowledgeable enough to appreciate its humor. That this audience existed is attested to by the repeated, and ever more ingenious, use of cartographic and geographic conventions in satirical literature from the last decades of the eighteenth century to the first decades of the nineteenth. By this time not only minor writers but also well-established literary figures like Hōseidō Kisanji (1735–1813) and Shikitei Sanba (1776–1822) began to manipulate the map image in more elaborate, and ultimately more political, ways.

Remapping the Pleasure Quarters: Hōseidō Kisanji's Dual Worlds

Hōseidō Kisanji was a privileged observer of the many dimensions of Edo culture. He was a high-ranking samurai from Satake domain in Akita province, but in addition to fulfilling the duties attendant to his rank and office, he was also a writer of popular comic fiction, both prose and poetry. Like other eighteenth-century *gesaku* and *kyōka* writers of samurai origin such as Hiraga Gennai and Ōta Nanpō, he was an "amphibious" intellectual, moving easily between the world of officialdom and that of the commoner quarters. In 1777, writing under the pen name Dōjarō Maa, he published *Shōhi jiriki,* a "geographical guide to the courtesans."[33]

In a manner similar to that used in the 1748 version of *Ka-ri tsūshō kō,* Kisanji remapped the pleasure quarters on the model of Gyōki-style maps of Japan. But Kisanji pushed the satirical boundaries further. Bringing together the conventions of history, geography, and comic fiction, he created a mock guide to an "unknown" land called Geppon-koku, the "Land of the Rising Moon," which on closer inspection turns out to be the Yoshiwara. The geo-history of Geppon, clearly meant to be the mirror image of Japan (Nippon-koku, the Land of the Rising Sun), plays on geographic and cartographic conventions stretching back to and including the ancient *fudoki* gazetteers and the Gyōki-style map of Japan.

The first lines of *Shōhi jiriki* manage to recall the rollicking language and playful etymologies of Hiraga Gennai's earlier works, as well as the sinicized four-character cadences of official documents: *"Cha iro no hyōshi ya shirabyōshi. Toki no chōshi wo toriaesu.* Shōhi jiriki *to dai su"* (Brown-cover books and dancing girls, I take, for now, the rhythm of time. I title this *Shōhi jiriki*).[34] In its depiction of the districts of the Yoshiwara as provinces, the text bears clear stylistic similarities to *Ka-ri tsūshō kō* and *Rokuchō ichiri,* as well as to *saiken* and urban guidebooks. But the most inventive aspect of Kisanji's new geography is his "creation myth" for Geppon, a wickedly funny takeoff on the official history of Japan as enshrined in the *Kojiki* (ca. 712). Kisanji's history of Geppon begins with the creation of land and humankind, but in Kisanji's hands numerous double entendres and visual puns render the making of the islands more a *pro*creation story than a myth of sacred origins.

As in the *Kojiki,* in the beginning there is nothingness, until the founding gods Izanagi (described as *"danna,"* the husband or male) and Izanami (described as *"shinzō,"* a term used for a young woman or bride, but which in the eighteenth century also referred to the second-highest rank of courtesan) create the islands of Japan by standing on the Floating Bridge of Heaven (Ama no ukihashi) and dipping the heavenly scepter *(ama no sakahoko)* into the primordial ooze. But instead of creating the islands simply by allowing the scepter's drippings to harden into landmasses, as described in the *Kojiki,* Izanagi inadvertently bumps the scepter against his groin. Because it tickles him he laughs, causing the drops from the scepter to scatter and harden, thus creating the island of "Nansembushū Toyo ashihara Dai Nihon koku," the "southern state of the abundant reed plain," the sacred land of "Great Japan."[35] The

sexualized imagery here, as it is in the original procreation scene in the
Kojiki, is too obvious to miss, and from this point on the "creation
story" departs from the *Kojiki* narrative and becomes increasingly outlandish, as Kisanji piles on the innuendo, wordplay, and imagery to create an entirely new take on mytho-history.

After describing the division of Great Japan into sixty-six provinces,
each of which is subdivided into districts, the narrator turns directly to
the reader and remarks in an aside that "this is a venerable fact that all
of you know" *(Kore minna gozonji no ongoto nari).*[36] Having made it
clear that he assumes his reader is familiar with the *Kojiki,* the *Nihon
shoki,* and the traditional geographic divisions of Japan, the author then
embarks on a hidden history, one that, he assumes, is unknown to the
reader. This part of the story concerns a pair of deities, again a male-
female couple, named Kozanagi and Kozanami. In contrast to their predecessors, Izanagi and Izanami, who are described as being of the "seventh generation of heavenly deities" *(tenshin shichidai me),* Kozanagi
and Kozanami are of a different lineage, dubbed the "seventh generation
of bizarre deities" *(henshin shichidai me).* As his first divine utterance,
Kozanagi, using rather rough colloquial language, says to himself, "I
think I'm going to make me some of those country-things, too" *(Ore
mo kuni to iu mono wo oshiraete min to omoimeshi).*[37] At Izanagi's urging, the couple then attempts to cross the Ama no ukihashi, but it makes
them dizzy and seasick, so they instead traverse the Imado-San'ya no
hashi, an actual bridge in Edo that linked the new Yoshiwara and its
surrounding neighborhood. From the top of this bridge, instead of bran-
dishing the gleaming sacred scepter *(ama no sakahoko),* they wave a
flabby shark-meat fishcake *(same no kamaboko).*[38] From the drippings
of the fishcake the deities create "Hokusen fushū Shin Yoshiwara Dai
Geppon-koku," roughly translatable as the "northern state of women,
new Yoshiwara, Great Land of the Rising Moon," a clear phonetic play
on "Nansembushū Dai Nippon-koku," one of the formal names for
"Great Japan" that was often used in Gyōki-style maps.

After creating this auspicious Land of the Rising Moon, the deities
divide it into five provinces (the five districts of the Yoshiwara), and sub-
divide those provinces into districts. But things are not altogether peace-
ful in the new realm, for the founding father figures of Nihon and
Geppon, Izanagi and Kozanagi, soon get into a quarrel over the boundaries between their two countries. Kozanagi eventually loses the fight
and this, the narrator informs the reader, is the reason that Nihon (Japan) came to control Geppon (Yoshiwara). Because their relationship

was born of this early animosity, the contrasts between the two lands are stark. Nihon, created by the drippings from a jeweled scepter, is ruled by sword-loving martial men, while Geppon, created from a fishcake, has a fish market at its center and is governed largely by women. Geppon's women serve as "elders" *(rōjō)*, also known as *yarite*.[39] The customs of the two countries differ considerably as well, a point that was not likely to be lost on many readers. Most striking is the fact that in Geppon, women are revered and men are looked down upon. Polygamy is forbidden, and women can initiate and break off relationships with men as they please. At the same time, however, women are extremely diligent and filial, even giving up food for themselves in order to support their parents and siblings, while men are dishonest and willing to live off the work of others.[40] Most importantly, the women officeholders of Geppon do not make rules arbitrarily; they accomplish everything through consensus, a trait "completely incomprehensible in the eyes of the people of Nihon."[41]

Despite their differences, one thing that both women and men share in Geppon is a love of the arts. Many are accomplished in artistic pursuits such as poetry writing (Chinese, Japanese, and linked verse), tea ceremony, incense collecting, and flower arranging. The Gepponese do not, however, follow fads mindlessly. They pursue their inclinations regardless of fashion, and this trait, the narrator remarks, marks their true wisdom:

> As Confucius said, "if what is here is the truth, what came before was also true; if you put a lie away, you must have taken one out before." But [in Geppon], one would translate this as "if it is refined *[tsū]* here, it was true before. If it's crude *[yabō]* here, then it was a lie before." Or, disregarding [the matter] of truth or lies . . . [one would say] "even if what came before was a lie, money will make it true; if what came before was true, if you haven't any money, it's meaningless here."[42]

This convoluted explanation indicates that in Geppon, absolute judgments of "true" virtue are worthless; the clear contrast is again to Nihon, where official pronouncements on the necessity of modesty, frugality, loyalty, and other undying virtues were frequent.

From this point, the text turns to a detailed description of the topography of Geppon. Like any country, Geppon has a distinct landscape, except in this case it is composed of the major man-made edifices of the Yoshiwara, which the author transforms into "natural" phenomena. Ageya man'ike (Teahouse Lake), Daimon nada (Main Gate Rapids), Kaijo shima (Cashier Island), and Rashōmon jima (Rashō Gate Island)

Figure 15. Dōjarō Maa (Hōseidō Kisanji), "Dai Geppon-koku no zu" (Map of Great Geppon), from *Shōhi jiriki*, 1777. Courtesy of the National Diet Library, Tokyo.

all stand as "naturalized" versions of well-known landmarks of the licensed quarter. The land of Geppon is divided into five provinces *(kuni)*, each of which corresponds to a street or area within the Yoshiwara: Edo-chō koku, Ni-chō koku (Edo-chō's second district), Kado-chō koku (another name for Sumi-chō), Kyōmachi-koku, and Shinchō koku (Kyōmachi's second district) (see fig. 15). The "provinces" are in turn divided into districts, each of which represents a single brothel. Under each district are listed numerous "sites," including natural wonders, famous places, or places of historical interest *(kyūseki)*. These sites represent individual courtesans, many of whom are described briefly in the manner of a travel account or gazetteer. The text's assessment of each place is, of course, a judgment of the individual courtesan's particular talents.

The "province" of Kyōmachi, for instance, contains sixteen "districts," or brothels (fig. 16). In Ōdawara district there are two "famous places," or courtesans, Wakama "Harbor" and Yoshi "Plain." The former is described as "a lively place, where the boats never cease to arrive; you could spend a year here and there would be plenty [to do]." The latter is, by contrast, "an old *meisho*; there's not much to see here." In Okamoto district, there is a famous "shrine," the Yoshitaka Daimyōjin, which is said to be "an extremely well built shrine whose grounds are beautiful—a sacred place." In Daimonji district there is Mitsuharu "Falls," whose "waves break through cracks in the rocks; the spray is something to look at." And in Yotsume district is "Mount" Tomi, "an unsurpassably large, finely shaped mountain. If you climb to its top you can see the route by which you came, and all the hills [you climbed] look flat. The view of surrounding mountains is difficult to describe in words." And so the "geographical guide" to the courtesans goes, as the author comments on which "places" (courtesans) are worth seeing, which are overtouristed ("this village is famous for its sunrise, but because of that, everyone wants to stay there"), and which are in need of repair or have outlived their formerly good reputations. Like any good guidebook, it makes note of every "village," "lake," "bridge," "forest," and even every "well," "pond," and "inlet" in the "Land of the Rising Moon." In doing so, it becomes a map of taste, in which the orderly cartographic schema articulates the hierarchy of Yoshiwara society.[43]

The genres combined to construct this elaborate parody are numerous and wide-ranging. Kisanji makes maps and other geographical texts work on many different levels, and he challenges the reader to "get" his

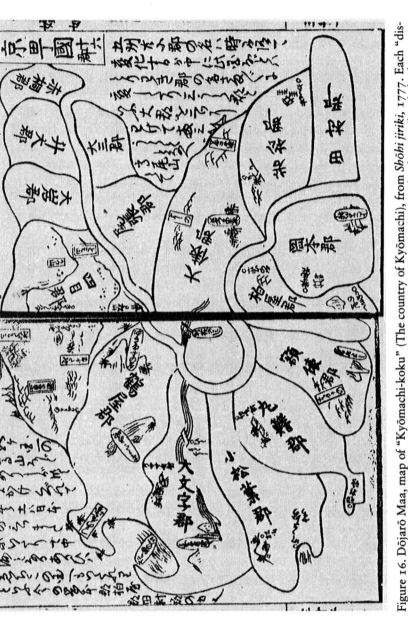

Figure 16. Dōjarō Maa, map of "Kyōmachi-koku" ("The country of Kyōmachi"), from *Shōbi jiriki*, 1777. Each "district" (*gun*) represents a brothel. Beginning at top center and moving clockwise, the districts/brothels shown are Yotsume-gun, Ōiwa-gun, Masudai-gun, Akagiri-gun, Daisan-gun, Owari-gun, Odawara-gun, Wakamatsu-gun, Tamura-gun, Okamoto-gun, Kashiwaya-gun, Gakudawara-gun, Maruei-gun, Komatsuba-gun, Daimonji-gun, and Tsuruya-gun. Courtesy of the National Diet Library, Tokyo.

multilayered joke. This satirical endeavor must have appealed to its audience, for later writers also adopted the map as a vehicle for parody, and they, even more than Kisanji, piled on the references, puns, and allusions to create bold pastiches of Edo culture, past and present.

Shikitei Sanba and the Mapping of Edo's Cultural History

For Shikitei Sanba, unlike Hōseidō Kisanji, writing fiction was not a sideline to more "serious" work. Born in Edo to a merchant family, he ran a variety of businesses, including a small printing concern and, more famously, a medicine shop, while making his name as a writer.[44] In 1802 Sanba took it upon himself to write what he called a "twisted history" of *kusazōshi,* popular illustrated fiction. In charting the development of a popular strain of literature and art, Sanba uses a different representational scheme than does Hōseidō Kisanji: the entertainment in Sanba's text is in the clever use of conventions ranging from Gyōki-style maps to *ukiyoe* (prints of the "floating world" of pleasure) to the popular histories known as *nendaiki.* By using these visual and textual metaphors, Sanba endeavors to describe the shifts in literary and artistic style from the Genroku period to the turn of the nineteenth century. His use of illustration, maps, and the diagrammatic form of the *nendaiki* allows him to show stylistic change graphically as well as verbally. In the opening lines to *[Mata yakinaosu Hachikazuki-hime] Kusazōshi kojitsuke nendaiki* ([Twice-cooked tale of Princess Pot-on-the-Head] The twisted history of popular fiction), he writes:

> This twisted history gathers together and summarizes the stylistic changes and trends [that have taken place] over time in popular fiction from its beginnings to the present time. However, dividing [this history] into [phases] of early, middle, and late takes up too many pages, and is not very detailed. To give better examples, Kitao-sensei [Kitao Masanobu][45] has produced pictures in the style of Torii Kiyomitsu,[46] Kiyotsune, and artists of the present time, altering the styles as they have changed over the years. [Masanobu] remakes the pictures [in their original style]. Still, one isn't able to include everything, so it's better to await the revised and expanded edition *[zōhō taizen]* [of this book] due next spring.[47]

Endeavoring to cover the peak years of production of popular literature in Edo, the text amounts to an offbeat survey of Edo print culture in the eighteenth century.[48] Its first part takes as its model a *nendaiki* by Kishida Tohō entitled *[Jūhō] Kusazōshi nendaiki* ([Great treasure] History of popular literature), published in 1783.[49] Whereas history on the classical model *(shi)* derived from the Chinese dynastic histories, *nendaiki* tended to be more accessible guides to past events, aimed toward readers more interested in calendars and horoscopes than in the weighty narratives of formal historical writing. *Nendaiki* were also much more visually oriented than classical histories, making heavy use of illustrations, maps (usually in the Gyōki style), and symbols. The *[Jūho] Kusazōshi nendaiki,* for instance, presented information in graphic form on the front of the page, while narrative explanations *(zassho)* and maps were printed on the back of the page.[50] Sanba follows the *nendaiki* model closely for the first section of the book, then gradually merges it into the plot of the folktale *Hachikazuki-hime* (Princess Pot-on-the-Head), which provides the satirical setting *(shukō)* for the remainder of the story. The present discussion will put aside discussion of the *Hachikazuki-hime* theme in order to focus on the blending of map imagery and what might loosely be termed cultural history in the *nendaiki* section of Shikitei Sanba's text.

Sanba opens his "twisted" history by replacing the original *nendaiki's* listing of information about important historical figures and events with a directory-like listing of the names, insignia *(mokuin),* and addresses of the guild-affiliated publishers in the city of Edo *(Edo jihon toiya).* In contrast to the original *nendaiki's* conventionalized subtitle "Great Treasure" *(jūho*—literally, "heavy treasure"), Sanba labels his history a "lightweight jewel" *(fujūho).* In doing so, he draws a distinction between the "official" information conveyed in conventional *nendaiki*— names of the shoguns, lists of famous religious figures—and his collection of the names of contemporary artists, writers, and their publishers. Sanba lists nineteen major Edo publishing houses that together produced the most widely read works of late-Edo-period fiction; the author notes that the list is not quite comprehensive, for there are "a few more [publishers] this year" that he has not included.[51] (Table 1 replicates the list of publishing houses.)

On the reverse of the page listing the publishers Sanba includes two "name-lists" *(nayose* or *nazukushi).* The first, a list of writers of comic fiction *(gesakusha nayose),* is in the *nendaiki* style, with the text set off in rectangular boxes. The names of eighteen authors from the late seventeenth through the early nineteenth century appear (see table 2 and fig. 17, top).[52] This list, Sanba notes, presents "works by authors who are familiar to you, without regard to new and old."[53]

The second name-list, which comprises the lower half of the page, is

TABLE I. LIST OF EDO'S GUILD PUBLISHERS
(JIHON TOIYA), FROM SHIKITEI SANBA,
KUSAZŌSHI KOJITSUKE NENDAIKI

Name	Location (in Edo)
Urokogataya Magobee	Tōri Abura-chō
Yamamoto Kubee	Tōri Abura-chō
Maruya Kanpachi	Tōri Abura-chō
Matsumura Yahee	Tōri Abura-chō
Murataya Jirōbee	Tōri Abura-chō
Tsutaya Jūsaburō	Tōri Abura-chō
Tsuruya Kiemon	Tōri Abura-chō
Iseya Jisuke	Yamashita-chō
Yoshiya Tahee	Bakurō-chō
Iwatoya Genpachi	Kaya-chō
Enokimoto Yoshibee	Yokoyama-chō
Yamaguchiya Tadasuke	Tōri Hatago-chō
Nishimura Yahachi	Bakurō-chō
Izumoya Ichibee	Bakurō-chō
Ōwada Shutten	Jinmyo-mae
Okumura Genroku	Ōdenma-chō
Nishinomiya Shinroku	Moto zaimoku-chō

of contemporary Japanese artists *(Yamato eshi)*. Sanba explains, "In addition to illustrators of *kusazōshi*, there are many famous artists, present and past, [who specialize in] single-sheet prints *[ichimai-e]*, and they are [also] listed here." This "list," however, unlike the former, is not in *nendaiki* style but in the form of a Gyōki-style map (fig. 17; see table 3 for a list of artists' names and their locations on the map). Sanba's choice of a map for this part of the history clearly derived in great part from his model text, for Kishida's *Kusazōshi nendaiki* contained a Gyōki-style regional map of the provinces of Ōmi, Minō, Shinano, and Kai, from which Sanba borrowed heavily. But there is perhaps another reason for the choice of a map, one that has more to do with the nature of the information being represented. The grouping of artists into schools, the members of which often shared a family name even if they were not related by blood, was particularly amenable to the representational schema of the Gyōki-style map. Like Hōseidō Kisanji's district/brothel, *meisho*/courtesan scheme, the map allowed for relative placement to represent familial or school ties. In Sanba's map of artists, each "island" generally represents a school and its style, and within it, each "province" stands for an individual artist, although some exceptional talents,

TABLE 2. NAME-LIST OF WRITERS OF COMIC
FICTION *(GESAKUSHA NAYOSE)*, FROM SHIKITEI
SANBA, *KUSAZŌSHI KOJITSUKE NENDAIKI*

Name	Genre
Wayō	*kurohon/aohon*
Hōrai Sanjin	*kibyōshi*
Tanaka Masunobu	*kurohon/aohon*
Jōa	*kurohon/aohon*
Moji	unknown
Tsūkō	unknown
[Hōseidō] Kisanji[1]	*kibyōshi*
Koikawa Harumachi[2]	*kibyōshi*
Shiba Zenkō[3]	*kibyōshi*
Manzō Tei[4]	*kibyōshi*
Tōrai Sanwa[5]	*kibyōshi*
Sakuragawa Kishida	*kibyōshi*
Tsūshō	*kibyōshi*
Kashō	*kibyōshi*
Shichihachi Manpo[6]	*kibyōshi*
Mihashi Kisanji	*kibyōshi*
Roku Sanjin Nobunami	*kibyōshi*
Shiba Kankō	*kibyōshi*

[1] Whereas only the names of the foregoing writers are listed, in the cluster of six larger boxes on the left-hand side of Sanba's list, the seals and alternate pen names of Kisanji and five other writers appear. The entry for Kisanji is as follows: "[seal] Hōseidō Kame Sanjin is also known as Tegara no Okamochi [seal]." KKN, p. 233.
[2] "[seal] Koikawa Harumachi, also known as Sake no ue no Furachi." Ibid.
[3] "[seal]." Ibid.
[4] "[seal] Shinra Banshō, his later *gō* is Manzō Tei, now known as Fūrai Sanjin, Keirin Sō, also Takesue no Sugaru." Ibid.
[5] "[seal] Tōrai Sanwa, also known as Tōrai Tei, Roku Sanjin." Ibid.
[6] "[seal] Shichichin Manpo, later *gō* Shinra Tei, now known as Nidai-me Manzō Tei [second-generation Manzō Tei]." This writer is obviously a disciple of Morishima Chūryō, a.k.a. Manzō Tei. Ibid.

like Hokusai, Utamarō, and Sharaku, have separate islands named after them.

Sanba's book, despite its general claim to be a "history" of popular literature, does not represent historical or temporal development, as do the *nendaiki*. The artists all stand in relationship to one another, but not to time. In fact, it is not until Sanba moves into the parody of the *Hachikazuki-hime* story that he begins to address the question of stylistic evolution over time via the illustrations cleverly executed by Kitao Moronobu in imitation of the styles of various artists. In contrast to the sequence of illustrations, the map allows him to show horizontal

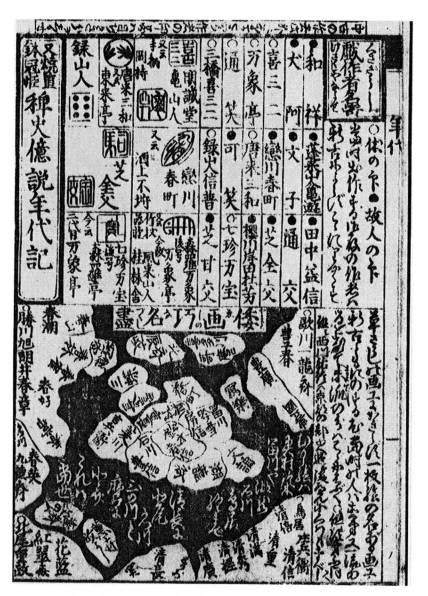

Figure 17. Shikitei Sanba, name-list of writers of comic fiction (gesakusha), top, and map of famous artists, bottom; from Kusazōshi kojitsuke nendaiki, 1802. Courtesy of the Kaga Collection, Tokyo Metropolitan Central Library.

TABLE 3. NAME-LIST OF JAPANESE ARTISTS (*YAMATO
ESHI NAZUKUSHI*), FROM SHIKITEI SANBA,
KUSAZŌSHI KOJITSUKE NENDAIKI

School or family name[1]	Artist's given name[2]
Utagawa	Ichiryūsai, Toyoharu, Toyohiro, Toyokuni
Torii (1)	Shohee Kiyonobu, Kiyomasu, Kiyoshige, Kiyomichi, Kiyohide, Kiyotsune, Kiyohiro
Torii (2)	Kiyonaga, Kiyoseki
Kitao (1)	Shigemasa, Kōsuisai, Karan
Kitao (2)	Tsūsai, Masanobu
Kitao (3)	[Kuwagata] Keisai Masayoshi
Katsukawa	Kyūtokusai, Shun'ei, Shuntō, Shunkō, Katsukawa Shunshō, Shunkaku, Shunrin, Shunchō, Shunsan, Rantokusai
Sanchō [and] Chōki	Sanchō, Chōki
Hokusai Tatsumasa	Hokusai Tatsumasa
Kitagawa Utamarō	Kitagawa Utamarō
Sharaku	Sharaku (large central island)[3] Harumachi, Tomigawa Ginsetsu, Fusanobu, Bunchō, Chōryūsai, Ishikawa Toyonobu, Hishikawa Yoshibee [Moronobu], Okumura Shigenaga, Suzuki Harunobu

[1] As names of "islands," reading clockwise from top right of map, moving to center.
[2] As names of "provinces" on "islands."
[3] Clockwise from top right, moving to center.

networks among contemporary practicing artists. In the absence of
other historical maps against which it could be compared, Sanba's "list"
of artists maps a space—and a moment—out of time.

A Cosmology of Pleasure:
Akatsuki Kanenari's "Insatiable Assets"

The last of the geographies of pleasure to be discussed is Akatsuki Kanenari's *Akan sanzai zue* (The insatiable illustrated three assets, 1821–50),
an extended parody of Terajima Ryōan's *Wakan sansai zue* (The illustrated Japanese-Chinese encyclopedia of the three elements, 1712).[54]
Completed in 1850, it sustains through multiple volumes its fusion of
maps, encyclopedias, and parodies of the pleasure quarters. In many
ways it represents the culmination of the process through which Edo
writers manipulated geographic, cartographic, and literary tropes and
images to refashion the relationship between place and culture.

Akan sanzai zue is not nearly as well known as the works by Sanba and Kisanji, nor is much known about the author. What we can discern from the text itself is that the author was, like most writers of satire, highly educated and very familiar with a wide range of texts, classical and contemporary, Chinese, Japanese, and perhaps, to some degree, European. He wrote and edited several published works, three of which are advertised at the end of the second volume of *Akan sanzai zue*.[55] Kanenari's intentions for the *Akan sanzai zue* are made clear in the preface *(hanrei)*, which is a parody of the preface of the *Wakan sansai zue*:

—This book makes fun of the way people throw away their money *[sanzai]* in the pleasure quarters and entertainment districts. It takes the three elements, heaven, earth, and man, [but] mixes them up and makes a joke out of them.

—Although [this book] contains rules of conduct for brothel patrons, it won't bring you bliss. . . . The book is neither poison nor cure.

—I have given the book the title *Akan sanzai zue* because it refers to the way brothel patrons scatter their money all over the pleasure quarters, but are never satisfied.

—I write the title "three assets" instead of "scattering money" because if a book came out in early spring with a title like [scattering money], it would be an inauspicious start, [or] so said the publisher, so I changed "scatter" to "three."

—[The book] doesn't include descriptions of all the pleasure quarters, because I want to describe them in detail. I wouldn't be able to convey the charm of the pleasure districts if I included everything.

—To call this an elegant book *[suisho]* would not be elegant *[sui]* at all. In it there is elegance, and there is nonelegance. [But] what is elegance, what is nonelegance? Even truth becomes a lie. If an elegant book sells, it becomes boorish. Then, because everything in the book starts to sound idiotic, [the author] has to hurry up and rewrite it, and apologize. When the readers *[ransuru kyaku]* find out about [the author's] apology, they won't apologize; if [the book] has got any sort of reputation, they'll say "this is the elegance [meant] for me."[56]

There are several points to note about this characterization of the book's contents. First is the author's concern with the marketability of the text, a sentiment no sooner articulated than it is undercut by his disdain for the whole idea of "selling" guides to elegance. Such contradictions were not unusual in writers of *gesaku,* but they are interesting for what they say about the relationship between artistic and literary creativity (which, to a considerable but not unlimited degree, valued innovation) and market value. More than the previous two authors discussed here, Kanenari seems to find the writer's pretense of pure artistic creativity and the demands of the market equally burdensome.

A brief comparison to the *Wakan sansai zue* preface makes this idea clearer. More than anything, the *Wakan sansai zue* professes to be a comprehensive, easy-to-use reference book. Terajima claims to have compiled the words of "many teachers," chosen the "appropriate" passages out of them, and cobbled them together. He notes that he has added numerous diagrams, and given several alternate names and readings for each entry: "on the right is *hiragana* for Japanese names, on the left is *katakana* for the Chinese names; it's easy enough for a child to read."[57] According to Kanenari's preface, by contrast, absolute truth is not nearly so easy to acquire. The author himself makes it clear that although the book may give some instruction on how to be stylish, it "won't bring you bliss." He seems to question why so many people exhaust their energies and money in the pleasure quarters in pursuit of an elusive elegance that can hardly be defined. This very elusiveness, though, is the key to this circuit of desire: the thing or person that gains a good reputation, however fleeting, gains in value whether or not that person or thing has any inherent worth. At the same time, simply selling in mass quantities seems to matter little to Kanenari, for "if a book sells, it becomes boorish." As in the disparity between a high-ranking courtesan and a "nighthawk," difference does not manifest itself only in visible, surface qualities; instead, the most telling differences lie in the evanescent and amorphous qualities of elegance, refinement, taste, or beauty. These qualities form the all-important determinant of success or failure in a world in which the boundaries among the marketplace, literary and intellectual life, and the pleasure quarters were frequently blurred.

The preface of *Akan sanzai zue* sets the reader up for a tour through Kanenari's topsy-turvy world, in which the fundaments of the cosmos are not the "three elements" of the *Wakan sansai zue*—heaven, earth, and humankind—but instead are the various "assets" that must be possessed by the pleasure-seeker, who will then "spend" them in the pleasure quarters. In the first volume of the first book of *Akan sanzai zue*, Kanenari begins with a diagram of the nine circuits or paths of the moon, entitled *Kontangi no zu* (fig. 18). The word *Kontangi* plays on *Kontengi*, an astronomical text of the Later Han (78–135 C.E.), in which the author observes that the heavens are constantly in motion, but it also puns on the term *kontan*, meaning "that which is hidden." The

Figure 18. Akatsuki Kanenari, "Kontangi no zu" (Map of the hidden [way]), from *Akan sanzai zue,* vol. 1:1, 1821. Courtesy of the National Diet Library, Tokyo.

diagram is a direct adaptation of one that appears in the first volume of
the first book of *Wakan sansai zue*. But instead of explaining the principles of lunar observation and astronomy, Akatsuki uses the diagram to
map the ways of love. In place of the yellow, red, white, green, and blue
circuits of the original astronomical diagram, Akatsuki graphs the "way
of the [brothel] patrons" *(kyakudō)*, the "way of love" *(shikidō)*, the
"horizontal way" *(yokodō)*, the "extreme way" *(gokudō)*, and the "way
to pay" *(kandō)*. Although Terajima Ryōan and the Chinese encyclope-
dists before him started with the cosmos in order to work down the
great chain of being to end with humans and their customs, Kanenari
disregards the hierarchical conventions of his model text. Instead, he begins and ends with the immediate and self-centered realm of pleasure.

Following the *Kontangi no zu* is a second diagram, also adapted from
the *Wakan sansai zue*, entitled *Kyūten no zu* (Map of the nine heavens).
Again, in place of astronomy one finds a diagram of the different kinds
of entertainments to be found in the various pleasure quarters (fig. 19).
The text in the diagram states that the "commonly used" name for the
nine heavens *(kyūten)* is *kugai* (another term for the pleasure quarters
and also a homonym for the nine heavens or worlds, *kūgai*).[58] In the
heavenly realms of the *kugai*, there are brilliant constellations to view
throughout the night. But this seemingly innocuous pun hides yet another set of "rankings" of the arts of pleasure. The hierarchy begins
from the "supreme heaven" of the outermost circuit, occupied by the
keisei ("courtesan star," a pun on a homonym used to refer to the highest ranking courtesans, the *tayū*). The neighboring orbit is the heaven
of the *sūgi* (or *shinzō*, a courtesan of high rank second to the *tayū*). Moving inward, there is the *shamisei* (*shamisen* [zither] star), located in the
heaven of song, and the *shōjo sei* (young girl star), located in the heaven
of dance; both of these represent artistic talents possessed by higher-
ranking courtesans. Next is the *dondon sei* (bang-bang star), whose
drumbeat is part of the heaven of attracting customers (literally, the
heaven of "head-turning"). Further inward is the *zōkyaku sei* (priest-
patron star), which orbits in the heaven of male love, in which priests
were notorious if illicit participants. The circuits move steadily inward
until we reach the smallest, least significant orbit, that of the *yahotsu
ten*, or streetwalker heaven. The remainder of the section on the heavens describes the key planets and constellations. For each entry there
is an illustration, most of which parody those of the *Wakan sansai zue*
by substituting the people, places, and things of the pleasure quarter for
astronomical or astrological phenomena: the moon is a brothel patron,

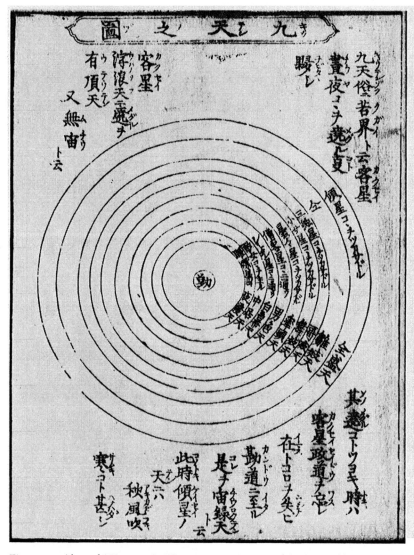

Figure 19. Akatsuki Kanenari, "Kyūten no zu" (Map of the insatiable nine heavens), from *Akan sanzai zue,* vol. 1:1, 1821. Courtesy of the National Diet Library, Tokyo.

the biggest star is the courtesan, thunder is a drum player, clouds are the embroidered pattern on a kimono sash, and wind comes from a hand fan.

The sections of the *Akan sanzai zue* centered on geography and on "foreign and civilized" *(ka-i)* peoples show more explicit uses of the

Figure 20. Akatsuki Kanenari, "Karyū betsu sekai no zu" (Map of the willowy other world), from *Akan sanzai zue*, vol. 1:2, 1821. Courtesy of the National Diet Library, Tokyo.

map. At the beginning of the geography section in book one, volume two is Kanenari's satirical take on a European-style globe entitled "Map of the Willowy Other World" *(Karyū betsu sekai no zu)* (fig. 20). The "Western" influence here is evident in the attempt to mimic an alphabetic script in the upper part of the right half of the two-page illustration. On the globe itself, the landmasses representing the "continents" are clearly shadowy outlines of human figures, which together form a scene of courtesans entertaining patrons in a brothel. The women are seated about the room, one playing a *shamisen,* one smoking a pipe, one pouring tea. Dishes and hibachi braziers are scattered about the room, as are the patrons, lounging on the floor in a relaxed manner. Each of the "continents" bears a name, two of which are fairly obvious phonetic puns on the names of foreign countries. "Korobia" which refers to the outline of the woman pouring sake, plays on the Japanese verb "to fall down [drunk]" *(korobu)* and likely refers to the actual country of Colombia. "Shaberia," located above and to the right of Korobia, plays on the verb "to chat" *(shaberu)* and puns on Siberia. All the other continent names, however, simply pun on the situation or activity they seem to be depicting. Each name is rendered only in *katakana,* the syllabary most often used for terms or names from foreign languages. To the left of Shaberia, below a screen blocking the view of what is going on behind it, is "Namekusari," or "raw odors," a not overly delicate hint at the type of activity taking place out of the reader's sight. At top center, next to the figure of what appears to be a person sleeping with his back turned, is "Muka[u]tsuki," or "looking away." At top left, next to the image of a man eagerly leaning toward a courtesan smoking a pipe, is "Yodareya," playing on the Japanese verb "to drool," which is clearly meant to characterize the ardor of the suitor. At middle right, next to a half-reclining figure of a man, is "Noroma," meaning dull-witted or slow, and just below him is "Suwaru to ba toru" ("when you sit there, you [only] take up space," probably an admonition to this dullard of a guest). Below the figure of the woman playing a *shamisen* in the middle of the globe is the label "Tsuntonya," a play on the term *tsunto,* referring to someone who is standoffish or prissy. And at far right, at the very ends of the earth, is a distant continent labeled only "Yume iro," or "dreams of love." The meanings of the parody are clear: unlike the modern globe, which seeks to make sense of space, Akatsuki's seeks to make nonsense of it.

The map puns become more acute when the author turns to the subject of the foreign. In the "foreign people" section, Akatsuki begins

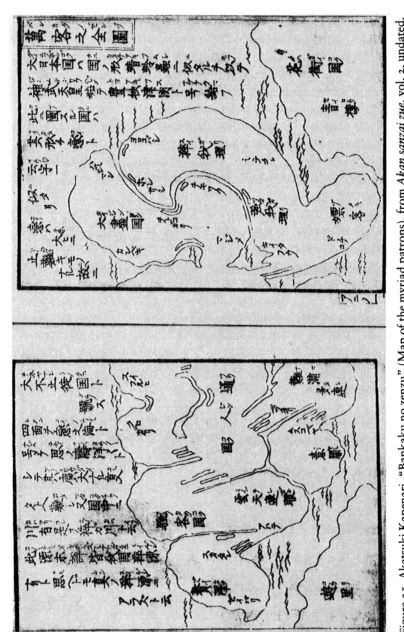

Figure 21. Akatsuki Kanenari, "Bankaku no zenzu" (Map of the myriad patrons), from *Akan sanzai zue*, vol. 2, undated. Courtesy of the National Diet Library, Tokyo.

a discussion of the peoples of the world by creating a "map of the myriad patrons," or *Bankaku no zenzu* (fig. 21). This is clearly a pun on the world maps, or "maps of myriad countries" *(bankoku no zu)*, included in most encyclopedias and gazetteers. The first thing that is evident about the map of the "myriad patrons" is that it is an archipelago of sorts, whose islands form the shape of the character for *koi*, or desire.[59] Within this land of desire are, once again, numerous countries, each of which represents a type of brothel patron. Major categories of clients are written in larger characters; some are represented as "countries," such as the Land of the Rich (Daijin-koku), the Land of the Refined Patron (Tsūjin-koku), and the Land of the Rowdy Patron (Sōkaku-koku). Other major types include posers *(suigari* and *tsuyogari)*, spendthrifts *(zeitaku)*, disruptive guests *(zomeki)*, idiots *(unteregan)*, and the hard-to-please *(na[n]ma[n]tare)*. Each "country" or region also contains smaller local places, which seem to represent variations on the dominant types of patron; sexual preference, for example, is acknowledged by the inclusion of "man-chasers" *(otokogari)*, located in the general vicinity of the Land of the Rich, and "show-offs" *(kiitafuu)*, who are placed in the region of posers. Two landmasses at bottom right and bottom left represent, respectively, the entertainment districts (Kagai-koku) and the pleasure quarters *(yūri)*. These, one presumes, are the destinations for visitors from the country of the "myriad guests," where the land itself literally *makes* love.[60] The almost complete fusion of image, icon, and written language to produce multiple meanings in this modified map is apparent.

The last of Akatsuki's maplike diagrams comes in the geography *(chi)* section of *Akan sanzai zue*. Here, he begins with a one-page map entitled *Shumisen no zu* (fig. 22), which he glosses as "Map of Nape-of-the-Neck Mountain."[61] When read phonetically, however, "Shumisen" puns on Mount Sumeru (also read "Shumisen"), the most sacred mountain in Buddhist cosmology, said to be the center of the entire universe. Visually, it is obvious at a glance that the "mountain" is the standing figure of a courtesan, viewed from behind. The pun here is at least twofold: first, it is one of substitution, placing a mere human being, and a courtesan no less, in Buddhism's most sacred place. In this case the pun works as a comparison of superlatives, on the one hand Mt. Sumeru, the most sacred of spaces, and on the other the nape of the neck, the most erotic of places on the female body. But the map is also and equally a play on meanings that would be known only to those familiar with the

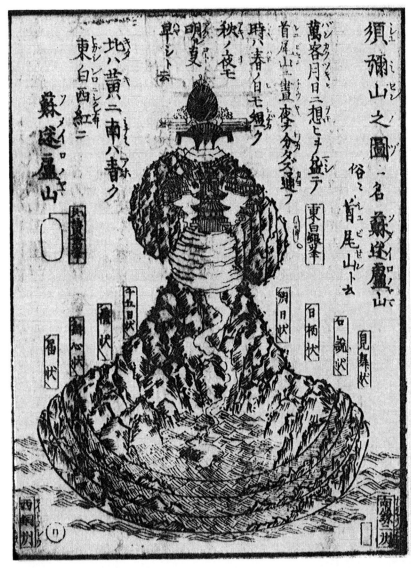

Figure 22. Akatsuki Kanenari, "Shumisen no zu" (Map of Nape-of-the-Neck Mountain), from *Akan sanzai zue,* vol. 3, 1850. Courtesy of the National Diet Library, Tokyo.

pleasure quarters. For in Yoshiwara *saiken* and other guidebooks the symbol *(aijirushi)* used to designate high-ranking courtesans was the double or single triangle, which resembles the shape of a mountain. By building on the courtesan-as-mountain visual pun, Akatsuki brings the semiotic process full circle, as the courtesan who had previously been symbolized *by* a mountain (as shorthand for the labels of rank and, ultimately, price) now *becomes* a mountain. Moreover, "Shumisen" is a label that—unlike the coded symbol of the *saiken*—embodies not the standards of the earthly (or fleshly) world, but those of the sublime and sacred.

In addition to referencing Mount Sumeru, the iconography of the map of Shumisen also plays on the convention of pilgrimage to sacred mountain peaks. Many maps were published in the early modern period to aid pilgrims in their journeys to mountainous sacred sites like Kumano, Kōya, and, of course, Fuji. In the *Akan sanzai zue* map, however, the "pilgrim" is the brothel patron, who must undertake the arduous climb toward the "summit" of the courtesan's body, symbolized by the nape of the neck. The spread-out skirt of the courtesan's robe thus becomes the route the patron must navigate on his climb toward the peak of pleasure. As on a pilgrimage route, each station along the route is clearly marked on the mountain path. But instead of measuring the distance covered during the trek, as road markers would do, in this map the stations mark the patron's progress in his pursuit of the courtesan's favors. He begins (on lower right) with a *mimai*, an initial introduction or "viewing" of courtesan by patron and vice versa; he then proceeds to the *kōsetsu*, or face-to-face meeting, and moves up to the *higara*, the day on which a patron buys out a courtesan's contract. This allows him access to the brothel, and from there, presumably, to the courtesan's body. Clearly, this is the path of success. By contrast, on the left is the path to failure. It begins with the sending of an initial appeal *(todoke)*, which is turned away *(mushin)* and is followed by an interminable period of waiting. An appearance in person, it seems, was the more direct route to a courtesan's heart.

The text surrounding the map of the "mountain" describes its location, in both geographic and geomantic terms. In the same way that Mount Sumeru stands at the center of Buddhist cosmological maps, here Shumisen occupies the central place, around which are arrayed the four directions. Each of the directions is assigned a color: north is yellow, south is blue, east is white, west is red. Thus is the mountain "dyed in color" *(some iro no yama)* or, to engage in an alternate reading of the characters of that phrase, "bathed in sex."[62] The explanation following the map explains that, like Mount Sumeru, Mount Nape-of-the-Neck is also surrounded by four states. To the north are the "new lands," sparkling with new construction; hence, north is golden. To the south are watery river lands; hence, south is green. To the east are brothels with their white curtains, so the east is white. Finally, to the west are the entertainment districts with their lights burning all night long, so the west is red. To anyone who was familiar with the basic geography of Edo, the references here are clear: Mount Nape-of-the-Neck and its surrounding "states" describe the Yoshiwara and its location within Edo.[63] It seems not coincidental that the Yoshiwara, the first and most sacred of pleasure quarters, should be the sacred center of the "other world" of pleasure. The contrast between sacred and profane is not only stark, it is telling, for in few other texts can we see so clearly the simultaneous exposure and explosion of the hierarchical functions of geography and of notions of class and status that prevailed in all of Tokugawa society, but took on particular valences in the Yoshiwara.

NOSTALGIA, THE BODY, AND THE MAP: THE ANTIPOLITICS OF PLEASURE

The foregoing discussion of various remappings of pleasure and place raises numerous questions. By the middle of the nineteenth century, when the last book of *Akan sanzai zue* was published, what did it really *mean* to reduce the cosmos to the body of a courtesan? Did the "insatiable" desire alluded to in the title of the text also characterize the demand for these types of texts? Or did maps and geography simply become grist for the mill of literary fashion? And what, if any, political implications did this popularization have? The development of geographical satire reveals at several levels the interwoven nature of the different dimensions of space: physical, social, discursive, and bodily.

As we have seen, the social structure of the Yoshiwara shifted along with the class dynamics of Edo. These changes were reflected in the mappings and remappings of the pleasure quarters themselves, in *saiken, sharebon,* and other texts, which in turn shaped the image of pleasure quarters in the minds of readers within and outside Edo.[64] By the beginning of the nineteenth century, satire's turn to focus on the insular culture of the pleasure quarters seemed to render it apolitical. But in yet

another ironic twist, in the context of turn-of-the-century politics—the
growing foreign threat, the struggle to once again institute reactionary
Confucian reforms, rising rural and urban unrest—the resolute focus
on the apolitical was, in itself, a political stance. In this sense, the
spatialized strategies of *sharebon*, which remapped the pleasure quarters
as the "other" Japan, made light of very serious issues concerning Japan's boundaries, sovereignty, and political integrity. *Sharebon* writers
did this by intertwining geographic and cartographic allusions with
the concrete image of the human body and the abstract metaphor of
the past.

The use of the past to poke fun at the present is most evident if we
compare historical and fictional perspectives on the Yoshiwara and its
high-ranking courtesans. While illicit pleasure quarters *(okabasho,* also
known colloquially as "hells," or *jigoku)* sprang up all over Edo in the
eighteenth century, until the turn of the nineteenth century the Yoshiwara retained its place at the apex of the hierarchy of pleasure quarters.
As one author put it in a guide to the licensed quarters published in
1778, "[The] accomplishments of the Yoshiwara are something that il-
legal prostitutes elsewhere could never compete with."[65] But this statement did not remain true for long. In 1811, Shikitei Sanba described the
Yoshiwara as "extremely quiet" and noted that the *saiken* at that time
listed few courtesans of high rank.[66] This was just the beginning of a
downhill slide that accelerated in the following decades. In the 1830s,
during the bakufu's Tenpō reforms, the government began to crack
down once again on prostitution and conspicuous consumption. By
1850, the Yoshiwara had become all but indistinguishable from Edo's
illicit pleasure quarters, its courtesans essentially prostitutes, gaudily
made-up and dependent not on their skills in the fine arts, but on the sale
of sexual services.

In the fictional works we have discussed here, this decline is not at all
apparent, at least on the surface. Rather, the various guides to the ways
of the pleasures quarters seem to depict a Yoshiwara frozen in a kind of
golden age, a world apart untouched by the passage of time. Even in the
last volume of *Akan sanzai zue,* published in 1850, the way to the courtesan's heart is a highly formalized one, redolent of the old Yoshiwara.
The initial meeting, the dispatch of letters, the buying-out of the contract: these were the practices of a time past, undertaken by an ever-
dwindling minority of brothel patrons. Those inclined to buy out a courtesan's contract were by this time more likely to choose a courtesan from

the newly thriving pleasure districts in the Fukugawa area east of the Sumida River, the new heart of the commoner downtown.[67] The image of the courtesan as mountain in the *Akan sanzai zue* played on the *saiken's* symbol for courtesans of rank and elegance, but by 1850 these were signs of the past. This seems odd in a genre (that of *sharebon*) that prided itself on being up-to-date. Perhaps, then, we might see this nostalgia for the Yoshiwara of old as a literary invention. In the same contradictory way that the Tokugawa bakufu's "reform" efforts were fundamentally reactionary, with their slogans urging disgruntled and underpaid samurai to "look back to Ieyasu," *sharebon's* longing for past times can be understood as a plea to recapture the Yoshiwara's faded glory, which itself became an increasingly elusive ideal. Yoshiwara, like other *meisho,* came to represent a place whose identity remained fixed, removed from or perhaps even defiant of change inflicted upon it.

Part of the humor of *sharebon* lay in its gamble with time; its authors and readers were involved in an endless race where novelty and invention lay just beyond the finish line. The use of geographic tropes and metaphors—even if they contributed to a nostalgic yearning for the past—was one way to use space to beat time. In order to make this work, however, the geography in *sharebon* had to differ from the satirical geographies that came before them. If we compare the uses of geography in the works discussed in this chapter to those discussed in the previous chapter, we can see how the function as well as the forms of mapping changed between the mid-eighteenth and the mid-nineteenth centuries. Whereas the fantastic fictions of Hiraga Gennai, Yū Koku Shi, and others created fantasy worlds out of foreign countries, *saiken* and *sharebon* identified new worlds within Japan, often within the city of Edo. There were many reasons to do so: pressures from outside (the foreign threat) made the foreign an unsuitable topic, while pressures from the inside such as crop failures and famines drove rural populations to the cities clamoring for aid, causing popular riots to break out even in the relatively tightly policed capital of Edo.[68] With these various and threatening strangers rattling the gates, urban culture, especially Edo culture, took an inward turn. Hayashiya Tatsusaburō has described Edo culture during the Bunka-Bunsei era (1804–30) as "overripe" *(ranjuku).*[69] This term conveys the image of a culture stewing in its own juices, so to speak, a convenient metaphor for the extremely self-referential nature of much late-Edo popular fiction.

The cultural turn inward heightened the attention to the self, specifically to the surface manifestations of that self, in early-nineteenth-century satirical writing. The *Akan sanzai zue,* instead of offering a single guide to the "way of the *tsū,*" as earlier texts did, offered multiple sites in which elegance could be exhibited. The true way, in other words, was the way that worked. Whereas in previous eras there was an underlying principle that organically guided "right" action, now the influences flowed in the reverse direction: that which *appeared* to be right *was* right. To tap into success, one therefore had to adjust appearances by following the guide and learning to read and replicate behavior. To the person aspiring to this sort of elegance, costuming and adornment of the body was everything. This was true not only of the *tsū,* but of the courtesan herself, who now played to an audience much more attracted by showiness than by suggestion. The women of the Fukugawa quarters not only dressed in a much flashier manner, but also made up their faces in ways older Yoshiwara courtesans would never have done. *Sharebon* aided and abetted this process by describing and diagramming the minutiae of the pleasure life. In true encyclopedic fashion, the *Akan sanzai zue* pictured life in the pleasure quarters from its broadest stereotypes (the spendthrift patron, the high-ranking courtesan, the priest patrons) to its tiniest objects (tea whisks, hair ornaments, drinking vessels, tobacco pipes, *shamisen* picks). The sum of these highly objectified people and things, it implies, made pleasure. And the culmination of this encyclopedic exhibition was the body of the courtesan.

In other words, between 1750 and 1850 the geographic imagination, as charted in satire, experienced a significant transition. Whereas in its early phases geography and cartography were the vehicles for criticizing Japan by engaging in fantasy about the "foreign," by the mid-nineteenth century they were much more about the immediate bodily and material realities readily available at home. This shift in focus was a shift in spatial scale from the unknown landscapes of the imagination to the highly knowable surfaces of the body. The narrowing focus of these geographies of pleasure reflects the larger history of mapping in the early modern period. For as with early modern mapping in general, the story of satirical maps is not one of "cartographic" change; the repeated use of the Gyōki model determined that the visual structure and vocabulary of maps varied little in the works under consideration here. What changed was the increase in what we might call the map's range of movement, its ability to encompass multiple meanings within its own iconic form. For as maps made their way from government document to accessory for travel, to creative inspiration, and to in-joke, the most significant change in them was their growing flexibility as forms of representation. This is not to say that maps started out "serious" and got "playful"; as we have seen in previous chapters, satire itself functioned as a form of serious play, and printed maps had from the beginning cultivated the pleasure of viewing and knowing. Moreover, the shogunate all along considered mapping a serious matter and renewed its official mapmaking efforts through the early nineteenth century. Maps had always been seen as serious documents with playful potential; this made them the perfect vehicles for comic fiction, as writers used them to reveal the hidden and upend conventional beliefs.

Recognizing the driving forces behind satire—its propensity for inversion, unmasking, disorder—leads us to the question of power. Satirical fiction about the pleasure quarters seems utterly frivolous, devoid of any political substance whatsoever, but this was precisely what constituted its political message. To understand the antipolitics of pleasure, however, we must look to the broader context of late-eighteenth-century satire. As part of the Kansei reform movement led by Matsudaira Sadanobu in the late 1780s and early 1790s, the shogunate began to more rigorously enforce an orthodox vision of culture. In political thought, Sadanobu sought to reinvigorate the study of Neo-Confucianism as it was taught by the Hayashi School, long one of the favored schools of the Tokugawa shogunate. As part of this narrowing of the definition of acceptable thinking, the study of "heterodox" ideas was formally banned and the study of the "cultural and military arts" *(bunbu)* was encouraged. Sadanobu also promoted frugality, a tactic utilized by earlier official reformers. Together, these restrictions and their unprecedentedly strict enforcement struck hard at writers and artists, especially those who produced satire or erotica. Erotica was targeted for eventual elimination; as for satire, although some writers, Hōseidō Kisanji among them, made orthodoxy itself the subject of their satirical barbs, they were in the minority, and they did not go unpunished. Kisanji's 1788 send-up of Sadanobu's zeal for the "military and cultural arts" entitled *Bunbu nidō mangoku dōshi* (The winnower of the two roads of *bun* and *bu*) was banned in 1789. More generally, regulations of consumption "interfered in the daily life of the people; prostitutes, hairdressers, gamblers, writers of popular literature, and expensive fashions fell victim to Sadanobu's moralistic zeal for austerity."[70] These prohibitions ultimately were among the bakufu's last and best-known official pronouncements on the relationship between play, pleasure, and politics. From the start it was very clear that in official discourse modesty, frugality, loyalty, and filial piety were essential characteristics of the elite, especially of those who held public office. Pleasure, while not offensive in and of itself, became problematic when it was gained at great financial cost, pursued to the detriment of one's official or familial duties, or the cause of public shame, disrepute, or conflict. In other words, the "way" of pleasure should not under any circumstances interfere with the interpretation and implementation of the "way" of good governance and moral exemplarity. Pitted against the public good, pleasure was a private matter.[71]

Read in this context, the mapping of pleasure might be seen as an act with a particular political valence. Not only did satire flaunt private matters in a public, published form, they did so in time- and energy-consuming detail. Satirical geographies, for their part, went further in that they used a discursive form usually reserved for "important" matters and places to map and remap the marginal space that was the pleasure quarters. Like the travel writers discussed in chapters 2 and 3, writers of *sharebon* exercised a certain cultural authority over the peoples and places they described; but they did so without the self-conscious seriousness of purpose exhibited by Furukawa Koshōken, Kaibara Ekiken, and others. Instead, they were apt to coyly disclaim their intent to write for an audience, and to disparage their own work. Hōseidō Kisanji, in the preface to *Shōhi jiriki*, complains that "it is difficult to resist the demands of a publisher." He goes on to relate to the reader how "Darasuke the bookseller" took home his Yoshiwara *saiken* to read, and then demanded that Kisanji produce a fictional variation upon it. In the end, Kisanji laments that all he has produced is "a mixed-up glowing red weave of lies, whose threads are made of dreams." Certainly the creation story of Geppon is a weave of lies, but it is also one that uses humor to poke fun at the mythology of its sacred model, the *Kojiki*. Likewise, although the "mountains," "lakes," and "historical sites" of Geppon are made up, the "geographical guide to the courtesans" is a highly usable introduction to the Yoshiwara circa 1777. *Sharebon* weren't simply frivolous discourses that skimmed only the surface of things and people; they were exercises in reading texts, symbols, signs, pictures, and maps. They also required reading between the lines, for, unlike Hiraga Gennai's *Fūryū Shidōken den*, *sharebou* had no omniscient narrator who magically appears to explain everything.

In sum, we might argue that the critical edge of *sharebon* on geographic themes was in their strategic deployment of form as meaning. They used every weapon in the narratological arsenal of both contemporary and canonical texts, regardless of original intended use. Although the authors of the fictions discussed here seem to lament the passing of a time when the way of pleasure was singular and pure, they encouraged the fragmenting of the way through its popularization and commodification. In remapping pleasure, *sharebon* writers contributed to the process whereby the famous place and the circumscribed culture that was the Yoshiwara became diffused throughout the country, in text, in pictures, and in practice.

Conclusion

Famous Places Are Not National Spaces

I began this book by suggesting that the history of mapping was a history of ideas. The preceding chapters have described a process through which those ideas came to be held, manipulated, and transformed by ever-greater numbers of people, and accrued multiple and multilayered meanings. In closing, I want to suggest how, in the mid-nineteenth century, the increasingly public ideas and images conveyed by mapping ultimately did not lead to political or social change on a grand scale. While early modern mapping inflected Meiji-period cartography and geography in distinctive ways, its amalgamation of famous places did not simply add up to an all-encompassing nation-space.[1]

In the mid- to late nineteenth century, the insularity of late-Tokugawa forms of mapping was confronted directly by the universalizing forces of modern geography and cartography. The move toward the latter began around 1800, in the climate of unrest surrounding the arrival of Russian envoys and traders in the Kuril Islands and in Ezo in the 1790s.[2] From about 1800 on, in large part because of the international crisis, the incentive to survey and make more accurate maps, especially of Japan's coastline, increased significantly. Inō Tadataka (1745–1818), a surveyor and mapmaker of merchant origins who eventually earned a shogunal post, undertook the first surveys of Japan's coastline beginning in 1800 and over a period of many years produced the first accurately measured maps of the Japanese islands from Ezo to Kyushu.[3] Unlike the shogunate's maps of Japan, these maps were guarded as state secrets. The furor that arose when the German doctor Philipp von Siebold tried to take them to Europe indicates that the security of boundaries, both geographical and political, was acquiring new meanings in the early nineteenth century.[4]

In the Meiji period, as part of the state's widespread reforms, surveying and mapmaking were undertaken as part of a comprehensive land-reform policy and the creation of a national defense system. This constituted Japan's modern "cartographic revolution." Concepts of land and boundaries were now directly tied to new notions of Japan as a nation-state within an international community. Japanese scholars went to Europe and imbibed the principles of the classical study of geography, which they then used to reconstruct Japan's notions of nation and, ultimately, of empire. The Cambridge-educated political economist Inagaki Manjirō (1861–1908) predicted in 1892 that the twentieth century would be the "Pacific Age."[5] Local historians, school administrators, and teachers began to reformulate the teaching of geography to emphasize the connection between region, nation, and world, lessons that were eventually adopted and standardized by the Ministry of Education and taught to schoolchildren in regions all across Japan.[6] The Meiji government and local officials thus eliminated much of the ambiguity that characterized early modern mapping; no longer was there much question about what constituted "a map" (chizu), nor about what purposes maps served. At the same time, just as it did in other realms of administration, the Meiji government centralized the geographic process, placing control of mapmaking in the hands of the state and establishing standardized procedures for the measuring and representation of land.

In this context, early modern forms of mapping became increasingly marginalized; and yet they were not completely subsumed by the new geographic and cartographic practices. Edo-period maps and travel accounts continued to be published well into the latter part of the nineteenth century, even as more accurate and comprehensive texts became available. The gradual nature of this shift from one geo-cultural practice to another throws into relief some key characteristics of early modern mapping, which stand out in greater contrast when juxtaposed to Meiji cartography.

First is the matter of "accuracy." In the early modern period there were no universal standards of accurate measurement. As is discussed in chapter 1, units of measurement were standardized, but not always reliably, and surveying practice varied considerably from place to place. Rather than accuracy, then, what was important in early modern mapping was *precision*. How the two differed can be seen in several practices described in the preceding chapters, including the repeated revising of the information on the face of a map whose boundaries never changed; the inclusion of exhaustive detail in descriptive travel accounts; the dense narration of maps and guidebooks to cities, towns, and roads; the careful depiction and description of the pleasure quarters in *saiken* and *sharebon*. Each of these finely etched discourses of space, place, and culture is highly precise in its own way, and each gives the lie to universalist assumptions equating increased accuracy with increased utility. Emphasizing precision encourages us to look at mapping not as a linear process of development, but as a horizontal process of relationships between space, place, culture, and identity. One only has to browse through the guidebooks in the travel section of any Japanese bookstore today to see the that these linkages are alive and well in the language of modern tourism, which continues to emphasize the conventionalized representation of timeworn routes and tours throughout the archipelago, leading the reader/traveler along the circuits of famous places on "historical walks" *(rekishiteki sanpō),* and advising him or her on what to select from the panoply of famous local products *(miyage)*. Mapping, it seems, still "works" at a meaningful cultural level.

Early and even premodern map images, too, managed to retain a presence, if a circumscribed one, in modern (i.e., Meiji and post-Meiji) visual culture. As geography and cartography grew in importance, the modern survey map became the dominant icon of political and geographic unification and standardization. Older map images, however, remained visible nonetheless as decorative or antiquarian objects. Gyōki-style maps continued to be produced as images on a variety of household items and personal accessories well into the Meiji period. They embellished a wide range of goods, including ceramic plates, *inrō* lacquer cases, sword guards, tobacco cases, and sash toggles, and personal items like fans. In this incarnation, Gyōki's map came to represent a timeless and perhaps sacred image of the archipelago in a time when Japan itself was being transformed both geographically and politically.

Furthermore, map-decorated objects, though made to be displayed, were intended not for exhibition in public places, but for viewing in small-scale settings. Ceramics and lacquer ware were household goods, and items like fans and sword guards were for individual use. Maps were inscribed on the tiniest and most personal items, such as medicine cases and *netsuke,* the toggles used to fasten the cords holding tobacco boxes or other implements to one's kimono sash. In general, the diminution of the map image indicates a trend toward the domestication of the map itself. The process of consumption transformed the map from a conspicuously public image into a symbol of private appreciation. As part of this transformation the map became less about making Japan highly legible and infinitely variable, and more about making it represent a condensed and concentrated—if somewhat obscure and antiquarian— essence of Japaneseness.

The rationalization of geographic practices in the Meiji period and their divergence from early modern mapping brings up the inevitable question regarding geography, spatial consciousness, and nationalism. In this study I have avoided the vocabulary of the "national," as I have avoided any teleological claims that mapping constituted a form of "proto"-geography or cartography. My interest, rather, has been in tracing the changes in mapping as a process, and in analyzing what this might tell us about the assumptions that bound people in the early modern period to their many and overlapping cultural and spatial communities. That early modern mapmakers, artists, and writers ultimately refrained from positioning themselves in overtly political ways does not negate their impact on or connection to the public discourse of their time. The challenge as I see it is to frame the problem historically, and to ask what it was about the Japanese early modern experience that inflected its maps and its mapping impulses in the particular ways described in the preceding chapters.

A first attempt at answering this question would be to say that I view Edo-period maps and the cultural mappings of fiction and travel writing as examples of "geosophy"—ways of thinking about the relationship between land, landscape, self, and culture. Although this approach in some ways recalls similar themes in the studies of Benedict Anderson and Thongchai Winichakul and other scholars of nationalism, colonialism, and geography, the present study differs in several ways.[7] In early modern Japan, neither "modernization" nor colonial interventions precipitated the growth of and changes in mapping. One can find hints of modern subjectivity in early modern maps, travel writing, and fiction only with the aid of hindsight, a privileged perspective that obscures as much as it reveals. Indeed, if anything it is inconsistency and ambivalence that characterizes early modern writers' apprehension of the cultural and physical landscapes of Japan. Mapmakers and writers before the early nineteenth century were only indirectly influenced by the rhetoric of authority and accuracy that made European and colonial maps and narratives of discovery in the early modern period documents of ideological and practical domination. Yet judging from the ubiquity of commercially published maps, the elaborate map images in art, and the use of map and travel metaphors in fiction, Japanese mapping nevertheless linked geographical knowledge with power; in Japan's case, though, it was the power of invention. I suggest that early modern Japanese mapping did not become ubiquitous *in spite of* Japan's lack of the technologies and experiences of exploration, but *because* of it. Mapping was not highly politicized, it was not dominated by governing authorities, nor was it the vehicle of hegemonic power. For these very reasons, maps and geographical texts were widely disseminated; and as they became commonly understood, their rich stores of information and their "logic"— the spatial syntaxes and the meanings they generated—became familiar as well. The power dynamic of the modern map as described by Anderson is thus inverted in the early modern Japanese map: in the former the map is a technology of centralization and consolidation utilized by the modern state. In the latter, however, meaning is not imposed by a singular authoritative source, but generated by the circulation of maps and the multiplication of mapping tropes. Instead of closing itself off as an elite political or scientific discourse, mapping in early modern Japan remained open to the diversity and occasional playfulness of the cultural practices of the everyday.

At the same time, it must be said that although mapping did a great deal to make space and spatial thinking accessible, it could not eliminate the very real boundaries separating people of different statuses and classes in the early modern period. As much as the picture of social and physical mobility in the Tokugawa period has been greatly enhanced by recent scholarship, the fact remains that even in a city like Edo, which was in large part run by commoners who comprised the vast majority of its population, it was the samurai and daimyo who lived behind the gated walls of the great mansions, and who had primary access to the perquisites of power, from education to office holding. Although mapping distributed a kind of power, its power did not and could not effect widespread political and social change: it could not be "national." Ernest Gellner has suggested that the nation emerges only when "the fusion of will, culture and polity becomes the norm, and one not easily or frequently defied. . . . It is nationalism which engenders nations, and not the other way round." [8] Writing in a way that very nearly endows political thinking with the characteristics of human agency, Gellner argues that nationalism very selectively and self-consciously appropriates the "shred[s]" and patch[es]" of the "historically inherited proliferation of cultures or cultural wealth" to manufacture an appearance so natural it fools itself.[9] For all that, nationalism, in Gellner's formulation, is a profoundly unnatural concept. The texts I have discussed here represent a conceptual world that predated, if not promoted, the "radical transformation" necessary for the emergence of nationalism. Early modern mapping clearly identified the disparate "shreds" and "patches" of knowledge, belief, and invention that constitute cultural difference, but it did not attempt to hide the seams binding, sometimes poorly, those irregular pieces together. What made mapping different from cartography and geography was not some essential ideological ingredient; rather, as a process it did not possess ideology's inclination to deceive, and, as a result, it did not produce the shared illusion of seamless incorporation that characterizes the garment of modern Japanese nationalism.

Notes

1. *"Zenkoku"* can also be read "all the provinces." As a consequence of what Mark Ravina calls the "polysemy of early modern Japanese," *kuni* and *koku*, the terms commonly used for the country of Japan, were also used to refer to individual daimyo domains and to provinces. See Ravina, *Land and Lordship in Early Modern Japan*, p. 33.

2. Concepts of "Japaneseness" will be addressed in chapter 4. For a summary of recent scholarship on the early modern polity and its boundaries (political and cultural, internal and external), see Tessa Morris-Suzuki, *Re-Inventing Japan*, esp. chapter 2, and Ronald P. Toby, "Rescuing the Nation from History: The State of the State in Early Modern Japan."

3. See in particular the work of J. B. Harley, especially "Deconstructing the Map," "Maps, Knowledge, and Power," and "Silences and Secrecy." See also Barbara Belyea, "Images of Power: Derrida/Foucault/Harley"; Matthew H. Edney, "Cartography Without 'Progress'"; Michel Foucault, "Questions on Geography" and "Space, Knowledge, and Power"; Robert A. Rundstrom, "Mapping, Postmodernism, Indigenous People and the Changing Direction of North American Cartography"; and Denis Wood, *The Power of Maps*. In spite of the growing awareness of the importance of mapping outside the West, David Woodward admits that he and J. B. Harley, as editors of the University of Chicago Press's recently published multivolume *History of Cartography* project, initially planned "to include the cartographies of all non-Western societies in volume 1. That volume was to include not only discussions of the maps of the prehistoric, ancient, and medieval West and the traditional cartographies of Asia, but also those of the indigenous societies of Africa, the Americas, the Arctic, Australia, and the Pacific islands. The utter impracticality of this view was soon apparent as the

richness and diversity of the non-Western mapping traditions emerged." See Woodward's preface to *The History of Cartography*, vol. 2, bk. 2, *Cartography in the Traditional East and Southeast Asian Societies*, p. xxiii.

4. Scholars working outside the field of Japanese studies have made the connection between maps and literature in various ways. See in particular Tom Conley's concept of "cartographic writing," in which "new modes of surveying and plotting the world influence representations of the private and public domains of the individual writer. . . . Writings can be called 'cartographic' insofar as tensions of space and of figuration inhere in the fields of printed discourse." Conley, *The Self-Made Map*, p. 2. See also Richard Helgerson, *Forms of Nationhood*, and Frank Lestringant, *Mapping the Renaissance World*.

5. Kären Wigen, *The Making of a Japanese Periphery, 1750–1920*, p. 268. On the spatial dimension of English-language historiography on early modern Japan, see Wigen, "The Geographic Imagination in Early Modern Japanese History."

6. Julia Adeney Thomas casts the relationship between spatiality and politics somewhat differently, arguing that "Tokugawa political thinkers mentally mapped the world, creating ideological diagrams that represented the pattern of power spatially. . . . Mental maps charted powerful emotions as well as physical places; they incorporated the society's fears and longings, its sense of identity and of history, as well as its sense of geography. . . . Their power was such that they defined, with considerable stringency, who had the space to become a political actor and the range of possible motion for that actor. In this way, geography imbued with value produced what one might call the 'topographic political imagination' of Tokugawa Japan." Thomas, *Reconfiguring Modernity*, pp. 35–38.

7. As Takashi Fujitani succinctly puts it, "During the earlier Tokugawa period the official discourse on ruling stressed that both society and polity were to be maintained by the accentuation of social, cultural, and even to some extent political differences, not by an ideology of social, cultural, and political sameness." Fujitani, *Splendid Monarchy*, p. 5. Fujitani's argument is similar to that made by Benedict Anderson in *Imagined Communities*, esp. pp. 163–85.

8. Morris-Suzuki calls this way of thinking the "logic of difference." Not until the Western imperialist powers began to threaten Japan at the turn of the nineteenth century did the government begin to consider forcibly absorbing ethnic groups living on the periphery into Japan and imposing on them the norms of "Japanese" culture; Morris-Suzuki refers to this latter process as the "logic of assimilation." In both cases, the figuring of difference or sameness has a distinct spatial inflection. See Morris-Suzuki, *Re-Inventing Japan*, pp. 17–20.

9. See Herman Ooms, *Tokugawa Village Practice*. Ooms also cites an instance of cartographic differentiation when he describes how mapmakers from the early Tokugawa period and later typically omitted from calculations of traveling distances stretches of road that passed through outcaste *(kawata)* villages. See ibid., p. 287.

10. "Parcellized sovereignty" originally appeared in Perry Anderson's *Lineages of the Absolutist State* and is applied to Japan under the rule of Toyotomi Hideyoshi by Mary Elizabeth Berry in *Hideyoshi*, p. 147. The tension inherent

in the term "parcellized sovereignty" characterizes many of the labels scholars have applied over the years to the early modern system. They range from "centralized feudalism" to "integral bureaucracy" and, more recently, "the compound state." "Centralized feudalism" appears in Edwin O. Reischauer, "Japanese Feudalism"; "integral bureaucracy" is used by Conrad Totman in *Japan Before Perry*, p. 133 ff.; "the compound state" is used by Mark Ravina, following Mizubayashi Takeshi, in *Land and Lordship in Early Modern Japan*. Recent detailed studies in English of domain and regional politics and economics also highlight the independence of domain administrations and their relationship to shogunal power; see Philip C. Brown, *Central Authority and Local Autonomy in the Formation of Early Modern Japan*; Mark Ravina, *Land and Lordship in Early Modern Japan*; Luke S. Roberts, *Mercantilism in a Japanese Domain*; David L. Howell, *Capitalism from Within*; Kären Wigen, *The Making of a Japanese Periphery, 1750–1920*.

11. See chapter 1 for details; maps of castles and, in the later Tokugawa period, survey maps of Japan's coastline were exceptional in that they were considered strategic and therefore "classified" information.

12. "Commoners" are defined here as those who belonged to neither the warrior nor the noble class.

13. The subject of visual culture and visuality has received considerable attention from scholars. The following works particularly influenced the present study: on maps and visual culture, Svetlana Alpers, "The Mapping Impulse in Dutch Art," in *The Art of Describing: Dutch Art in the Seventeenth Century*, pp. 119–68; on visuality in the early modern Chinese context, Craig Clunas, *Pictures and Visuality in Early Modern China*; on visuality and visual culture and its relationship to artistic production and consumption, Michael Baxandall, *Painting and Experience in Fifteenth-Century Italy*; on ways of seeing in early modern Japanese culture, Timon Screech, *The Western Scientific Gaze and Popular Imagery in Later Edo Japan*; Sumie Jones, "William Hogarth and Kitao Masanobu"; J. Scott Miller, "The Hybrid Nature of Kyōden's *Sharebon*"; Henry D. Smith II, "World Without Walls," and also his *Ukiyōe ni miru Edo meisho*; Kobayashi Tadashi, *Edo no e wo yomu*; and Tanaka Yūko, *Edo no sōzōryoku*.

14. On the development of Japan as a geopolitical and cultural entity (with an emphasis on localities and regions), see Amino Yoshihiko, "Deconstructing: 'Japan'"; like Amino, Oguma Eiji also criticizes the "myth" of homogenous Japan in his best-selling books *Tan'itsu minzoku shinwa no kigen* and *"Nihonjin" no kyōkai*. For a historical survey of the construction of boundaries, see Bruce Batten, "Frontiers and Boundaries of Pre-Modern Japan"; Ronald Toby also discusses the various definitions of Japan in "Rescuing the Nation from History."

15. Lefebvre draws a distinction between "representational space," that is, space as it is lived and experienced, and "representations of space," or space as it is conceptualized. The former tends to be expressed or understood nonverbally ("the city," "the church"), while the latter tends to be conveyed verbally, often textually (a map, a painting, a travel account). See Lefebvre, *The Production of Space*, esp. pp. 39–46.

16. Turnbull, *Maps are Territories, Science Is an Atlas*, p. 42. For a broadly

comparative interpretation of geographies "at work" in the construction of po-
litical and cultural identities in early modern and modern Asia, see Marcia
Yonemoto, Thongchai Winichakul, and Kären Wigen, eds., "Geographies at
Work in Asia," a special issue of *The Journal of Asian Studies.*

17. This estimate is based on the number of titles appearing in Tokyo
Daigaku Shiryō Hensanjo, ed., *Henshū chishi biyō tenseki kaidai.*

18. On mapping as a "spatial vernacular," see Marcia Yonemoto, "The
'Spatial Vernacular' in Tokugawa Maps," and chapter 1.

CHAPTER ONE

1. Muehrcke, *Map Use: Reading, Analysis and Interpretation,* cited in J. B.
Harley, "Silences and Secrecy," p. 71. Muehrcke's point echoes that of Bene-
dict Anderson in *Imagined Communities,* pp. 170–78; see also Thongchai
Winichakul, *Siam Mapped,* pp. 14–16.

2. According to the *Nihon shoki* (a.k.a. *Nihongi*), in 645 the court ordered
provincial governors to "regulate the myriad provinces. When you proceed to
your posts, prepare registers of all the free subjects of the State and of the people
under the control of others, whether great or small. Take account of the acreage
of cultivated land." W. G. Aston, trans. and ed., *Nihongi,* p. 200. In the following year another proclamation specifically indicated to provincial governors that
"the boundaries of the provinces should be examined and a description or map
prepared, which should be brought here and produced for our inspection."
Ibid., p. 225. The *Nihongi* also records the submission of maps of Tanegashima
and Shinano provinces in 691 and 694, respectively. Ibid., p. 352.

3. According to the *Zoku Nihongi,* on the second day of the fifth month
of 713 (Wadō 6) the imperial government issued an edict to all the provinces to
collect detailed geographic information at the district and village levels, listing
"all precious metals, plant life, animal, fish, insect, and other life forms," and
assessing the fertility of all lands. See Akimoto Kichirō, ed., *Fudoki,* vol. 2,
pp. 9–10.

4. On Gyōki-style maps, see Unno Kazutaka, "Cartography in Japan,"
pp. 366–71; Hugh Cortazzi, *Isles of Gold,* pp. 3–10 and pl. 2, 3, 4, 5, and 6.
On Gyōki's life, see Janet R. Goodwin, *Alms and Vagabonds,* esp. pp. 23–25.

5. The most common impetus for making *shōen* maps was the disparate and
often conflicting interests of absentee proprietors, military officials, resident land
managers, and individual cultivators, which manifested themselves in the form
of frequent and contentious disputes over boundaries and resource allocation.
The aggrieved parties, usually under the supervision of the shogunate's judiciary,
often used maps to illustrate, negotiate, or dictate a settlement. There are between 150 and 200 *shōen* maps in existence today; the earliest examples were
made in the late eighth century, but the bulk of the maps date from the Kamakura and Muromachi periods (from approximately the twelfth through the
fifteenth centuries). A comprehensive overview of different types of *shōen* maps
can be found in Kokuritsu Rekishi Minzoku Hakubutsukan, *Shōen ezu to sono
sekai;* concise analyses of individual maps can be found in Koyama Yasunori and
Satō Kazuhiko, eds., *Ezu ni miru shōen no sekai.* For a theoretically informed,

critical reading of *shōen* maps, see in particular Katsurakawa Ezu Kenkyūkai, "'Katsurakawa ezu' ni miru kūkan ninshiki to sono hyōgen," and Katsurakawa Ezu Kenkyūkai, "Ezu wo yomu." For a more general theoretical study of the *shōen* in English, see Thomas Keirstead, *The Geography of Power in Medieval Japan.*

6. On Oda Nobunaga's land surveys, see Mary Elizabeth Berry, *Hideyoshi,* pp. 29–32; on Hideyoshi's land surveys see ibid., pp. 112–13. Regarding maps made during Hideyoshi's reign, the abbot of the Kōfukuji in Nara wrote in the *Tamon'in nikki* in 1591, "[I hear that] orders have been given to all the districts in the country to map *[sashizue ni kaki]* paddy fields as well as seas, mountains, rivers, villages, temples and shrines . . . [and] render [them] to the court in due haste." Quoted in Kawamura Hirotada, *Edo bakufu-sen kuniezu no kenkyū,* p. 22. On provincial mapmaking under Hideyoshi, including reproductions of two extant district maps from the province of Echigo dating from 1596 or 1597, see Kazutaka Unno, "Government Cartography in Sixteenth-Century Japan."

7. On European influences on Japanese mapmaking in the unification and Tokugawa periods, see Kawamura Hirotada, "Kinsei shoto Nihon no kaigai chishiki," and Shintarō Ayusawa, "Japanese Knowledge of World Geography"; for reports by European missionaries and traders regarding early Tokugawa leaders' interests in world geography, see Michael Cooper, ed., *They Came to Japan,* pp. 122–23; for a detailed analysis of Japanese world maps and representations of foreign lands and peoples in the later Tokugawa period, see Robert Eskildsen, "Telling Differences."

8. Precisely because maps and geographic knowledge were embedded in a larger framework of political and intellectual order, geography and cartography were never separated out as separate disciplines or fields of study in imperial China. This was one reason militating against the development of a class of specialists in mapmaking. Another reason was the amateur tradition among Chinese literati, which dismissed narrow specialization and instead stressed broad learning in literature, the arts, and the sciences. For these reasons no class of specialists in cartography emerged until the late Qing period. See Cordell D. K. Yee, "Cartography in China," pp. 71–73; Richard J. Smith also discusses Chinese cartography in its political and cultural context in *Chinese Maps.* On the cultural politics of mapping under the Qing, see Laura Hostetler, *Qing Colonial Enterprise,* and Mark C. Elliott, "The Limits of Tartary." Although Cordell Yee criticizes Joseph Needham's reliance on a scientific paradigm for interpreting maps, the locus classicus for the study of Chinese cartography is Needham's *Science and Civilisation in China,* vol. 3, pp. 497–502. On the influence on early modern Japanese mapping of the comprehensive maps of China made during the Qing dynasty with assistance from Jesuit missionaries, see Funakoshi Akio, *Sakoku Nihon ni kita "Kōki zu" no chirigakuteki kenkyū.* Ronald P. Toby has argued that in the Tokugawa lexicon of "foreign" concepts, Chinese ideas not only served as models for change, they functioned as a default mode in times of transition or stasis; see Toby, "The 'Indianness' of Iberia and Changing Japanese Iconographies of Other."

9. The most comprehensive account of the shogunal mapmaking projects is Kawamura Hirotada, *Edo bakufu-sen kuniezu no kenkyū;* references to this

work are abbreviated below as *EBSKK*. See also Kuroda Hideo, "Edo bakufu kuniezu, gōchō kanken (1)" and "Genson Keichō, Shōhō, Genroku kuniezu no tokuchō ni tsuite"; Sugimoto Fumiko, "Kuniezu"; Marcia Yonemoto, "Surveying the Realm: Administrative Cartography by the Tokugawa Shogunate (1603–1868)," translated and published in Dutch as *"Het rijk in kaart gebracht: Bestuurlijke cartografie van het Tokugawa-shogunaat (1603–1868)."* In English, see Unno Kazutaka, "Cartography in Japan," esp. pp. 394–404. For large color reproductions of shogunal maps of the provinces, cities, and Japan (and for commercially printed maps as well), see Unno Kazutaka, ed., *Nihon kochizu taisei,* and Akioka Takejirō, ed., *Nihon kochizu shūsei.* Generously illustrated general introductions to premodern Japanese maps include Nanba Matsutarō, ed., *Kochizu no sekai;* Oda Takeo, *Chizu no rekishi* and *Kochizu no sekai;* and Yamori Kazuhiko, *Kochizu to fūkei.* In English see Nanba Matsutarō, Muroga Nobuo, and Unno Kazutaka, eds., *Old Maps in Japan.*

10. See Sugimoto Fumiko, "Kuniezu," for a discussion that supports the argument for the use of mapmaking as an expression of state power.

11. This argument is similar to that adopted in recent English-language studies of domain politics, economics, and land-tenure policies, especially the work of Philip C. Brown. See Brown, *Central Authority and Local Autonomy in the Formation of Early Modern Japan,* esp. pp. 39–112, "The Mismeasure of Land," and "State, Cultivator, Land." See also Mark Ravina, *Land and Lordship in Early Modern Japan,* and Luke S. Roberts, *Mercantilism in a Japanese Domain.*

12. Repeated queries from confused local officials resulted in the shogunate's not altogether helpful answer that it was advisable to use color in addition to black ink, for overuse of the latter would make it difficult to discern text on the map. It suggested the use of "blues and yellows when drawing mountains to make them easily visible," and encouraged the application of other colors to make roads and river networks stand out. Kawamura, *EBSKK,* p. 37.

13. *EBSKK,* p. 89.

14. This equates to a scale of 1:260,000.

15. *EBSKK,* pp. 98–99.

16. *EBSKK,* pp. 98–99.

17. On these disputes, see *EBSKK,* pp. 127–28.

18. *EBSKK,* p. 200.

19. Three were settled locally, and two were resolved in bakufu courts. *EBSKK,* pp. 204–5.

20. The resolution involved drawing a detailed map of the boundary itself, which included the exact location and orientation of fifty-nine wooden boundary markers. For a partial reproduction of the 1854 maps and an analysis of the dispute between Chikuzen and Chikugo, see Kawamura Hirotada, "Ezu ni egakareta kyōkai no fūkei."

21. *EBSKK,* p. 249.

22. For color reproductions of this map, which is in the collection of the National Diet Library, Tokyo, see J. B. Harley and David Woodward, eds., *The History of Cartography,* vol. 2, bk. 2, pl. 26; and Cortazzi, *Isles of Gold,* pp. 96–97. A second large-scale shogunal map of Japan made in the early seventeenth

century exists in the collection of the Saga Prefectural Library; it measures roughly nineteen by nineteen feet, and it is thought to have been compiled from either the first or the second set of provincial maps. There is some debate as to which of these two maps was compiled from the first set of provincial maps, and which from the second set. See Unno, "Cartography in Japan," p. 397.

23. On the notion of the "map-as-logo" of the modern nation-state, see Benedict Anderson, *Imagined Communities,* pp. 175–77.

24. Primary sources include the records of publishing guilds, such as those collected in Higuchi Hideo and Asakura Haruhiko, eds., *(Kyōhō ikō) Edo shuppan shomoku;* Inoue Takaakira, ed., *Kinsei shorin hanmoto sōran;* and Sakamoto Muneko, ed., *(Kyōhō ikō) Hanmoto betsu shoseki mokuroku.* Compilations of publishers' advertisements can be found in Asakura Haruhiko, ed., *Kinsei shuppan hōkoku shiryō shūsei.* The secondary scholarship is voluminous. For a general introduction, see the following works: Konta Yōzō, "Genroku-Kyōhō ki ni okeru shuppan shihon no keisei to sono rekishiteki igi ni tsuite," "Edo shuppan gyō no tenkai to sono tokushitsu," *Edo no hon'ya san,* and "Edo no shuppan shihon"; Nagatomo Chiyoji, "Edo no hon'ya," *Kinsei kashihon'ya no kenkyū,* and *Kinsei no dokusho;* Suwa Haruo, *Shuppan kotohajime;* Suzuki Toshio, *Edo no hon'ya;* Yoshiwara Ken'ichirō, "Edo chōnin bunka to hon'ya." See also the special editions of the journal *Edo bungaku,* Nakano Mitsutoshi, ed.: vol. 15, *Edo no shuppan, I,* and vol. 16, *Edo no shuppan, II.*

25. See in particular Peter Kornicki, *The Book in Japan;* Henry D. Smith II, "The History of the Book in Edo and Paris."

26. Because of the increased availability of education to non-elites, literacy rates rose during the early modern period, and tended to be especially high in the cities. Although literacy rates are notoriously difficult to assess, Ronald Dore and Herbert Passin estimate that by the mid-nineteenth century overall literacy rates in Japan approached those in Britain and France at the same time. Dore estimates that by 1868 about 43 percent of boys and 15 percent of girls of school age (between ages six and thirteen) were attending school outside the home. See Ronald P. Dore, *Education in Tokugawa Japan,* pp. 320–21, 291. Passin breaks down his data by class and arrives at overall figures of 80 percent literacy for men and 50 percent for women. See Passin, *Society and Education in Japan,* p. 57. Henry D. Smith II cites Daniel Roche's comparative data for early modern France, which indicate that by the time of the French Revolution, about 90 percent of men and 80 percent of women were able to sign wills; see Smith, "History of the Book in Edo and Paris," p. 336. On the combination of bookselling and education, see Nagatomo Chiyōji, "Edo no hon'ya," p. 103. On the difficulty of assessing literacy rates in the early modern period, and on the importance of distinguishing urban from rural populations, see Kornicki, *The Book in Japan,* pp. 269–76. On assessing literacy in the Meiji period, see Richard Rubinger, "Who Can't Read and Write? Illiteracy in Meiji Japan," and Kornicki's response, "Literacy Revisited: Some Reflections on Richard Rubinger's Findings."

27. On the history of printing, see David Chibbett, *The History of Japanese Printing and Book Illustration.*

28. For these figures, see Kornicki, *The Book in Japan,* pp. 171–75. The

figure of five hundred titles is derived from the catalogs kept by Japanese publishers and booksellers beginning in the mid-seventeenth century.

29. Ibid., p. 140.

30. Ibid.

31. Smith, "The History of the Book in Edo and Paris," p. 350.

32. Unno, "Cartography in Japan," pp. 411–12.

33. Mary Elizabeth Berry, "Was Early Modern Japan Culturally Integrated?"

34. Several of the maps discussed in this chapter were published by Suharaya Mohee. On maps as "ephemeral" printed goods, see Peter Kornicki, *The Book in Japan*, pp. 60–63 and 210–12.

35. Numbers of samurai fluctuated with the constant movement of daimyo and retainers in and out of the city on official duty; neither samurai nor the floating population appears in the urban registries. These figures, along with a concise discussion of urbanization in early modern Japan, can be found in Susan B. Hanley, "Urban Sanitation in Preindustrial Japan," pp. 3–5. Edo's commoner quarters were especially densely populated; land surveys of Edo-Tokyo taken just after the Meiji Restoration in 1868 show that housing for the samurai class occupied roughly 69 percent of the city's land, commoner housing 16 percent. Earlier, around the turn of the eighteenth century, more than half of Edo's total population was housed in about one-sixth of the city's land area. For the latter figures, see Takeuchi Makoto, *Edo to Osaka*, p. 212.

36. On the development of Edo maps, see Iida Ryūichi and Tawara Motoaki, *Edo zu no rekishi;* see also Yamori Kazuhiko, *Toshizu no rekishi*, vol. 1.

37. For a reproduction of Hōjō's map, see Unno, "Cartography in Japan," p. 402.

38. Some sources indicate that Hōjō himself revised the map; see *Kokushi daijiten*, vol. 12, pp. 592–93. Yamori Kazuo and Unno Kazutaka both claim the work was Fujii's. See Unno, "Cartography in Japan," p. 420, and Yamori, *Kochizu e no tabi*, p. 107.

39. Ochikochi Dōin, *Shinpan Edo ō-ezu*.

40. The wealth of daimyo was measured in terms of the total assessed annual productivity of lands under their control, expressed in *koku* of rice (one *koku* equals approximately five bushels or 180 liters). The assessed productivity figure was referred to as *kokudaka*.

41. See the version of *Edo zukan kōmoku* reproduced in Lutz Walter, ed., *Japan, A Cartographic Vision*, pl. 88.

42. See Nishiyama Matsunosuke et al., eds., *Edogaku jiten*, pp. 470–71; see also Fujizane Kumiko, "*Bukan* no shuppan to shomotsu shi Izumodera."

43. When Ryūsen's maps of Edo were copied by European mapmakers, who could not read the colophon, this inset map was misinterpreted so that the Honjo area depicted in the inset was grafted onto the southeastern portion of the map as if it were a peninsular protuberance extending into Edo Bay.

44. In the late Edo period broadsides, or *kawaraban*, circulated widely in the major cities and functioned as a sort of parodic commentary on current events. On this and other types of ephemeral print media, see Kornicki, *The Book in Japan*, pp. 62–65; see also Minami Kazuo, *Isshin zen'ya to Edo no shōmin*.

45. Gesshin refers to Edo maps as *Edo no chizu,* but *chizu,* the modern term for map, was seldom used in the actual titles of the earlier Edo maps that he consults.

46. Saitō Gesshin, *Bukō nenpyō,* vol. 2, p. 41.

47. Ibid., p. 81.

48. These areas constitute the flatlands that were to become the heart of the city's "downtown."

49. Note that text within parentheses is from Gesshin's original. My emendations, as well as dates and translations, are in brackets. See Saitō Gesshin, *Bukō nenpyō,* vol.2, p. 57.

50. *Honchō zukan kōmoku* seems to have been the original title for the map; often, however, alternate titles such as *Nihon zukan kōmoku* were used on the thick paper cover into which the folded map was inserted.

51. Numerous copies of both maps exist in public and private archive and library collections inside and outside Japan, and inexpensive reprints are available for purchase in many large Japanese bookstores.

52. On the influence of Ryūsen maps on European cartography, see Marcia Yonemoto, "Envisioning Japan in Eighteenth-Century Europe."

53. For a reproduction of this map, see Akioka Takejirō, ed., *Nihon kochizu shūsei,* pl. 28; for discussion of the map, see Akioka, *Nihon chizu sakusei shi,* insert to *Nihon kochizu shūsei,* pp. 87–88.

54. For reproductions of these maps, see both works by Akioka, ed., cited in the previous note.

55. For a reproduction, see Unno, "Cartography in Japan," p. 368.

56. In most copies of Ryūsen maps each province appears in a different color. Although many of Ryūsen's maps were printed in black and white and hand-colored, and although color schemes are not identical from map to map, color usage consistently emphasizes the provincial divisions.

57. Nagato and Suō provinces were governed by members of the powerful daimyo family the Mōri, but the Nagato branch married into the Tokugawa house in the early seventeenth century and thereafter took the name Matsudaira.

58. In both of Ryūsen's maps of Japan, cumulative produce of the various provinces and districts is also recorded in table form (see fig. 3, bottom right, and fig. 4, bottom center).

59. On Japan's early modern road system, see Constantine Nomikos Vaporis, *Breaking Barriers.*

60. Julia Adeney Thomas describes the phenomenon of decentralization in political thought in *Reconfiguring Modernity,* pp. 39–59.

61. The cultural concept of foreignness will be addressed at greater length in chapter 4. On Tokugawa diplomatic relations, see Ronald P. Toby, *State and Diplomacy in Early Modern Japan;* see also Arano Yasunori et al., eds., *Ajia no naka no Nihon shi,* vol. 5, *Ji'isshiki to sōgo rikai.*

62. On Korean embassies to Japan in the Tokugawa period, see Ronald P. Toby, "Carnival of the Aliens"; on Tokugawa relations with the Ryūkyū Islands, see Gregory Smits, *Visions of Ryukyu;* on Tokugawa relations with Ezo and the Ainu people, see Brett L. Walker, *The Conquest of Ainu Lands.*

63. Unno, "Cartography in Japan," p. 414.

64. On Western influences on eighteenth- and nineteenth-century Japanese mapmaking, see Unno, "Cartography in Japan," pp. 432–43.

65. Sekisui also may have been influenced by the shogunate's Shōhō map of Japan, but this map is not extant.

66. Nanba Matsutarō et al., eds., *Old Maps in Japan*, p. 172.

67. The Ise Road was a flat and easily traveled highway.

68. For a partial reproduction of Sekisui's *Dai Shin kōyozu*, see Unno, "Cartography in Japan," p. 430.

69. The mythical places on Sekisui's world maps include the Land of the Giants, the Land of Dwarves, the Land of the Night, and the Land of Cannibals. On Sekisui's world maps and their representations of oceanic space, see Marcia Yonemoto, "Maps and Metaphors of the 'Small Eastern Sea' in Tokugawa Japan (1603–1868)."

70. On the distinction between space and place, see Yi-Fu Tuan, *Space and Place: The Perspective of Experience,* and Cordell D. K. Yee, *Space & Place: Mapmaking East and West,* p. 25.

71. *Sekisho* were established, developed, and expanded by Japanese governments, both imperial and military, beginning in 646, as surveillance mechanisms. On early modern *sekisho,* see Vaporis, *Breaking Barriers,* pp. 99–133.

72. As Ravina notes, the ambiguity of the term "state" (which *kuni,* in its modern variant, also connotes) was not limited to Japan; it also characterized the language of statehood in early modern England and Prussia. Mark Ravina, *Land and Lordship in Early Modern Japan,* pp. 32–33.

73. See Matthew Edney, "Cartography Without 'Progress.'"

CHAPTER TWO

1. On the connection between maps and ethnography in general, see Benedict Anderson, *Imagined Communities,* pp. 163–85. On cartography and ethnography in Qing China, see Laura Hostetler, *Qing Colonial Enterprise.*

2. Reflecting on the relationship of place to poem, the late-seventeenth-century philologist Keichū wrote, "When there is a place-name *[meisho]* in a Japanese poem, it does for that poem what a pillow does for us in sleep. When we rest on a pillow, we have lavish dreams. When we refer to famous places, we make fine poems. Is this not why we call them *'utamakura'* [poem-pillows]?" Quoted in Edward Kamens, *Utamakura, Allusion, and Intertextuality in Traditional Japanese Poetry,* p. 1.

3. See Thomas Rimer, "The Theme of Pilgrimage in Japanese Literature," p. 117.

4. Later medieval poets often moved from place to place seeking patronage from local notables. For the poems of Saigyō, see Kawada Jun, ed., *Sanetomo shū, Saigyō shū, Ryōkan shū;* Kubota Jun, *Sankashū;* for English translations of Saigyō, see Burton Watson, trans., *Saigyō: Poems of a Mountain Home.* For the poems of Sōgi, see Morozumi Sōichi, *Sōgi renga no kenkyū;* Kaneko Kinjirō, *Rengashi Sōgi no jitsuzō* and "Sōgi and the Imperial House"; Steven D. Carter,

Three Poets at Yuyama and "Sōgi in the East Country"; Eileen Katō, "Pilgrimage to Dazaifu." For Sōchō, see Shigematsu Hiromi, ed., *Sōchō sakuhin shū;* in English, see H. Mack Horton, *Song in an Age of Discord,* and "Saikokuen Sōchō and Imagawa Daimyo Patronage"; H. Mack Horton, ed., *The Journal of Sōchō.*

5. Watanabe Kenji, "Daimyo no kikōbun," p. 5. See also his study of daimyo culture and regional difference, *Kinsei daimyo no bungeiken kenkyū.*

6. Itasaka Yōko, *Edo no tabi to bungaku,* p. 151. On women's travel diaries in the early modern period, see Shiba Keiko, *Kinsei onna tabi nikki.* It should be noted that one important extant medieval travel diary was written by a woman: the *Towazugatari* of Lady Nijō. See Karen Brazell, trans., *The Confessions of Lady Nijō.* Also, the aforementioned poet Sōgi was of humble birth; see Eileen Katō, "Pilgrimage to Dazaifu," p. 334.

7. See Itasaka Yōko, *Edo no tabi to bungaku;* for more detailed discussion of each of these individual topics, see the following articles by Itasaka Yōko: "Yama no kikō," "Hana no kikō," and "Kinsei Tōkaidō kikō no shōmondai."

8. It should be noted that some texts were published because their authors paid for the printing themselves.

9. The merchant diary is Hishiya Heishichi, "Chikushi kikō."

10. Itasaka Yōko provides the estimate for the *Kokusho sōmokuroku* in Itasaka, ed., *Kinsei kikō shūsei,* p. 426; Watanabe Kenji counts over 800 titles in the holdings of the National Research Institute for Japanese Literature (Kokuritusu Bungaku Kenkyū Shiryōkan). See Watanabe Kenji, "Kinsei kikō bungaku no saihyōka," p. 153.

11. See Haruo Shirane, *Traces of Dreams,* pp. 2, 194–95.

12. See Asai Ryōi, *Tōkaidō meisho no ki;* Ihara Saikaku, *Saikaku shōkoku banashi.*

13. On the recycling of text in famous place guidebooks, see Jurgis Elisonas, "Notorious Places."

14. One of Sorai's travel accounts is translated into English by Olof J. Lidin in *Ogyū Sorai's Journey to Kai.*

15. For the full text of Shiba Kōkan's illustrated diary of his trip to Nagasaki, see Shiba Kōkan, *Kōkan saiyū nikki;* for a study of Ike no Taiga's life and painting, see Melinda Takeuchi, *Taiga's True Views.*

16. On the relationship of urban culture to provincial culture, especially in the late eighteenth century, see Nishiyama Matsunosuke, *"Edo bunka to chihō bunka";* the main arguments are presented in English translation in Nishiyama, *Edo Culture,* pp. 95–100 and 104–12.

17. These two trends in thought have been characterized, respectively, as "practicality" and "principle" by scholars of Neo-Confucianism. See Wm. Theodore de Bary and Irene Bloom, eds., *Principle and Practicality.*

18. On the relationship between the writings of Kaibara Ekiken, Kumazawa Banzan, and Miyazaki Antei, see Tessa Morris-Suzuki, "Concepts of Nature and Technology in Early Modern Japan," pp. 81–97.

19. On Ekiken's travel writing, see Itasaka Yōko, "Kaibara Ekiken no kikōbun" and *"Kishi kikō no baai."*

20. For a biography of Ekiken, see Inoue Tadashi, *Kaibara Ekiken.*

21. Mary Evelyn Tucker, *Moral and Spiritual Cultivation in Japanese Neo-Confucianism,* pp. 32–33.

22. For a timeline of events *(nenpyō)* in Ekiken's life, see Inoue, *Kaibara Ekiken,* pp. 343–66.

23. Tucker, *Moral and Spiritual Cultivation in Japanese Neo-Confucianism,* p. 41.

24. Itasaka Yōko, "Kaisetsu," in *Kinsei kikō shūsei,* p. 423.

25. Tucker, *Moral and Spiritual Cultivation in Japanese Neo-Confucianism,* pp. 3–29.

26. Minamoto Ryōen, "*Jitsugaku* and Empirical Rationalism in the First Half of the Tokugawa Period," pp. 375–456.

27. There is some speculation that Ekiken did not actually write *Onna daigaku;* see Yokota Fuyuhiko, "Imagining Working Women in Early Modern Japan," p. 166, n. 2.

28. Quoted in Tucker, *Moral and Spiritual Cultivation in Japanese Neo-Confucianism,* p. 44. *Yamato honzō* was an updated Japanese version of the *Ben cao kang mu* by Li Shichen, published in China in 1596. A copy of this text had been obtained by Hayashi Razan in Nagasaki, and was subsequently presented to Tokugawa Ieyasu; Razan wrote commentary on it and translated the plant names. Ekiken in turn published a revised edition of the text in 1672, then republished it as *Yamato honzō* in 1709. In *Yamato honzō* he lists 1,550 objects in thirty-seven categories, each described in detail and copiously illustrated. The text is generally recognized as the forerunner to subsequent scholarly efforts to compile definitive encyclopedias of Japan's flora and fauna.

29. *Analects,* 25:13:3; this translation can be found in Richard E. Strassberg, *Inscribed Landscapes,* p. 431, n. 44.

30. Kaibara Ekiken, *Jinshin kikō,* in Itasaka Yōko, ed., *Kinsei kikō shūsei,* pp. 5–48. All references to this text are abbreviated below as *JK.*

31. All of Ekiken's travel accounts were published by two Kyoto houses, Ryūshiken and Ibarakiya Tazaemon; see Itasaka Yōko, *Edo no tabi to bungaku,* p. 105. In his *Sugagasa nikki* (1772) Norinaga cited Ekiken's travel account of the Kinai area, *Washū junranki;* Nanpō cited Ekiken's *Kisoji no kikō* in his *Jinshū kikō* (1802). See ibid., p. 9.

32. Ibid.

33. Itasaka is arguing against the canonical view of early modern travel writing as marginal, or, as one leading critic of Edo literature has put it, "uncategorizable" *(kengai).* See Nakamura Yukihiko, "Kengai bungaku."

34. See Itasaka, *Edo no tabi to bungaku,* esp. pp. 106–22.

35. "Lyric" travel account is the translation of *"yūki"* (in Chinese, *yu-chi*) devised by Strassberg in *Inscribed Landscapes,* p. 4.

36. See Mary Louise Pratt, "Fieldwork in Common Places"; see also her *Imperial Eyes,* p. 78.

37. *JK,* p. 6.

38. *JK,* p. 6.

39. The travel accounts of the geographer Furukawa Koshōken, discussed in chapter 5, are one exception.

40. Nariai is located in the northern part of present-day Kyoto-fu; the peak called Nariai-san is said to be the northern end of the Ama no hashidate, the Bridge of Heaven in Japanese Shinto mythology. At the top of the mountain is a Shingon temple, Nariaiji, which is the twenty-eighth stop on the thirty-three-site pilgrimage of the western provinces.

41. Shōkū (ca. 917–1007) was a mid-Heian priest who founded the Enkyōji on Shoshazan.

42. *JK*, p. 7.

43. *JK*, p. 9.

44. One standard *chō* equaled sixty *ken,* or approximately 109 meters; it is not clear, however, what exactly constituted a "long" *chō.*

45. *JK*, pp. 20–21.

46. *JK*, p. 22–23.

47. *JK*, p. 23.

48. *JK*, p. 23.

49. *JK*, p. 33.

50. *JK*, p. 12.

51. *JK*, p. 18–19.

52. *JK*, p. 19. The original poem by Saigyō reads: "*Sabishisa ni / aware mo itodo / masarikeri / hitori zo tsuki wa / mirubekarikeru.*"

53. The term "memoryscape" is from Lisa Yoneyama, "Taming the Memoryscape."

54. *JK*, p. 11.

55. *JK*, p. 14.

56. *JK*, p. 46.

57. *JK*, pp. 35, 40.

58. *JK*, pp. 47–48.

59. *JK*, p. 48.

60. Itasaka Yōko, *Edo no tabi to bungaku*, p. 123.

61. "Jinnan" and "Kaminami" are alternate readings of the same character compound.

62. *JK*, p. 16.

63. *JK*, p. 14.

64. *JK*, p. 15.

65. *JK*, p. 17.

66. *JK*, p. 22.

67. *JK*, p. 29; Ekiken's words are "*Sōjimono no ashiki wo kuwase*"; Sei Shōnagon's original reads "*Sōjimono no ito ashiki wo uchi kui.*"

68. *JK*, p. 33.

69. *JK*, p. 43.

70. Itasaka, "Kaisetsu," in *Kinsei kikō shūsei*, p. 434.

71. Quoted in Georges Van Den Abeele, *Travel as Metaphor*, p. viii.

72. Mary Louise Pratt, "Scratches on the Face of the Country," p. 140.

73. Tzvetan Todorov, *The Conquest of America*, p. 28.

74. The exceptions here would be the accounts of shipwrecked "drifters" (*hyōryūmin*), and accounts written by members of the first embassies to Europe and the United States in the 1860s, just before the Meiji Restoration. For an ed-

ited collection of writings by hyōryūmin, see Katō Atsushi, ed., *Hyōryū kidan shūsei*.

75. The term "geo-body" is from Thongchai Winichakul, *Siam Mapped*.

76. Munemasa Isoo, ed., *Tōzaiyūki*, vol. 1, p. xv.

CHAPTER THREE

1. *Tō-oku kikō*, a record of Sekisui's short journey to the northeast as far as Matsushima, can be found as *Sekisui sensei Tō-oku kikō*, in Nagakubo Sekisui, *Nihon jūrin sōsho*, vol. 4. *Nagasaki kōeki nikki* can be found in Nagakubo Sekisui, *Nihon kikōbun shūsei*; all further references to *Nagasaki kōeki nikki* will be to this text, abbreviated *NKN*. Donald Keene briefly discusses the *Nagasaki kōeki nikki* (he translates the title somewhat oddly as "The Diary of the Nagasaki Border Guard") in *Travelers of a Hundred Ages*, pp. 354–58.

2. Like Kaibara Ekiken, he refrains from including maps in his travel account.

3. We might recall here Joseph Levenson's definition of the "amateur ideal" in the Chinese tradition. Such an ideal would have been particularly appealing to a sinophile like Sekisui. See Levenson, "The Amateur Ideal in Ming and Early Ch'ing Society," pp. 15–43.

4. Annam corresponds to the central part of present-day Vietnam.

5. *NKN*, p. 222.

6. Although other accounts of "sea drifters" *(hyōryūmin)* had been collected at the time, such individuals possessed information about foreign countries that was deemed sensitive by the shogunate, and their contact with others was strictly controlled until they could be debriefed by shogunal officials. It is possible that Sekisui avoids mentioning the drifters in the *Kōeki nikki* because he had aspirations to publish his diary, and such controversial material would have been a barrier to publication.

7. *NKN*, pp. 224, 229.

8. *NKN*, p. 225.

9. *NKN*, p. 248.

10. For a detailed study of Michizane in English, see Robert Borgen, *Sugawara no Michizane and The Early Heian Court*.

11. Kakinomoto Hitomaru (ca. 687–707), whose name is abbreviated as *kaki* (or, in an alternative reading, *shi*) in the poem's text, was the most famous of the poets whose work appears in the *Man'yōshū* (759), the first Japanese imperial poetry collection. Yama (also read *san* or *zan*) most likely refers to Yamabe no Akabito (dates unknown), a poet active in the Nara period (608–794) who was well represented in the *Man'yōshū*.

12. "Gen" refers to the prominent Chinese poet Yuan Zhen (in Japanese, Gen Jin, 779–831); "Haku" refers to Bo Juyi (in Japanese, Haku Kyōi, 772–846), perhaps the best-known poet of the Tang represented in the *Man'yōshū*. Another possible referent is the poet Yamanoue no Okura (660–733).

13. Michizane's malevolent spirit was said to haunt the court after his death, and so many misfortunes were ascribed to him that he was eventually posthumously promoted to high office as a means of satisfying his ghost.

14. For the original text, see *NKN*, p. 234.

15. See Clifford Geertz, "I-Witnessing: Malinowski's Children," pp. 73–101.

16. *Karuwaza* were popular street performers, acrobats of a sort.

17. *NKN*, p. 237.

18. *NKN*, p. 237.

19. *NKN*, p. 237.

20. *NKN*, p. 238. In a separate section, Sekisui includes lists of "Nagasaki *miyage*," or distinctive local products. These include products of European origin, such as glasses, "astronomical instruments" *(tenmon dōgu)*, wool fabrics, and various types of food products such as butter cake *(kasutera)* and tobacco, but also numerous regional products such as inlaid sword guards, jewelry cut from precious stones, pumpkins *(kabocha)*, and watermelon. For these lists, see *NKN*, pp. 246–47.

21. *NKN*, p. 238.

22. *NKN*, pp. 240–41.

23. *NKN*, p. 241.

24. This "foreign" style of eating was much remarked upon by observers and scholars of European culture in early modern Japan. The communal table was also used at the so-called "Oranda shōgatsu," or "Dutch-style New Year's gatherings" of Edo literati that took place at Ōtsuki Gentaku's academy in the 1780s.

25. The Fukusaiji was built by and for people from Hobei and Fujian provinces, the Sōfukuji served the Fujian community, and the Kōfukuji served Nanjing natives. See *NKN*, p. 243.

26. *NKN*, p. 242; the Four Books are *The Great Learning, The Doctrine of the Mean,* the *Analects* of Confucius, and the *Mencius;* the Five Classics are *The Book of Songs, The Book of History, The Book of Changes, The Spring and Autumn Annals,* and *The Book of Rituals.*

27. *NKN*, p. 243.

28. All references to *Tōyū zakki* are to Furukawa Koshōken, *Toyū zakki,* Ōtō Tokihiko, ed., abbreviated hereafter as *TZ*. All references to *Saiyū zakki* are to Furukawa Koshōken, *Saiyū zakki,* Yanagida Kunio, ed., *Nihon kikōbun shūsei,* vol. 1, abbreviated hereafter as *SZ*.

29. For details on Koshōken's background, see Ōtō Tokihiko's essay following his translation, *TZ*, p. 283; see also Kuromasa Iwao, "Furukawa Koshōken no chōjutsu ni tsuite."

30. Ōtake Shigehiko, *Tabi to chiri shisō*, pp. 13–21.

31. Ibid.

32. For example, in Matsushima on the northeast coast of Honshu, site of one of the most famous views in all of Japan, Koshōken offers first a Chinese poem of Sekisui's, and then a Japanese poem of his own. The extraordinary nature of the place, it seems, compels him to adopt a poetic voice; simple narrative does not suffice in this case. He explains, "In the entire realm, Matsushima's superior views have no peer. Truly, even the mythical mountain realm of Hōraizan and the West Lake of the Great Tang have difficulty equaling this region." *TZ*, p. 244.

33. See Hayashi Shihei, *Sangoku tsūran zusetsu*, in Yamagishi Tokubei and Sano Masami, eds., *Shinpen Hayashi Shihei zenshū*, vol. 2, pp. 1–80.

34. The original reads, *"Hayashi Shihei jikoku no chiri wo shirazu, iwan ya tōki ikoku ni tsuite wo ya."* Quoted in Itasaka Yōko, "Koshōken no Hayashi Shihei hihan," p. 24.

35. In the fifth month of 1792, Shihei was put under house arrest, and all of his manuscripts and books were confiscated. He died shortly thereafter, in 1793, at the age of fifty-six.

36. See Itasaka Yōko, "Kyūshū kikō shokō," p. 22.

37. *TZ*, p. 115.

38. This map is missing from the surviving text.

39. *SZ*, p. 318.

40. When pressed for information as to why this type of construction is prevalent, Koshōken's local informants respond simply that "it's been this way for ages." They add that since farmers in the area have nothing worth stealing, theft and the security of homes is not a problem. *SZ*, p. 334.

41. *SZ*, p. 354.

42. *SZ*, p. 354.

43. *SZ*, p. 354.

44. *SZ*, p. 355.

45. *SZ*, p. 355.

46. *SZ*, p. 355. For prints of the sort referred to by Koshōken, see Masanobu Hosono, *Nagasaki Prints and Copperplates*.

47. *SZ*, p. 355.

48. The Dutch were commonly referred to either as *"Oranda-jin"* ("Hollanders") or *"kōmō-jin"* ("red hairs").

49. *SZ*, p. 356.

50. *SZ*, p. 357.

51. On defining cultural and ethnic boundaries in the far northeast, see David L. Howell, "Ainu Ethnicity and the Boundaries of the Modern Japanese State"; Tessa Morris-Suzuki, "Creating the Frontier."

52. *TZ*, p. 135.

53. Koshōken does not comment on the longstanding practice of polygamy among the Japanese elite.

54. *TZ*, p. 169.

55. *TZ*, p. 170.

56. Nagakubo Sekisui adopted a similar tactic in his emphasis on the Dutch servants' clothing and appearance; the difference is that Sekisui depicted the entire person nonetheless.

57. See Mary Louise Pratt, *Imperial Eyes*, p. 39.

58. This is not to say that the Japanese coveted only knowledge about the Ainu. Brett Walker focuses on the unequal relationship between Japanese and Ainu that resulted from political and trade policies pursued in Ezo by both domain and shogunal governments. See Walker, *The Conquest of Ainu Lands*.

59. Cited in Harold Bolitho, "Travelers' Tales," p. 489.

60. Shirado Kinkichi, "Go-junkenshi gogekō ni tsuki shogoto kokoroe narabi ofuregaki."

61. All references to *Saiyūki* are to Tachibana Nankei, *Saiyūki*, in Itasaka Yōko and Munemasa Isoo, eds., *Azuma ji no ki, Kishi kikō, Saiyūki*, abbreviated hereafter as *SK*. All references to *Tōyūki* are to Tachibana Nankei, *Tōyūki*, in Munemasa Isoo, ed., *Tōzaiyūki*, vol. 1, abbreviated hereafter as *TK*.

62. On Nankei's life, see Sakuma Shōken, *Tachibana Nankei*.

63. Munemasa Isoo, "Tachibana Nankei *Saiyūki* to Edo kōki no kikō bungaku," pp. 437–46.

64. Ibid., 446.

65. *SK*, pp. 437–38.

66. Itasaka Yōko argues that Nankei's penchant for the odd and interesting detail makes his travel accounts read more like tales of the supernatural *(kidanshū)*; Itasaka, "Sengō e no tabi," p. 89.

67. *TZ*, p. 131.

68. *TK*, p. 59.

69. *TK*, p. 59.

70. *SK*, pp. 353–54. An alternate translation of this passage can be found in the epigraph to Timon Screech, *The Western Scientific Gaze and Popular Imagery in Later Edo Japan*. Screech discusses Nankei throughout his study, in the context of the development of visual technology in the Edo period.

71. *SK*, p. 355.

72. *SK*, p. 356.

73. *SK*, pp. 356–57.

74. *SK*, p. 356. The notion of the Dutch as "lukewarm" stands in contrast to Furukawa Koshōken's description, quoted above, of the Dutch as "very emotional" people given to month-long crying spells.

75. *SK*, p. 356. The description of the Ryūkyūans as "too warm" is left unexplained; it most likely refers to the differences between the social customs and relative levels of social reserve of "mainland" Japanese as compared to the indigenous people of the Ryūkyūs. The Ryūkyūans, for their part, view Nankei as an oddity. Although they are in frequent contact with the Japanese of the southern Kyushu domain of Satsuma, Nankei is a "person from the capital" *(miyakobito)*, the likes of which the Ryūkyūans seldom encounter. Nankei's sense of himself as a "person of the capital" no doubt informed his sense of his own authority on matters of culture.

76. *SK*, p. 373.

77. *SK*, p. 375.

78. *TK*, p. 198.

79. Nankei's statements about the lack of a money economy are exaggerated; see David L. Howell, *Capitalism from Within*, on the "proto-capitalist" development of the fishing industry in Hokkaido.

80. For an Ainu-centered perspective on this issue, see Brett Walker, *The Conquest of Ainu Lands*.

81. Both Uteshi and Tsugaru are on the far northern tip of Honshu, near but not on the island of Ezo. Hence their culture, according to Nankei, resembles that of Ezo but is not identical to it.

82. *TK*, p. 107. The character used here, as below, for *ka* is "flower," the same as is used in *chūka*, the "central civilization," an alternate name for China.

I hyphenate the term to distinguish it from the modern Japanese term *bunka*, which also means "culture."

83. *Mōreki* are also known as Tayama *reki* or Morioka *reki* in reference to the places in which they were originally produced. Tayama *reki* were banned by the Meiji government in the late nineteenth century, but Morioka *reki* continued to be actively used in Morioka until the 1950s, and are produced as local cultural artifacts to the present day. The *mōreki* reproduced by Tachibana Nankei is his own slightly flawed facsimile of an unidentified original text. For reproductions and explanation, see Kokushi Daijiten Henshū Iinkai, ed., *Kokushi daijiten*, vol. 13, insert between pp. 780–81.

84. *TK*, p. 118.

85. *SK*, p. 207. Nankei gives as an example a long and involved account of the adjudication of a crime involving several Satsuma residents, the gist of which is that even among commoners, the self-sacrifice of the guilty and the ready acceptance of blame and punishment due are characteristic of the moral quality of the local residents. See *SK*, pp. 221–26.

86. *SZ*, pp. 229–31.

87. *TK*, p. 118.

88. *TK*, p. 119.

89. *NKN*, p. 221.

90. On Sorai's diaries and his *ex post facto* editing of them, see Olof G. Lidin, *Ogyū Sorai's Journey to Kai*.

91. Hayden White, "The Forms of Wildness," p. 5.

92. Expressions connoting peripheral, rural, or out-of-the-way locations such as *henchi, hekichi, henpi,* and *henkyō naru* (on the border) are commonly and frequently used in the accounts I have discussed here. Expressions denoting inside and outside included *kono kata,* or *kono hō* ("this side," or "our people"), denoting Japan, and *sono kata,* or *sono hō* ("that side," or "their people"), indicating the foreign.

93. The phrase is from Norbert Elias's classic study of manners and social control, *The Civilizing Process.*

94. Karatani Kōjin, *Origins of Modern Japanese Literature,* pp. 18–34, 52–54.

95. Ibid., p. 27.

96. Ibid., pp. 52–53.

97. Karatani, too, of course, is wary of linear trajectories, and he means in his writings to problematize every aspect of the "origins of modern Japanese literature."

CHAPTER FOUR

1. This term, which began to come into use in the early nineteenth century, encompasses the many subgenres of comic fiction, from *sharebon* ("books of style") and *kibyōshi* ("yellow-cover books") popular in the mid- to late eighteenth century, to the lengthy *gōkan* ("multivolume") texts of the early nineteenth century. See Nobuhiro Shinji and Tanahashi Masahiro, "Gesaku kenkyū

no shin chihei e," pp. 2–8. For a definition of each of the separate genres, see Murata Yūji, "Gesaku kenkyū wo yomu tame ni kiwaado," pp. 10–15, and Okamoto Masaru and Kira Sueo, eds., *Kinsei bungaku kenkyū jiten*, pp. 155–60. A classic discussion of *gesaku* as a genre is Nakamura Yukihiko, *Gesaku ron*.

2. For a succinct summary of these issues see Ronald P. Toby, "Contesting the Centre"; see also his monograph, *State and Diplomacy in Early Modern Japan*.

3. Hayashi Gahō (1618–80), son of Hayashi Razan, wrote in 1689 that "the barbarians have snatched the flower *[ryakka]* ... but our country is at peace, the waves of the ocean are gentle, and the winds of virtue blow broadly, summoning merchant ships to Nagasaki from Tang [China]." Quoted in Toby, "Contesting the Centre," p. 355. On the treatment of Koreans, a subject not discussed here, see Ronald P. Toby, "Carnival of the Aliens."

4. See Marius Jansen, *China in the Tokugawa World*, pp. 33–34.

5. Toby, "Contesting the Centre," pp. 360–61.

6. Ibid., p. 361, and Jansen, *China in the Tokugawa World*, pp. 85–86. Nagakubo Sekisui, sinophile that he was, preferred to use the term "Great Qing" for China and "Qing guests" for the Chinese. On the reversion to "Chinese" tropes in the representation of "others" in early modern Japan, see Ronald P. Toby, "The 'Indianness' of Iberia and Changing Japanese Iconographies of Other."

7. For an excellent discussion of the *San cai tu hui* in the context of early modern Chinese visual culture, see Craig Clunas, *Pictures and Visuality in Early Modern China*, pp. 77–101.

8. Marius Jansen gives a figure of 412 new gazetteers in the bakufu archives as of 1735; see *China in the Tokugawa World*, p. 37.

9. The subject of Western learning and its influence on Japanese intellectual and cultural life has been discussed in detail in both English and Japanese; I will not address it in depth here. In English, see Leonard Blussé, Willem Remmelink, and Ivo Smits, eds., *Bridging the Divide*; Beatrice Bodart-Bailey, ed. and trans., *Kaempfer's Japan*; Donald Keene, *The Japanese Discovery of Europe, 1720–1880*; Beatrice M. Bodart-Bailey and Derek Massarella, eds., *The Furthest Goal*; Grant K. Goodman, *Japan: The Dutch Experience*; Derek Massarella, *A World Elsewhere*; A. Querido, "Dutch Transfer of Knowledge Through Deshima"; Timon Screech, *The Western Scientific Gaze and Popular Imagery in Later Edo Japan*; Haga Tōru, "The Western World and Japan in the Eighteenth Century."

10. Nishikawa Jōken, *[Zōhō] Ka'i tsūshō kō*, hereafter cited as *KTK;* Terajima Ryōan, *Wakan sansai zue*, hereafter cited as *WSZ*.

11. The "fifteen provinces" consisted of the "two capitals" of Beijing and Nanjing and the "thirteen circuits" of Shandong, Shanxi, Henan, Shaanxi, Huguang (Hubei and Hunan), Jiangxi, Zhejiang, Fujian, Guangdong, Gansu, Guizhou, Sichuan, and Yunnan.

12. Tonkin referred to the area roughly corresponding to the central part of present-day Vietnam. The early Tokugawa shoguns exchanged diplomatic correspondence with Tonkin, and had good relations and trade with the country, importing copper, raw silk, woven silks, and medicines. After the restrictions

on trade were implemented in the 1630s, trade was suspended. See Kokushi Daijiten Henshū Iinkai, ed., *Kokushi daijiten,* vol. 10, p. 488. The country is also listed in the *WSZ,* pp. 280–81.

13. Cochin referred to the area roughly corresponding to the southern part of present-day Vietnam. The people are described in the *Wakan sansai zue* as being descended from "mountain monkeys" and being "wickedly cunning," resembling in that regard malign spirits. See *WSZ,* pp. 277–79.

14. Champa, also known as Rinyū, was located in what is now central Vietnam. The country was part of the early Chinese empire, but gained independence in the second century C.E.; see Kokushi Daijiten Henshū Iinkai, ed., *Kokushi daijiten,* vol. 14, p. 678. The *Wakan sansai zue* describes Champa as facing the sea on the east, and bordering the Chinese province of Yunnan to the west, Annam (northern Vietnam) to the north, Shinrō (Cambodia/Thailand) to the south, and Guangdong to the northeast, which would put it closer to present-day northern Laos. See *WSZ,* pp. 281–84.

15. This country is described in the *Wakan sansai zue* as being a small country in southern India, "whose people resemble the Cambodians." They trade with China and, through China, with the Japanese; see *WSZ,* p. 286.

16. Rokkon is described in the *Wakan sansai zue* as being Tani's smaller southern neighbor. Rokkon also traded with the Chinese and, through them, with the Japanese. See *WSZ,* p. 287.

17. Malacca referred to the western coast of the Malaysian peninsula, which was colonized in 1522 by the Portuguese and became their Asian trading base. See Kokushi Daijiten Henshū Iinkai, ed., *Kokushi daijiten,* vol. 13, p. 201.

18. Bantan (presently known as Banten) is located on the northwest coast of Java, in Indonesia. During the Tokugawa period it was an active trading port.

19. Mogul referred to the territory of the former Mogul empire in northern India.

20. *KTK,* pp. 568–80. It should be noted that conditions in Japan itself are not discussed in *Kai'i tsūshō kō.*

21. The modeling of relations between the "civilized" and the "barbaric" as nested concentric circles was formulated by early Chinese imperial rulers themselves. See Needham, *Science and Civilisation in China,* vol. 3, p. 502.

22. *KTK,* p. 278.

23. *KTK,* p. 279.

24. *WKS,* pp. 15, 41.

25. The grouping of Japan, China, and India together as countries that practice Buddhism has roots in cosmological mapping and the religious iconography of mandala. On Buddhist world maps, see Kazutaka Unno, "Cartography in Japan," pp. 371–76; on mandala, see Elizabeth ten Grotenhuis, *Japanese Mandalas;* Allan G. Grapard, "Flying Mountains and Walkers of Emptiness."

26. Mori's diary is especially valuable because the author records the prices he paid to buy and to borrow books. He spent the considerable sum of 120 *monme* in silver for *Wakan sansai zue,* but he paid much less for other works of short fiction, and less still—only 6 *fun*—to borrow texts like the parody of the writings of the Taoist sage Zhuangxi, entitled *Rustic Zhuangxi* (Inaka Sōji, 1727). By comparison, his diary notes that in the same years he paid

5 *monme,* 5 *fun* for two ceramic water vessels and 5 *fun* for three ladles, which leads one to believe that the prices for cheaper books were in the same range as those for small household goods. See Konta Yōzō, *Edo no hon'ya san,* pp. 45–48.

27. See Ichiko Teiji, ed., *Otogizōshishū.*

28. The term "poaching" is a translation of Michel de Certeau's term *"braconnage,"* which Roger Chartier explains most clearly as the idea that "reading is not simply submission to textual machinery. Whatever it may be, reading is a creative practice, which invents singular meanings and significations that are not reducible to the intentions of authors of texts or producers of books. Reading is a response, a labor, or . . . an act of 'poaching' *[braconnage]."* See Chartier, "Texts, Printing, Reading," p. 156. For de Certeau's original text in English translation, see Michel de Certeau, "Reading as Poaching," pp. 165–76.

29. The first attempt at an account of Gennai's life was Chikusō Rekisai's *True Record of Hiraga Kyūkei (Hiraga Kyūkei jikki)* of 1789; Takizawa (Kyokutei) Bakin included Gennai in his catalog of Edo writers, *Kinsei mono no hon sakusha burui* of 1834, reprinted in Takizawa Bakin, *Kinsei mono no hon sakusha burui.* The most comprehensive twentieth-century scholarly biographies of Gennai are Haga Tōru, *Hiraga Gennai;* Inagaki Takeshi, *Hiraga Gennai no Edo no yume;* Jōfuku Isamu, *Hiraga Gennai no kenkyū;* and Noda Hisao, *Hiraga Gennai no hito to shōgai.* Gennai studies became a small industry in the 1980s with the so-called "Edo boom," an upsurge of popular and scholarly interest in Edo-period literature, culture, and history that produced a spate of books aimed at nonspecialist readers. Most of these popular books are of questionable scholarly merit; one exception is Tanaka Yūko's *Edo no sōzōryoku.* Gennai has been studied far less extensively outside Japan. The only full-length English-language biography of him is Stanleigh H. Jones's dissertation, "Scholar, Scientist, Popular Author Hiraga Gennai, 1728–1780." Gennai also figures in Sumie Amikura Jones, "Comic Fiction in Japan During the Later Edo Period." In French, Hubert Maës has written in detail about Gennai. His comprehensive biography is entitled *Hiraga Gennai et son temps;* his study and translation of *Shidōken* is *Histoire Galante de Shidōken.*

30. For comprehensive biographical detail, see Jones, "Scholar, Scientist, Popular Author Hiraga Gennai, 1728–1780," pp. 6–26. See also the year-by-year timeline of Gennai's activities in the supplement to his collected works: Hiraga Gennai Sensei Kenshōkai, ed., *Hiraga Gennai zenshū.*

31. Jones, "Scholar, Scientist, Popular Author Hiraga Gennai, 1728–1780," p. 10.

32. The plates date from the 1760s; three of them are still in existence. In addition to the plate embellished with a map of Japan, one depicts a map of the world on the model of late-seventeenth-century printed world maps, and another depicts North and South America. For reproductions, see Kanagawa Kenritsu Rekishi Hakubutsukan, ed., *Sekai no katachi, Nihon no katachi,* pp. 60, 72.

33. Morishima Chūryō was also known by his pen names Shinra Banshō, Shinra Manzō, and Manzō Tei. He fashioned himself the "second-generation Fūrai Sanjin" *(Nisei Fūrai Sanjin)* in honor of Gennai. For his writings, see Ishigami Satoshi, ed., *Morishima Chūryō shū.*

34. Again, I wish to credit and draw attention to the translations that do exist. Interested readers should consult Stanleigh H. Jones's partial English translation of *Shidōken* in "Scholar, Scientist, Popular Author Hiraga Gennai, 1728–1780," or Hubert Maës's French translation, *L'Histoire Galante de Shidōken.*

35. Hiraga Gennai, *Nenashigusa,* p. 224.

36. The influences on the plot of *Shidōken* were many. Foremost among them were the encyclopedias *Wakan sansai zue* and *Ka'i tsūshō kō.* In addition, an *otogizōshi* entitled *Onzōshi shima watari* (Onzōshi's island crossings), which was included in an eighteenth-century collection of popular tales, is often cited as an influence, as it tells the story of visits to distant islands. In particular, in *Onzōshi shima watari* there is a passage in which the protagonist visits an island populated by centaurlike creatures who are so tall and spindly that, like the Long-Legs of Gennai's story, they wear small drums at their waists to summon help in case they fall down and are unable to upright themselves without aid from others. See Ichiko Teiji, ed., *Otogizoshishū,* pp. 102–23. On the eighteenth-century publication of *otogizōshi,* see Fujikake Kazuyoshi, "Kyōho ki ni okeru Shibukawa-ban *Otogizōshi* no itchi," pp. 25–36. Less certain is the recurring assertion that Gennai was familiar with the plot of Swift's *Gulliver's Travels* through connections in the Dutch community in Nagasaki, and that this influenced the world travel motif of *The Tale of Dashing Shidōken;* the most recent variation on this argument is Uda Toshihiko, "Daijin koku yobun—Hiraga Gennai to *Garibuaa ryokōki.*"

37. Hiraga Gennai, *Fūryū Shidōken den,* in Nakamura Yukihiko, ed., *Fūrai Sanjin shū,* p. 159. Hereafter cited as FSD.

38. Quoted in FSD, p. 159, n. 4.

39. See Nanpo, *Ichiwa ichigen,* in Hamada Giichirō, ed., *Ōta Nanpo zenshū,* p. 424; Nanpo is also cited in Noda Hisao, *Kinsei shōsetsu shi ronkō,* pp. 274 and 333.

40. Fūrai Senjin is both a play on Gennai's pen name Fūrai Sanjin, and an allusion to the *sennin,* the reclusive mountain sage of Taoist lore. The term *sennin* derives from the Chinese *(xianren),* and was originally used to refer to individuals who were thought to have attained supernatural powers, especially those of immortality, by engaging in Taoist ascetic practices in remote mountain regions. The character *sen* combines the radicals for "person" and "mountain" to describe beings that Kristofer Schipper likens to "liberated elves, who, like the Old Child (Laozi), know neither parents nor children, neither lineage, nor country. . . . They do not fit into any system and it is impossible to place them into any framework whatsoever." See Schipper, *The Taoist Body,* p. 166.

41. Asanoshin's innocence is likely a jab at Buddhist priests, who were notorious for indulging freely in all manner of worldly vices, including drinking, carousing, and especially frequenting brothels. The diarist Kitagawa Morisada wrote that of all the social classes, priests were the main patrons of male prostitutes. From *Morisada mankō,* quoted in Hanasaki Kazuo, *Edo no kagemajaya,* p. 58. On the Buddhist clergy and same-sex relationships, see Gregory M. Pflugfelder, *Cartographies of Desire,* esp. pp. 73–76.

42. FSD, pp. 174–75.

43. While Gennai's *Rootless Grass* contains a protracted debate on the mer-

its of female versus male love, here the matter is bypassed quickly. Gennai him-self was a great lover of both the kabuki theater and its young male actors; see Haga Tōru, *Hiraga Gennai*, pp. 284–301. On male-male sexuality and the the-ater, see Pflugfelder, *Cartographies of Desire*, pp. 113–20; see also Hanasaki Kazuo, *Edo no kagemajaya*, pp. 100–124.

44. The *Chōsen nagaya*, or Korean tenements, provided housing for low-ranking attendants to the Korean embassies on visits to Edo. See Toby, "Con-testing the Centre," pp. 347–63.

45. *FSD*, pp. 187–88; Nasu no Yōichi was the famous Minamoto warrior who, during the Battle of Yajima in the Genpei War (1180–85), successfully re-sponded to the enemy's challenge of shooting an arrow through a white fan painted with a red circle held aloft on a Heike boat. His exploits were recorded in *The Tale of the Heike*. See *FSD*, p. 188, n. 5; for a translation of this episode, see Helen C. McCullough, trans., *The Tale of the Heike*, pp. 366–68.

46. On early modern Japanese "ocean fears," see Marcia Yonemoto, "Maps and Metaphors of the 'Small Eastern Sea' in Tokugawa Japan (1603–1868)."

47. The text gives a height of "two *jō*," which is slightly over six meters, or twenty feet (1 *jō* = 10 *shaku* = 3.03 meters = 10 feet). The Giants described in *Shidōken* in much the same way as they appear in the *Wakan sansai zue*.

48. This, too, was a land described in the *Wakan sansai zue*.

49. For a similar description of these people in the *Wakan sansai zue*, see *WSZ*, vol. 3, p. 334.

50. The pun here is that one whose "arms are long" *(te ga nagai)* is one in-clined to thievery. See *FSD*, p. 195, n. 12.

51. For a similar description in the *Wakan sansai zue*, see *WSZ*, vol. 3, p. 331.

52. This is most likely an absurdist take on the Tokugawa concern with status-appropriate characteristics and behaviors.

53. The name used in the text is "Somondara." See *FSD*, p. 199, n. 15.

54. The name used in the text is "Borunera." See *FSD*, p. 199, n. 16.

55. The name used in the text is "Harusha." See *FSD*, p. 199, n. 17.

56. The name used in the text is "Muscovia." See *FSD*, p. 199, n. 18.

57. The *Wakan sansai zue* describes this country, located in what is now Burma, as being in south-central India, three or four days' journey from Siam (Thailand). It was said to be the site of a former residence of the historical Bud-dha, and contained many sacred sites and temples. See *WSZ*, p. 339.

58. Arakan is not among the countries listed in the *Wakan sansai zue*, but it is described in Nishikawa Jōken's *Ka'i tsūshō kō* as being in the western part of Burma; *FSD*, p. 199, n. 20.

59. The name used in the text is "Arumenia." See *FSD*, p. 199, n. 21.

60. The term used here is Tenjiku, referring to the entire Indian subcontinent.

61. The name used is "Oranda." See *FSD*, p. 199, n. 23.

62. The dates for the Qing dynasty are 1644–1911.

63. Male brothels *(kodomoya)* and teahouses specializing in assignations with male prostitutes *(kagemajaya)* were numerous in Edo. Most of the clients were men, especially Buddhist priests, but women also patronized male brothels. These women were often ladies-in-waiting or economically independent women,

such as pawnbrokers or other merchants. See Hanasaki Kazuo, *Edo no kage-majaya*; see also Gregory M. Pflugfelder, *Cartographies of Desire*, pp. 120–22.

64. *FSD*, p. 219.

65. *FSD*, p. 174.

66. The equation of vision with knowledge is a metaphor that is threaded throughout the story. Gennai had a strong interest in visual technologies such as telescopes, perspective print viewers *(nozoki* or *ukie)*, and magnifying glasses and microscopes *(mushimegane)*, which, as we have seen in chapter 3, were then becoming a fad among artists and intellectuals in Edo and elsewhere. In his other major satirical work, *Nenashigusa* (Rootless grass), published the same year as *The Tale of Dashing Shidōken*, Gennai lists the perspective print viewers among *misemono* exhibited in the bustling commercial and entertainment district around the Ryōgoku bridge. The narrator comments that "those who look into the *ukie* feel [themselves] transported to another world." See Hiraga Gennai, *Nenashigusa*, p. 77. For a detailed discussion of visual technology and its relationship to artistic representation, see Timon Screech, *The Western Scientific Gaze and Popular Imagery in Later Edo Japan.*

67. One root of the term *"okabasho"* was in the expression *"hoka [no] basho,"* or "other places," that is, private brothel districts outside the licensed quarters. Shinagawa, Naitō Shinjuku, and Itabashi were places mentioned by Gennai.

68. During Gennai's time, only courtesans of the highest class *(chūsan)* were allowed to be on display in the latticed rooms for the inspection of prospective clients (excepting the *yobidashi chūsan*, the highest-ranking of the *chūsan* class, who were allowed the luxury of being available only by appointment). On ranks and roles of courtesans, see Cecilia Segawa Seigle, *Yoshiwara*, esp. pp. 230–32.

69. *FSD*, p. 185.

70. The god of marriages *(en musubi no kami)* at Izumo Shrine is said to enter into his register all one's relationships. See *FSD*, p. 185, n. 44–45.

71. Fujimoto (Hatakeyama) Kizan's *Shikidō ōkagami* was completed in 1678. Its eighteen volumes of text and diagrams described in detail many of the major pleasure quarters of Japan, their rules and etiquette, language, dress, and rituals; it also listed names and crests of courtesans found there. It also proposed strategies for (male) clients to implement in order to assure successful liaisons, such as setting up elaborate (but discreet) ruses in order to play hard-to-get. For original text, see Noma Kōshin, ed., *[Kanpon] Shikidō ōkagami.* See also Cecilia Segawa Seigle, *Yoshiwara*, pp. 132–33.

72. *FSD*, p. 191.

73. Temples would periodically hold *kaichō* to exhibit relics or statuary not usually on public display. These religious events were often the occasion for great public gatherings that attracted a variety of secular, profit-making endeavors in the form of temporary vendors, *misemono*, and outdoor performances. On temples as popular spaces, see Nam-lin Hur, *Prayer and Play in Late Tokugawa Japan*; on *misemono*, see Andrew L. Markus, "The Carnival of Edo."

74. See Saitō Gesshin, *Bukō nenpyō*, vol. 1, p. 200. See also Andrew L. Markus, "The Carnival of Edo," p. 516.

75. Nakamura Yukihiko argues that this incident represents nostalgia on Gennai's part for a traditional sense of duty among officials; see *FSD*, p. 193, n. 13. It also might conceivably be a poke at the mania among scholars (especially the inept doctors Gennai so often railed against) for collecting and gathering specimens about which they knew little.

76. As the son of a low-ranking provincial samurai, Gennai was familiar with the prejudices of rank; and as one who made numerous attempts to make a name for himself (and attract official approbation) through the display of his unique talents, he believed that individuals should be recognized for their merit and was frustrated at the arbitrariness of the status system. See Jōfuku Isamu, *Hiraga Gennai no kenkyū*, pp. 47–78; on samurai complaints about heredity versus merit, see Thomas C. Smith, "'Merit' as Ideology in the Tokugawa Period."

77. Gennai entered the academy of the preeminent nativist scholar of the eighteenth century, Kamo no Mabuchi, in the ninth month of 1763. In the eleventh month of the same year *Fūryū Shidōken den* and *Nenashigusa* were published. See Haga Tōru, *Hiraga Gennai*, pp. 426–27. See also Jones, "Scholar, Scientist, Popular Author Hiraga Gennai, 1728–1780," p. 15 and n. 34.

78. *FSD*, p. 201.

79. His clothes and even the magic fan had been burned up in the skirmish with palace guards.

80. *FSD*, p. 203.

81. *FSD*, p. 204; *"Nihonjin no negoto"* is a play on the phrase *"Tōjin no negoto,"* or "sleep talk of a Chinese," which meant gibberish. See *FSD*, p. 204, n. 2.

82. *FSD*, p. 204. The Five Sacred Mountains of China represent the cardinal direction points in traditional geo-cosmography and derive from a history of mountain worship dating from as early as the Chou period (ca. 1027–1256 B.C.E.). They are also often associated with Taoism. The mountains and their representative directions are: Mount Tai (east), Mount Hua (west), Mount Heng (north), Mount Heng (south), and Mount Song (center). The composition of the group of five mountains was altered slightly by the emperor Wu of Han, who changed the southern Mount Heng to Mount Tianzhu in Anhui province; some of the later Han emperors followed suit. See Munakata Kiyohiko, *Sacred Mountains in Chinese Art*, p. 5.

83. The embedded quotation is an allusion to a poem by Ishikawa Jōzan (1583–1672). See *FSD*, p. 204, n. 8.

84. The pun here is in the use of the term *"yamashi"* (literally "mountain experts"), which referred to contractors involved in entrepreneurial mining exploration who turned to speculation, hence the pejorative connotation of the term. Gennai himself was involved in such mining ventures.

85. "Fuji" here is rendered with the characters meaning "not to die."

86. *FSD*, p. 205.

87. *FSD*, pp. 214–15.

88. Yū Koku Shi, *[Ikoku kidan] Wasōbyōe*.

89. The earliest derivative is said to be *Shōchū Resshi* (Humorously an-

notated Resshi), a mock biography of the Taoist philosopher's world travels written by Shōshi Tei in 1782; see Noda Hisao, *Kinsei shosetsu shi ronkō*, pp. 281–83.

90. For a plot summary, see Noda, *Kinsei shōsetsu shi ronkō*, p. 282.

91. The character *"sō"* in Sōemon, as in Wasōbyōe, here may also connote Sōshi, the Japanese reading of Zhuangxi, the Chinese Taoist sage. The author of the story is Hokushū Sanjin Kajimaru; see Noda, *Kinsei shōsetsu shi ronkō*, p. 283.

92. This difficult-to-translate title suggests, as do so many titles of satirical works, slovenliness and unreliability. The bracketed phrase means roughly "slovenly conceit," the main title literally "mud broom." The whole title, when considered along with the story's content, connotes the tidying up of a dissolute life.

93. Noda, *Kinsei shōsetsu shi ronkō*, p. 283.

94. Quoted in ibid., p. 258.

CHAPTER FIVE

1. Peter Stallybrass and Allon White, *The Politics and Poetics of Transgression*, p. 80.

2. On prostitution in early Japan, see Janet R. Goodwin, "Shadows of Transgression."

3. It should be noted that prostitution and nonsexual entertainment, as defined here and as represented in historical documents and literary texts, refers almost exclusively to a situation in which female prostitutes or courtesans serve male patrons. For a brief summary of prostitution before the early modern period, see Cecilia Segawa Seigle, *Yoshiwara*, pp. 1–13. A discussion of the theoretical issues regarding concepts of sex, gender, and sexuality (same-sex and heterosexual) in classical and early modern Japan is beyond the scope of the present discussion; for a detailed analysis focusing on male-male sexuality, see Gregory M. Pflugfelder, *Cartographies of Desire*, esp. pp. 1–145. This chapter treats the brothel districts and the performing arts and sexual services provided in them as a study in the creation and manipulation of highly localized cultural and spatial identities. This is not to slight the importance of the overarching history of sexuality, prostitution, or women. On the contrary, following the lead of Watanabe Kenji and other scholars who approach the history of pleasure quarters as cultural history, I see the development of a "pleasure industry" as part and parcel of early modern society. That is, prostitution was not an exceptional, or exceptionally dark, aspect of Edo culture and history, but one instance of the many and often highly unbalanced relationships of social and economic power that characterized the Tokugawa system. See Watanabe Kenji, *Edo yūri seisuiki*.

4. For a translation of these laws, see Seigle, *Yoshiwara*, pp. 23–24.

5. Yoshiwara courtesans famously devised a particular manner of speaking, marked by unique verb endings that transformed, for example, the verb meaning "be," *"aru,"* into *"arinsu"*; as a result, the Yoshiwara became known colloquially as "Arinsu-koku," the "land of *arinsu*."

6. These figures are from Seigle, *Yoshiwara*, pp. 34–35.

7. Watanabe Kenji, *Edo yūri seisuiki*, esp. pp. 12–39.

8. Stallybrass and White, *The Politics and Poetics of Transgression*, p. 25.

9. On *yūjo hyōbanki*, see Nakano Mitsutoshi, *Edo bunka hyōbanki*.

10. Nishiyama Matsunosuke et al., eds., *Edogaku jiten*, pp. 548–52.

11. Emphasis in original; quoted in Nakano Mitsutoshi, "Yoshiwara saiken," p. 7.

12. Emphasis in original; from an undated *saiken* published by Urokogataya Magobee. Quoted in ibid.

13. On Tsutaya's publication of *saiken*, see Suzuki Toshiyuki, "Tsutaya-han saiken to sono fuzai kōkoku"; see also Nishiyama et al., eds., *Edogaku jiten*, p. 556.

14. On Tsutaya's *saiken* advertisements, see Suzuki Toshiyuki, "Tsutaya-han saiken to sono fuzai kōkoku."

15. For a detailed discussion of these changes, see Yamashiro Yūkiko, "Yoshiwara saiken no kenkyū," pp. 121–31.

16. Satō Yōjin, "Yoshiwara saiken shuppan jijō," p. 116.

17. This writer was also known as Tanba-ya Rihee. For the full edited text of this work, see Inaka Rōjin Tada Okina, *Yushi hōgen*, in Mizuno Minoru, ed., *Kibyōshi, Sharebon shū*, pp. 269–94.

18. For the full edited text of Santō Kyōden's *Edo umare uwaki no kabayaki*, see Hamada Gi'ichirō, Suzuki Katsutada, and Mizuno Minoru, eds., *Kibyōshi, senryū, kyōka*, pp. 117–37; for Kyōden's *Tsūgen sōmagaki*, see Mizuno Minoru, ed., *Kibyōshi, sharebon shū*, pp. 353–86.

19. For a discussion, in English, of the functions of *shukō* in Edo literature, see Haruko Iwasaki, "The Literature of Wit and Humor in Late-Eighteenth-Century Edo."

20. Tenjiku Rōnin was one of the pen names of the *rangaku* (Dutch studies) scholar Morishima Chūryō, in imitation of his mentor, Hiraga Gennai, who used the same name. For the complete text, see Tenjiku Rōnin, *Tōsei dōtsūki*, in Takagi Kōji, Yamamoto Testsuzō, and Watanabe Yoshi, eds., *Sharebon taikei*, vol. 1, pp. 251–88.

21. A less literal but perhaps more felicitous translation of this phrase might be "all you need is love."

22. Tenjiku Rōnin, *Tōsei dōtsūki*, p. 251.

23. Whereas the "*tsūshō*" in Jōken's title connoted "trade and commerce," in Ishijima's title it makes more sense in its alternate reading, "the marketing of [the] *tsū*." Two versions of this text exist: the earlier (1748) text can be found in Ishijima Masatane (Sanjin), *Ka-ri tsūshō kō*, in Mizuno Minoru et al., eds., *Sharebon taisei*, vol. 1, pp. 223–33; the later (1754) text was published as an appendix to *Kontan sōkanjō* under Ishijima's pseudonym An Gyūsai. This version can be found in Ishijima Masatane, *Kontan sōkanjō*, Takagi, Yamamoto, and Watanabe, eds., *Sharebon taisei*, vol. 1, pp. 151–57. On themes of male-male love in the latter text, see Gregory M. Pflugfelder, *Cartographies of Desire*, p. 67.

24. For a reproduction, see Ishijima, *Ka-ri tsūshō kō*, p. 233

25. Ibid.

26. Ibid.

27. For a reproduction of this map, see Ishijima, *Ka-ri tsūshō kō*, p. 153.

28. Ibid.

29. Ibid., pp. 154–55.

30. Ibid., p. 156.

31. The editors of *Sharebon taikei* state that *Rokuchō ichiri* was a sequel to *Ka-ri tsūshō kō*; see Takagi, Yamamoto, and Watanabe, eds., *Sharebon taikei*, vol. 2, pp. 6–7. Mizuno Minoru, however, argues that there is no direct correlation between the two texts. See Mizuno Minoru, ed., *Sharebon taisei*, vol. 1, p. 391.

32. Manji Kōkaisen, *Rokuchō ichiri*, p. 48.

33. Dō Jarō Maa, *Shōji jiriki*, Mizuno Minoru et al., eds. All references to this text will be abbreviated hereafter as *SJ*. Kisanji's pen name, read aloud phonetically, mimics the uncertainty of the phrase *Dō darō? Maa* . . . ("What could it be? Hmm . . .").

34. *SJ*, p. 209.

35. *SJ*, p. 210.

36. *SJ*, p. 211.

37. *SJ*, p. 211.

38. The pun here is also a visual one, for *kamaboko,* a plebeian sort of food, typically came in long cylindrical shapes. Its glutinous consistency and fishy odor made it a good contrast to the shining jeweled scepter the deities use to create Japan in the *Kojiki.*

39. In the actual Yoshiwara, *yarite* were women who supervised the day-to-day running of brothels. The repeated references to fish may also connote the scent often associated with female sexuality.

40. Each of these characteristics stands in direct opposition to the Neo-Confucian view of women, in which disorderly women are a threat to familial and societal harmony.

41. *SJ*, p. 213. This is an obvious jab at the bakufu's tendency toward inconsistency and arbitrariness in its policy making.

42. *SJ*, p. 214.

43. *SJ*, pp. 221–23.

44. For an English-language study of Sanba's life and work, see Robert Leutner, *Shikitei Sanba and the Comic Tradition in Edo Fiction.*

45. This is the artistic name used by the writer Santō Kyōden.

46. Torii Kiyomitsu (1735–85) was of the third generation of the well-known family of *ukiyoe* artists. He was most famous for his prints of actors and "beautiful women" *(bijin-e).*

47. Shikitei Sanba, *[Mata yakinaosu Hachikazuki-hime] Kusazōshi kojitsuke nendaiki*, p. 231. Hereafter, this source will be abbreviated *KKN.* The "revised and expanded edition" never was published. *"Kojitsuke"* (twisted or distorted) is the idiosyncratic reading Sanba assigned to two characters in the title of the work that can also be read "millions of explanations." Likewise, the characters assigned the reading of *"kusazōshi"* (popular literature) can also be read *"haishi,"* which was a fictionalized form of popular history.

48. Sanba adopts a fairly conventional timeline for his survey. Most schol-

ars date the emergence of *akahon* (red-cover books), the first genre of literature included in the umbrella term *kusazōshi* (here translated as "popular" literature), from the appearance of *Shoshun no iwai* in 1678. Subsequent subgenres of *aohon* (blue-cover books), *kurohon* (black-cover books), and *kibyōshi* (yellow-cover books) blend together, but in general *kurohon* and *aohon* were dominant in the 1740s to 1770s and *kibyōshi* from the 1770s through the first years of the nineteenth century. The publication of Shikitei Sanba's *Ikazura Tarō kyōaku monogatari* in 1806 is given as one ending point for *kibyōshi*. These were terms widely known to writers and readers of Edo fiction; Sanba himself uses these categorizations in his text. See Okamoto Masaru and Kira Sueo, eds., *Kinsei bungaku kenkyū jiten,* pp. 155–60.

49. The original *nendaiki* was a historical encyclopedia of sorts, containing lists of the birth and death dates of all the shoguns, from Minamoto Yoritomo forward, and a list of the death dates of famous Buddhist monks.

50. For a fuller discussion of *nendaiki*, see Nakayama Yūshō, "Kaisetsu," in Koike et al., eds., *Edo no gesaku ehon,* vol. 4, p. 264; for reproductions of a map and a page of text from the *[Jūho] Kusazōshi nendaiki,* see *KKN,* p. 233.

51. *KKN,* p. 232.

52. I have added to this list dates for individual authors, when available, and an indication of the genre in which each wrote.

53. *KKN,* p. 233.

54. See Akatsuki Kanenari, *Akan sanzai zue.* All further references to this work are to the version in the collection of the National Diet Library, Tokyo, and will be abbreviated *ASZ.*

55. The titles include a five-volume text he has edited, *Harugasumi iru no saigen;* a three-volume text called *Ogura hyaku shurui daibanashi;* and the six-volume *Shunsei yuki no aizuchi. ASZ,* bk. 2, vol. 2, p. 14.

56. *ASZ,* bk. 1, vol. 1, p. 6.

57. Terajima Ryōan, *Wakan sansai zue,* vol. 1, pp. 11–12.

58. An alternate reading of *kugai* would be "nine streets," perhaps a reference to the geography of the Yoshiwara. The term is also, perhaps, a play on *kugai,* "public space" or the "general public," also a term used in medieval times to denote a space free from the laws and constraints of everyday life. On the latter meaning, see Amino Yoshihiko, *Muen, Kugai, Raku.*

59. *Koi* connotes carnal desire, in contrast to *ai,* another common character for love, which carries more benign connotations such as love for family or for humanity in general. This map is also reproduced in Kazutaka Unno, "Cartography in Japan," p. 431, along with another map of "islands" formed by Japanese script. The latter is from a text entitled *Zen'aku meisho zue* (Illustrated famous places, good and evil, 1846), by Ippitsuan Eisen (1790–1848) and spells out, in *hiragana* syllabary, the phrases *"satorubeshi"* ("you should be spiritually awakened") and *"mayōnna"* ("don't go astray"). See ibid., pp. 431–32.

60. Again mirroring the format of the *Wakan sansai zue,* the map is followed by detailed descriptions and illustrations of the "inhabitants" of the various countries. Most of them rehearse stereotypes and images that are by now familiar, so I omit them here.

61. The nape of the neck, left intentionally exposed and framed by the folded collar of a kimono, as can be seen in the map itself, was said to be the most alluring part of a woman's body.

62. The single character *iro* (also read *kō*) literally meant color, but it also connoted sexuality, as in the titles of the many fictional tales of *kōshoku,* or the "love of love."

63. In geomantic terms, Edo was thought by the early Tokugawa shoguns to be a fortuitous location because it had a mountain to the north (the Kōjimachi highlands), a body of water to the south (Edo Bay), a river to the east (the Sumida River), and a road to the west (the Tōkaidō). These natural or manmade features corresponded to the directional colors yellow, blue, white, and red, respectively. See Naitō Akira, "Edo no toshi kōzo."

64. Although publishing was largely Edo-based by the late eighteenth century, texts such as *Akan sanzai zue* were published simultaneously by houses in Edo, Kyoto, and Osaka.

65. Quoted in Seigle, *Yoshiwara,* p. 202.

66. Ibid., p. 206.

67. On the shift from Nihonbashi to Fukugawa, see Henry D. Smith II, "The Floating World in Its Edo Locale"; see also Marcia Yonemoto, "Nihonbashi: Edo's Contested Center."

68. See Anne Walthall, "Edo Riots." On popular protest in general, see Walthall, *Social Protest and Popular Culture in Eighteenth-Century Japan.*

69. See Hayashiya Tatsusaburō, "Ka-sei bunka no rekishiteki itchi." On Bunka-Bunsei culture outside the cities, see Sugi Hiroshi, "Kasei ki no shakai to bunka: zaison bunka no tenkai to kinseiteki bunka kōzō no kaitai."

70. Quote is from Herman Ooms, *Charismatic Bureaucrat,* p. 84; on Matsudaira Sadanobu's reform vision, see ibid., pp. 122–50. On the effects of the Kansei reforms on literature and art, see Sarah E. Thompson, "The Politics of Japanese Prints," pp. 56–72. For a recent study of erotic prints in English, see Timon Screech, *Sex and the Floating World.*

71. In Tokugawa official discourse the term I translate as "public" *(ōyake,* or *kō)* most often referred to the shogun himself or the shogunate; occasionally it referred to high-ranking officials as well.

CONCLUSION

1. On the concept of the "nation-space," see Homi K. Bhabha, *Nation and Narration.*

2. See George Alexander Lensen, *The Russian Push Toward Japan,* and John J. Stephan, *The Russian Far East.*

3. On Inō's work, see Tokyo Chigaku Kyōkai, ed., *Inō zu ni manabu.*

4. On the "Siebold incident," see Lutz Walter, "Philipp Franz von Siebold," and Itazawa Takeo, *Shiiboruto, Rekishi jinbutsu sosho.*

5. Inagaki was inspired by the theories of Carl Ritter, which he had studied through his Cambridge mentor John Robert Seeley. See Pekka Korhonen, *Japan and Asia Pacific Integration,* pp. 87–92.

6. On the teaching of geography in the Meiji period, see Kären Wigen, "Teaching About Home."

7. See Benedict Anderson, *Imagined Communities,* rev. ed., and Thongchai Winichakul, *Siam Mapped.* See also David Hooson, ed., *Geography and National Identity.*

8. See Ernest Gellner, *Nations and Nationalism,* p. 55 ff.

9. Ibid., pp. 55–56. Gellner's elliptical formulation is, "Nationalism is not what it seems, and above all is not what it seems to itself." Ibid., p. 56.

Bibliography

UNPUBLISHED SOURCES

Maps

Ishikawa Ryūsen. *Edo zukan komoku, ken.* Edo: Sagamiya Tahee, Genroku 2 (1689). Mitsui Collection, East Asian Library, University of California, Berkeley.

———. *Edo zukan komoku, kon.* Edo: Sagamiya Tahee (Genroku period, after 1694). Mitsui Collection, East Asian Library, University of California, Berkeley.

———. *Honchō zukan komoku.* Kyoto: Hayashi Yoshinaga (n.d.). Mitsui Collection, East Asian Library, University of California, Berkeley.

———. *Nihon kaisan chōriku zu.* Edo: Sagamiya Tahee, Genroku 4 (1691). Mitsui Collection, East Asian Library, University of California, Berkeley.

Matsumoto Yasuoki. *Dōsen Nihon yochi saizu.* N.p.: Seika Shujin, 1835. Mitsui Collection, East Asian Library, University of California, Berkeley.

Nagakubo Sekisui [Genshū, pseud.]. *Kaisei Nihon yochi rotei zenzu.* Naniwa: Asano Yahee, Kansei 3 (1791).

Ochikochi Dōin. *Shinpan Edo ōezu, eiri.* Edo: Hyōshiya Ichirōbee, Enpo 4 (1674). The George H. Beans Collection, University of British Columbia Library, Special Collections Division.

Manuscripts

Akatsuki Kanenari. *Akan sanzai zue,* 5 vols., 6 bks. Vols. 1:1, 1:2, 2, 3:1, 3:2. Tōto: Chōshiya Heibee; Kyoto: Kabuya Kanbee, Maruya Zenbee; Naniwa:

Kawachiya Heishichi (1821–50). Collection of the National Diet Library, Tokyo.

Nagakubo Sekisui. *Sekisui Chō Sensei Nagasaki kikō*. Tōbu: Ogura Jinbee; Kyoto: Hayashi Ihee, Fujii Magobee; Setsujo: Morimoto Tasuke, Tashiki Kyūbee, Asano Yahee, Bunka 2 (1805). Mitsui Collection, University of California, Berkeley, East Asian Library.

Shikitei Sanba. *[Mata yakinaosu Hachikazuki-hime] Kusazoshi kojitsuke nendaiki*. Tōto: Nishinomiya Shinroku, Kyōwa 2 (1802). Collection of Tokyo Metropolitan Central Library.

PUBLISHED SOURCES

Akimoto, Kichirō, ed. *Fudoki*. Vol. 2, *Nihon koten bungaku taikei*. Tokyo: Iwanami Shoten, 1958.

Akioka, Takejiro, ed. *Nihon kochizu shūsei*. Tokyo: Kajima Kenkyūjo Shuppankai, 1971.

Alpers, Svetlana. *The Art of Describing: Dutch Art in the Seventeenth Century*. Chicago: University of Chicago Press, 1986.

Amino Yoshihiko. "Deconstructing 'Japan.'" *East Asian History* 3 (1992): 121–42.

———. *Muen, kugai, raku*. Tokyo: Heibonsha, 1978.

Anderson, Benedict. *Imagined Communities*. Rev. ed. London: Verso, 1991 [1983].

Anderson, Perry. *Lineages of the Absolutist State*. London: Verso, 1979.

Arano, Yasunori, Ishii Masatoshi, and Murai Shōsuke, eds. *Ajia no naka no Nihon shi: Ji'isshiki to sōgo rikai*. Vol. 5. Tokyo: Tokyo Daigaku Shuppankai, 1993.

Asai Ryōi. *Tōkaidō meisho no ki*. Edited by Asakura Haruhiko. Tokyo: Heibonsha, 1979.

Asakura Haruhiko, ed. *Kinsei shuppan hōkoku shiryō shūsei*. Tokyo: Yumani Shobo, 1983.

Aston, W. G., trans. and ed. *Nihongi: Chronicles of Japan from the Earliest Times to A.D. 697*. Rutland, Vt.: Charles E. Tuttle, 1972.

Ayusawa, Shintarō. "Japanese Knowledge of World Geography." *Monumenta Nipponica* 19, no. 3–4 (1964).

Batten, Bruce. "Frontiers and Boundaries of Pre-Modern Japan." *Journal of Historical Geography* 25, no. 2 (1999): 166–82.

Baxandall, Michael. *Painting and Experience in Fifteenth-Century Italy: A Primer in the Social History of Pictorial Style*. 2nd ed. Oxford: Oxford University Press, 1988.

Belyea, Barbara. "Images of Power: Derrida/Foucault/Harley." *Cartographica* 29, no. 2 (1992): 1–9.

Berry, Mary Elizabeth. *Hideyoshi*. Cambridge, Mass.: Harvard University Press, 1982.

———. "Was Early Modern Japan Culturally Integrated?" *Modern Asian Studies* 31, no. 3 (1997): 547–81.

Bhabha, Homi K., ed. *Nation and Narration*. London: Routledge, 1990.

Blussé, Leonard, Willem Remmelink, and Ivo Smits, eds. *Bridging the Divide: 400 Years, The Netherlands–Japan.* Hilversum and Leiden: Teleac/NOT and Hotei Publishing, 2000.

Bodart-Bailey, Beatrice M., and Derek Massarella, eds. *The Furthest Goal: Englebert Kaempfer's Encounter with Tokugawa Japan.* Folkestone, Eng.: Japan Library, 1995.

Bolitho, Harold. "Traveler's Tales: Three Eighteenth-Century Travel Journals." *Harvard Journal of Asiatic Studies* 50, no. 2 (1990): 485–504.

Borgen, Robert. *Sugawara no Michizane and the Early Heian Court.* Princeton, N.J.: Princeton University Press, 1982.

Brazell, Karen, trans. *The Confessions of Lady Nijō.* Garden City, N.Y.: Anchor Books, 1973.

Brown, Philip C. *Central Authority and Local Autonomy in the Formation of Early Modern Japan: The Case of Kaga Domain.* Stanford, Calif.: Stanford University Press, 1993.

———. "The Mismeasure of Land: Land Surveying in the Tokugawa Period." *Monumenta Nipponica* 42, no. 2 (1987): 115–55.

———. "State, Cultivator, Land: Determination of Land Tenures in Early Modern Japan Reconsidered." *The Journal of Asian Studies* 56, no. 2 (1997): 421–44.

Carter, Steven D. "Sōgi in the East Country: Shirakawa Kikō." *Monumenta Nipponica* 42, no. 2 (1987): 167–209.

———. *Three Poets at Yuyama.* Berkeley: Institute of East Asian Studies, University of California, Berkeley, Center for Japanese Studies, 1983.

Chartier, Roger. "Texts, Printing, Reading." In *The New Cultural History,* edited by Lynn Hunt, 154–75. Berkeley: University of California Press, 1989.

Chibbett, David. *The History of Japanese Printing and Book Illustration.* Tokyo: Kōdansha International, 1977.

Clifford, James. *Routes: Travel and Translation in the Late Twentieth Century.* Cambridge, Mass.: Harvard University Press, 1997.

Clunas, Craig. *Pictures and Visuality in Early Modern China.* Princeton, N.J.: Princeton University Press, 1997.

Conley, Tom. *The Self-Made Map: Cartographic Writing in Early Modern France.* Minneapolis: University of Minnesota Press, 1996.

Cooper, Michael, ed. *They Came to Japan: An Anthology of European Reports on Japan, 1543–1640.* Berkeley: University of California Press, 1965.

Cortazzi, Hugh. *Isles of Gold: Antique Maps of Japan.* Tokyo: Weatherhill, 1983.

de Certeau, Michel. "Reading as Poaching." In *The Practice of Everyday Life,* translated by Steven Rendell, 165–76. Berkeley: University of California Press, 1984.

deBary, Wm. Theodore, and Irene Bloom, eds. *Principle and Practicality: Essays in Neo-Confucianism and Practical Learning.* New York: Columbia University Press, 1979.

Dō Jarō Maa [Hōseidō Kisanji]. "Shōhi jiriki." In *Sharebon taisei,* edited by Mizuno Minoru et al., 209–28. Tokyo: Chūō Kōronshi, 1980.

———. "Shōhi jiriki." In *Sharebon taikei,* edited by Takagi Koji, Yamamoto

Tetsuzō, and Watanabe Yoshi, 23–67. Tokyo: Kabushiki Gaisha Rinpei Shoten, 1931.

Dore, Ronald P. *Education in Tokugawa Japan*. Berkeley: University of California Press, 1965.

Edney, Matthew H. "Cartography Without 'Progress': Reinterpreting the Nature and Historical Development of Mapmaking." *Cartographica* 30, no. 2–3 (1993): 54–68.

Elias, Norbert. *The Civilizing Process*. 3 vols. New York: Pantheon, 1978.

Elisonas, Jurgis. "Notorious Places: A Brief Excursion into the Narrative Topography of Early Edo." In *Edo & Paris: Urban Life and the State in the Early Modern Period,* edited by James L. McClain, John M. Merriman, and Ugawa Kaoru, 253–91. Ithaca, N.Y.: Cornell University Press, 1994.

Elliott, Mark. "The Limits of Tartary: Manchuria in Imperial and National Geographies." *The Journal of Asian Studies* 59, no. 3 (2000): 603–46.

Eskildsen, Robert. "Telling Differences: The Imagery of Civilization and Nationality in Nineteenth-Century Japan." Ph.D. diss., Stanford University, 1998.

Foucault, Michel. *The Order of Things: An Archaeology of the Human Sciences*. New York: Vintage Books, 1973.

———. "Questions on Geography." In *Power/Knowledge: Selected Interviews and Other Writings, 1972–77,* 63–77. New York: Pantheon, 1980.

———. "Space, Knowledge, and Power." In *The Foucault Reader,* edited by Paul Rabinow, 239–56. New York: Pantheon, 1984.

Fujikake Kazuyoshi. "Kyōho ni okeru Shibukawa-ban *Otogizōshi* no itchi." *Niihon bungaku* 31 (1982): 25–36.

Fujitani, T. *Splendid Monarchy: Power and Pageantry in Modern Japan*. Berkeley: University of California Press, 1996.

Fujizane Kumiko. "*Bukan* no shuppan to shomotsu shi Izumodera." *Edo bungaku* 16 (1996): 108–23.

Funakoshi Akio. *Sakoku Nihon ni kita "Kōki zu" no chirigakuteki kenkyū*. Tokyo: Hōsei Daigaku Shuppankyoku, 1986.

Furukawa Koshōken. *Saiyū zakki*. In *Nihon kikōbun shūsei,* edited by Yanagida Kunio, 263–375. Tokyo: Nihon Tosho Sentaa, 1979.

———.*Tōyū zakki*. Edited by Ōtō Toyohiko. Tokyo: Heibonsha, 1964.

Geertz, Clifford. "I-Witnessing: Malinowski's Children." In *Works and Lives: The Anthropologist as Author,* 73–101. Stanford, Calif.: Stanford University Press, 1988.

Gellner, Ernest. *Nations and Nationalism*. Ithaca, N.Y.: Cornell University Press, 1985.

Goodman, Grant K. *Japan: The Dutch Experience*. London: Athlone Press, 1986.

Goodwin, Janet R. *Alms and Vagabonds: Buddhist Temples and Popular Patronage in Medieval Japan*. Honolulu: University of Hawai'i Press, 1994.

———. "Shadows of Transgression: Heian and Kamakura Constructions of Prostitution." *Monumenta Nipponica* 55, no. 3 (2000): 327–68.

Grapard, Allan G. "Flying Mountains and Walkers of Emptiness: Toward a Definition of Sacred Spaces in Japan." *History of Religions* 21, no. 3 (1982): 195–221.

Haga Tōru. *Hiraga Gennai.* Tokyo: Asahi Shinbunsha, 1989.

———. "The Western World and Japan in the Eighteenth Century." *Comparative Studies of Culture (University of Tokyo College of General Education)* 16 (1977).

Hanasaki Kazuo. *Edo no kagemajaya.* Rev. ed. Tokyo: Mitsugi Shobō, 1992.

Hanley, Susan B. "Urban Sanitation in Preindustrial Japan." *Journal of Interdisciplinary History* 18, no. 1 (1987): 1–26.

Harley, J. B. "Deconstructing the Map." *Cartographica* 26, no. 2 (1989): 1–20.

———. "Maps, Knowledge, and Power." In *The Iconography of Landscape,* edited by Denis Cosgrove and Stephen Daniels, 277–312. Cambridge: Cambridge University Press, 1988.

———. "Silences and Secrecy: The Hidden Agenda of Cartography in Early Modern Europe." *Imago Mundi* 40: 57–76.

Harley, J. B., and David Woodward, eds. *The History of Cartography: Cartography in the Traditional East and Southeast Asian Societies.* Vol. 2:2. Chicago: University of Chicago Press, 1994.

Hayashi Shihei. "Sangoku tsūran zusetsu." In *Shinpen Hayashi Shihei zenshū* vol. 2, edited by Yamagishi Tokubei and Sano Masami, 1–80. Tokyo: Daiichi Shobō, 1979.

Hayashiya Tatsusaburō. "Ka-sei bunka no rekishiteki itchi." In *Ka-sei bunka no kenkyū,* edited by Hayashiya Tatsusaburō. Tokyo: Iwanami Shoten, 1976.

Helgerson, Richard. *Forms of Nationhood: The Elizabethan Writing of England.* Chicago: University of Chicago Press, 1992.

Higuchi Hideo and Asakura Haruhiko, eds. *(Kyōho ikō) Edo shuppan shomoku.* Tokyo: Mikan Kokubun Shiryō Kankōkai, 1962.

Hiraga Gennai [Fūrai Sanjin, pseud.]. "Fūryū Shidōken den." In *Fūrai Sanjin shū,* edited by Nakamura Yukihiko, 155–224. Tokyo: Iwanami Shoten, 1961.

———. "Nenashigusa." In *Fūrai Sanjin shū,* edited by Nakamura Yukihiko, 35–94. Tokyo: Iwanami Shoten, 1968.

———. "Nenashigusa kōhen." In *Fūrai Sanjin shū,* edited by Nakamura Yukihiko, 95–151. Tokyo: Iwanami Shoten, 1961.

Hiraga Gennai Sensei Kenshōkai, ed. *Hiraga Gennai zenshū.* 2 vols. Tokyo: Hiraga Gennai Sensei Kenshōkai, 1932–34.

Hishiya Heishichi. "Chikushi kikō." In *Nihon kikōbun shūsei,* edited by Yanagida Kunio, 587–672. Tokyo: Nihon Tosho Sentaa, 1979.

Hooson, David, ed. *Geography and National Identity.* Oxford: Blackwell, 1994.

Horton, H. Mack. "Saiokuen Sōchō and Imagawa Daimyo Patronage." In *Literary Patronage in Medieval Japan,* edited by Steven D. Carter. Ann Arbor: University of Michigan Press, 1993.

———. *Song in an Age of Discord: "The Journal of Sōchō" and Poetic Life in Late Medieval Japan.* Stanford, Calif.: Stanford University Press, forthcoming.

Horton, H. Mack, ed. *The Journal of Sōchō.* Stanford, Calif.: Stanford University Press, forthcoming.

Hosono, Masanobu. *Nagasaki Prints and Early Copperplates.* Tokyo: Kodansha International and Shibundo, 1978.

Hostetler, Laura. *Qing Colonial Enterprise: Ethnography and Cartography in Early Modern China.* Chicago: University of Chicago Press, 2001.

Howell, David L. "Ainu Ethnicity and the Boundaries of the Early Modern Japanese State." *Past & Present* 142 (1994): 69–93.

———. *Capitalism from Within: Economy, Society, and the State in a Japanese Fishery.* Princeton, N.J.: Princeton University Press, 1995.

Hur, Nam-lin. *Prayer and Play in Late Tokugawa Japan: Asakusa Sensōji and Edo Society.* Cambridge, Mass.: Harvard University Asia Center and Harvard University Press, 2000.

Ichiko Teiji, ed. *Otogizōshishū.* Vol. 38, *Nihon koten bungaku taikei.* Tokyo: Iwanami Shoten, 1958.

Ihara Saikaku. *Saikaku shôkoku banashi.* In *Kōshoku nidai otoko, Saikaku shōkoku banashi, Honchō nijū fukō,* edited by Fuji Akio, Inoue Toshiyuki, and Satake Akihiro, 261–385. Tokyo: Iwanami Shoten, 1991.

Iida Ryūichi and Tawara Motoaki. *Edo zu no rekishi.* 2 vols. Tokyo: Tsukiji Shokan, 1988.

Inagaki Takeshi. *Hiraga Gennai no Edo no yume.* Tokyo: Shinchōsha, 1989.

Inaka Rōjin Tada Okina. "Yūshi hōgen." In *Kibyōshi, sharebon shū,* edited by Mizuno Minoru et al., 269–94. Tokyo: Iwanami Shoten, 1958.

Inoue Tadashi. *Kaibara Ekiken.* Tokyo: Yoshikawa Kōbunkan, 1963.

Inoue Takaakira, ed. *Kinsei shorin hanmoto sōran.* Tokyo: Aoshōdō, 1981.

Ishigami Satoshi, ed. *Morishima Chūryō shū.* Vol. 32, *Sosho Edo bunkō.* Tokyo: Kabushiki Gaisha Kokusho Kankōkai, 1994.

Ishijima Masatane [An Gyūsai, pseud.]. "Kontan sōkanjō." In *Sharebon taikei,* vol. I, edited by Takagi Koji, Yamamoto Tetsuzō, and Watanabe Yoshi, 113–57. Tokyo: Kabushiki Gaisha Rinpei Shoten, 1931.

Ishijima Masatane [Sanjin, pseud.]. "Ka ri tsūshō kō." In *Sharebon taisei,* edited by Mizuno Minoru et al., 223–33. Tokyo: Chūo Kōronsha, 1978.

Itasaka Yōko. *Edo no tabi to bungaku.* Tokyo: Pericansha, 1993.

———. "Hana no kikō." *Edo jidai bungaku shi* 7 (1990): 46–59.

———. "Kaibara Ekiken to kikōbun." *Aichi Kenritsu Daigaku Bungakubu ronshū* 28 (1974).

———. "Kinsei Tōkaidō kikō no shōmondai." *Fukuoka Kyōiku Daigaku kiyō* 36, no. 1 (1986): 1–11.

———. "Kishi kikō no baai." *Edo jidai bungaku shi* 4 (1985).

———. "Koshōken no Hayashi Shihei hihan." *Kinsei bungei* 31 (1979).

———. "Kyūshū kikō shōkō." *Gobun kenkyū* 62 (1986): 13–26.

———. "Sengō e no tabi: Tachibana Nankei *Tōzaiyūki* wo yomu." *Edo jidai bungaku shi* 8 (1991): 89–101.

———. "Yama no kikō." *Kyūshū Daigaku gobun kenkyū* 63 (1987): 1–12.

Itasaka Yōko, ed. *Kinsei kikō bunshū.* Vol. 17, *Sosho Edo bunkō.* Tokyo: Kabushiki Gaisha Kokusho Kankōkai, 1991.

Itazawa Takeo. *Shiiboruto, Rekishi jinbutsu sosho.* Tokyo: Yoshikawa Kōbunkan, 1988.

Iwasaki, Haruko. "The Literature of Wit and Humor in Late-Eighteenth-Century Edo." In *The Floating World Revisited,* edited by Donald Jenkins,

47–61. Portland and Honolulu: Portland Art Museum and University of Hawai'i Press, 1993.

Jansen, Marius B. *China in the Tokugawa World.* Cambridge, Mass.: Harvard University Press, 1992.

Jōfuku Isamu. *Hiraga Gennai no kenkyū.* Osaka: Sōgensha, 1976.

Jones, Stanleigh H. "Scholar, Scientist, and Popular Author Hiraga Gennai, 1728–1780." Ph.D. diss., Columbia University, 1968.

Jones, Sumie. "William Hogarth and Kitao Masanobu: Reading Eighteenth-Century Pictorial Narratives." *Yearbook of Comparative and General Literature* 34 (1985): 37–73.

Jones, Sumie Amikura. "Comic Fiction in Japan During the Later Edo Period." Ph.D. diss., University of Washington, 1979.

Kaempfer, Englebert. *Kaempfer's Japan: Tokugawa Culture Observed.* Edited and translated by Beatrice M. Bodart-Bailey. Honolulu: University of Hawai'i Press, 1999.

Kaibara Ekiken. "Jinshin kikō." In *Kinsei kikō shūsei,* edited by Itasaka Yōko, 5–48. Tokyo: Kabushiki Gaisha Kokusho Kankōkai, 1991.

Kain, Roger J. P. and Elizabeth Baigent. *The Cadastral Map in the Service of the State.* Chicago: University of Chicago Press, 1992.

Kamens, Edward. *Utamakura, Allusion, and Intertextuality in Traditional Japanese Poetry.* New Haven, Conn.: Yale University Press, 1997.

Kanagawa Kenritsu Rekishi Hakubutsukan, ed. *Sekai no katachi, Nihon no katachi: Watanabe Shin'ichirō kochizu korekushon wo chūshin ni.* Yokohama: Kanagawa Kenritsu Rekishi Hakubutsukan, 1997.

Kaneko Kinjirō. *Rengashi Sōgi no jitsuzō.* Tokyo: Kadokawa Shuppan, 1999.

———. "Sōgi and the Imperial House." In *Literary Patronage in Medieval Japan,* edited by Steven D. Carter. Ann Arbor: University of Michigan Press, 1993.

Karatani Kōjin. *The Origins of Modern Japanese Literature.* Translated by Brett DeBary. Durham, N.C.: Duke University Press, 1993.

Katō, Eileen. "Pilgrimage to Dazaifu: Sōgi's Tsukushi no Michi no Ki." *Monumenta Nipponica* 34, no. 3 (1979): 333–67.

Katō Takashi, ed. *Hyōryū kidan shūsei.* Vol. 1, *Sōsho Edo bunko.* Tokyo: Kokusho Kankōkai, 1990.

Katsurakawa Ezu Kenkyūkai. "Ezu wo yomu." *Chiri* 29, no. 1–5, 7 (1984).

———. "'Katsurakawa ezu' ni miru kūkan ninshiki to sono hyōgen." *Nihonshi kenkyū* 244 (1982).

Kawada Jun, ed. *Sanetomo shū, Saigyō shū, Ryōkan shū.* Vol. 21, *Koten Nihon bungaku zenshū.* Tokyo: Chikuma Shobō, 1960.

Kawamura Hirotada. *Edo bakufu-sen kuniezu no kenkyū.* Tokyo: Kokon Shoin, 1984.

———. "Ezu ni egakareta kyōkai no fūkei." *Chiri* 37, no. 12 (1992): 40–47.

———. "Kinsei shoto Nihonjin no kaigai chishiki: Kan'ei jūsannen shojo no sekai zu wo tōshite." *Yamaguchi Daigaku Kyōikugakubu kenkyū ronso* 44, no. 1 (1994): 9–26.

Keene, Donald. *The Japanese Discovery of Europe, 1720–1880.* Rev. ed. Stanford, Calif.: Stanford University Press, 1969.

———. *Travelers of a Hundred Ages: The Japanese as Revealed Through 1,000 Years of Diaries*. New York: Henry Holt, 1989.

Keirstead, Thomas. *The Geography of Power in Medieval Japan*. Princeton, N.J.: Princeton University Press, 1992.

Kobayashi Tadashi. *Edo no e wo yomu*. Tokyo: Pericansha, 1989.

Koike Masatane, Uda Toshihiko, Nakayama Yūshō, and Tanahashi Masahiro, eds. *Edo no gesaku ehon*. 5 vols. Tokyo: Shakai Shisōsha, 1983.

Kokuritsu Rekishi Minzoku Hakubutsukan, ed. *Shōen ezu to sono sekai*. Chiba: Kokuritsu Rekishi Minzoku Hakubutsukan Shinkōkai, 1993.

Kokushi Daijiten Henshū Iinkai, ed. *Kokushi daijiten*. 14 vols. Tokyo: Yoshikawa Kōbunkan, 1979–93.

Konta Yōzō. *Edo no hon'ya san*. Tokyo: Nippon Hōsō Shuppan Kyōkai, 1977.

———. "Edo no shuppan shihon." In *Edo chōnin no kenkyū*, vol. 3, edited by Nishiyama Matsunosuke, 109–95. Tokyo: Yoshikawa Kōbunkan, 1974.

———. "Edo shuppan gyō no tenkai to sono tokushitsu." *Shuppan kenkyū* 3 (1972): 22–55.

———. "Genroku-Kyōho ni okeru shuppan shihon no keisei to sono rekishiteki igi ni tsuite." *Hisutoria* 19 (1957): 48–66.

Korhonen, Pekka. *Japan and Asia Pacific Integration: Pacific Romances 1968–1996*. London: Routledge, 1998.

Kornicki, Peter. *The Book in Japan: A Cultural History from the Beginnings to the Nineteenth Century*. Leiden: Brill, 1998.

———. "Literacy Revisited: Some Reflections on Richard Rubinger's Findings." *Monumenta Nipponica* 56, no. 3 (2001): 381–94.

Koyama Yasunori and Satō Kazuhiko, eds. *Ezu ni miru shōen no sekai*. Tokyo: Heibonsha, 1987.

Kubota Jun. *Sankashū*. Tokyo: Iwanami Shoten, 1983.

Kuroda Hideo. "Edo bakufu kuniezu, gōchō kanken (1)." *Rekishi chiri* 93, no. 2 (1977).

———. "Genson Keichō, Shōhō, Genroku kuniezu no tokuchō ni tsuite—Edo bakufu kuniezu, gōchō kanken (2)." *Tokyo Daigaku Shiryō Hensanjohō* 15 (1980).

Kuromasa Iwao. "Furukawa Koshōken no chōjutsu ni tsuite." *Kyoto Teikoku Daigaku keizai gakkai: Keizai ronsō* 14, no. 6 (1925): 1065–71.

Lefebvre, Henri. *The Production of Space*. Translated by Donald Nicholson-Smith. Oxford: Blackwell Publishers, 1991.

Lensen, George Alexander. *The Russian Push Toward Japan*. Princeton, N.J.: Princeton University Press, 1959.

Lestringant, Frank. *Mapping the Renaissance World*. Berkeley: University of California Press, 1994.

Leutner, Robert W. *Shikitei Sanba and the Comic Tradition in Edo Fiction*. Cambridge, Mass.: Harvard University Press, 1985.

Levenson, Joseph. "The Amateur Ideal in Ming and Early Ch'ing Society: Evidence from Painting." In *Confucian China and Its Modern Fate: A Trilogy*, 15–43. Berkeley: University of California Press, 1968.

Lidin, Olof G. *Ogyū Sorai's Journey to Kai in 1706*. London: Curzon Press, 1983.

McCullough, Helen C., trans. *The Tale of the Heike*. Stanford, Calif.: Stanford University Press, 1988.

Maës, Hubert. *Hiraga Gennai et son temps*. Paris: École Française d'Extreme-Orient, 1979.

———. *Histoire Galante de Shidōken*. Paris: L'Asiatheque, 1979.

Manji Kōkaisen. "Rokuchō ichiri." In *Sharebon taikei*, vol. 2, edited by Takagi Koji, Yamamoto Tetsuzō, and Watanabe Yoshi, 48–67. Tokyo: Rinpei Shoten, 1933.

Markus, Andrew L. "The Carnival of Edo: Misemono Spectacles from Contemporary Accounts." *Harvard Journal of Asiatic Studies* 45 (1986): 489–541.

Massarella, Derek. *A World Elsewhere: Europe's Encounter with Japan in the Sixteenth and Seventeenth Centuries*. New Haven, Conn.: Yale University Press, 1990.

Miller, J. Scott. "The Hybrid Narrative of Kyōden's *Sharebon*." *Monumenta Nipponica* 34, no. 2 (1979): 133–52.

Minami Kazuo. *Isshin zen'ya no Edo no shōmin*. Tokyho: Kyōikusha, 1985.

Minamoto Ryōen. "*Jitsugaku* and Empirical Rationalism in the First Half of the Tokugawa Period." In *Principle and Practicality: Essays in Neo-Confucianism and Practical Learning*, edited by Wm. Theodore de Bary and Irene Bloom, 375–469. New York: Columbia University Press, 1979.

Montaigne, Michel de. "Of Cannibals." In *The Complete Essays of Montaigne*, translated by Donald M. Frame, 150–59. Stanford, Calif.: Stanford University Press, 1958.

Morozumi Sōichi. *Sōgi renga no kenkyū*. Tokyo: Benseisha, 1985.

Morris-Suzuki, Tessa. "Concepts of Nature and Technology in Early Modern Japan." *East Asian History* 1 (1991): 81–97.

———. "Creating the Frontier: Border, Identity and History in Japan's Far North." *East Asian History* 7 (1994): 1–24.

———. *Re-Inventing Japan: Time, Space, Nation*. Armonk, N.Y.: M. E. Sharpe, 1998.

Munakata, Kiyohiko. *Sacred Mountains in Chinese Art*. Urbana: University of Illinois Press, 1991.

Munemasa Isoo. "Tachibana Nankei *Saiyūki* to Edo kōki no kikō bungaku." In *Azuma ji no ki, Kishi kikō, Saiyūki*, edited by Itasaka Yōko and Munemasa Isoo, 437–48. Tokyo: Iwanami Shoten, 1991.

Munemasa Isoo, ed. *Tōzaiyūki*. 2 vols. Tokyo: Heibonsha, 1974.

Murata Yūji. "Gesaku kenkyū no tame no kiiwaado." *Edo bungaku* 19 (1998): 10–15.

Nagakubo Sekisui. "Nagasaki kōeki nikki." In *Nihon kikōbun shūsei*, edited by Yanagida Kunio, 222–60. Tokyo: Nihon Tosho Sentaa, 1979.

———. "Tō-oku kiko." In *Nihon jūrin soshō*, vol. 4. Tokyo: Ohtori Shuppan, 1970.

Nagatomo Chiyoji. "Edo no hon'ya." *Kokubungaku Kenkyū Shiryōkan kōen shū* 9 (1988): 99–129.

———. *Kinsei kashihon'ya no kenkyū*. Tokyo: Tokyodō, 1982.

———. *Kinsei no dokusho*. Musashi Murayama-shi: Seishōdō, 1987.

Naitō Akira. "Edo no toshi kōzō." In *Edo jidai zushi*, vol. 4, edited by Nishi-yama Matsunosuke and Yoshiwara Ken'ichirō, 32–54. Tokyo: Chikuma Shobō, 1975.

Nakamura Yukihiko. *Gesaku ron*. Tokyo: Kadokawa Shoten, 1966.

———. "Kengai bungaku." In *Nakamura Yukihiko chōjutsu shū*. Tokyo: Chūō Kōronsha, 1984.

Nakano Mitsutoshi. *Edo bunka hyōbanki*. Tokyo: Chūō Kōronsha, 1992.

———. "Yoshiwara saiken." In *Edo bijo kurabe: Yoshiwara saiken*, edited by Hiraki Ukiyōe Zaidan, 6–10. Yokohama: Hiraki Ukiyōe Foundation, 1995.

Nakano Mitsutoshi, ed. "Tokushū: Edo no shuppan, I." *Edo bungaku* 15 (1996).

———. "Tokushū: Edo no shuppan, II." *Edo bungaku* 16 (1996).

Nakayama Yūshō. "Kaisetsu: Kusazōshi kojitsuke nendaiki." In *Edo no gesaku ehon*, vol. 4: *Makki kibyōshi shū*. Edited by Koike Masatane, Uda Toshihiko, Nakayama Yūshō, and Tanahashi Masahiro, 264–66. Tokyo: Shakai Shisō-sha, 1997.

Nanba Matsutarō, ed. *Kochizu no sekai*. Kobe: Kobe Shiritsu Hakubutsukan, 1983.

Nanba Matsutarō, Muroga Nobuo, and Unno Kazutaka, eds. *Old Maps in Japan*. Translated by Patricia Murray. Osaka: Sogensha, 1972.

Needham, Joseph, with Wang Ling. *Science and Civilisation in China*. Vol. 3, *Mathematics and the Sciences of the Heavens and the Earth*. Cambridge: Cambridge University Press, 1959.

Nishikawa Jōken. "[Zōho] Ka'i tsūshō kō." In *Nihon keizai taiten*, edited by Takimoto Seiichi, 277–384. Tokyo: Haimeisha, 1928.

Nishiyama Matsunosuke. "Edo bunka to chihō bunka." In *Iwanami kōza Nihon rekishi*, vol. 13: Kinsei 5, 161–207. Tokyo: Iwanami Shoten, 1964.

———. *Edo Culture: Daily Life and Diversions in Urban Japan, 1600–1868*. Translated by Gerald Groemer. Honolulu: University of Hawai'i Press, 1997.

Nishiyama Matsunosuke et al., eds. *Edogaku jiten*. Tokyo: Kōbunkan, 1994.

Nobuhiro Shinji and Tanahashi Masahiro. "Gesaku kenkyū no shin chihei e." *Tokushū: Gesaku no jidai I, Edo bungaku* 19 (1998): 2–9.

Nobuhiro Shinji and Tanahashi Masahiro, eds. *Edo bungaku* 19 (1998).

Noda Hisao. *Hiraga Gennai no hito to shōgai*. Tokyo: Kōseikaku, 1944.

———. *Kinsei shōsetsu shi ronkō*. Tokyo: Kaku Shobō, 1961.

Noma Kōshin, ed. <Kanpon> *Shikidō ōkagami*. Tokyo: Yūsan Bunko, 1961.

Oda Takeo. *Chizu no rekishi*. Tokyo: Kōdansha, 1972.

———. *Kochizu no sekai*. Tokyo: Kōdansha, 1981.

Oguma Eiji. "*Nihonjin*" *no kyōkai: Okinawa, Ainu, Taiwan, Chōsen, shoku-minchi shihai kara fukki undō made*. Tokyo: Shinyōsha, 1998.

———. *Tan'itsu minzoku shinwa no kigen: "Nihonjin" no jigazō no keifu*. Tokyo: Shinyōsha, 1995.

Okamoto Masaru and Kira Sueo, eds. *Kinsei bungaku kenkyū jiten*. Tokyo: Oufūsha, 1986.

Ooms, Herman. *Charismatic Bureaucrat: A Political Biography of Matsudaira Sadanobu, 1758–1829*. Chicago: University of Chicago Press, 1975.

———. *Tokugawa Village Practice: Class, Status, Power, Law.* Berkeley: University of California Press, 1996.

Ōta Nanpō. *Ichiwa ichigen.* In *Nihon zuihitsu taisei bekkan,* vols. 1–6. Tokyo: Yoshikawa Kōbunkan, 1978–79.

Ōtake Shigehiko. *Tabi to chiri shisō.* Tokyo: Daimeidō, 1990.

Passin, Herbert. *Society and Education in Japan.* New York: Teachers College Press, 1965.

Pflugfelder, Gregory M. *Cartographies of Desire: Male-Male Sexuality in Japanese Discourse, 1600–1950.* Berkeley: University of California Press, 1999.

Pratt, Mary Louise. "Fieldwork in Common Places." In *Writing Culture,* edited by James Clifford and George Marcus, 27–50. Berkeley: University of California Press, 1992.

———. *Imperial Eyes: Travel Writing and Transculturation.* London: Routledge, 1992.

———. "Scratches on the Face of the Country: or, What Mr. Barrow Saw in the Land of the Bushmen." In *"Race," Writing, and Difference,* edited by Henry Louis Gates Jr. Chicago: University of Chicago Press, 1985.

Querido, A. "Dutch Transfer of Knowledge Through Deshima." *Transactions of the Asiatic Society of Japan* 18, Third Series (1983): 17–37.

Ravina, Mark. *Land and Lordship in Early Modern Japan.* Stanford, Calif.: Stanford University Press, 1999.

Reischauer, Edwin O. "Japanese Feudalism." In *Feudalism in History,* edited by Rushton Coulborn, 26–48. Princeton, N.J.: Princeton University Press, 1956.

Rimer, J. Thomas. "The Theme of Pilgrimage in Japanese Literature." In *Pilgrimages: Aspects of Japanese Literature and Culture,* 113–33. Honolulu: University of Hawai'i Press, 1988.

Roberts, Luke S. *Mercantilism in a Japanese Domain: The Merchant Origins of Economic Nationalism in Eighteenth-Century Tosa.* Cambridge: Cambridge University Press, 1998.

Rubinger, Richard. "Who Can't Read and Write? Illiteracy in Meiji Japan." *Monumenta Nipponica* 55 (2000): 163–98.

Rundstrom, Robert A. "Mapping, Postmodernism, Indigenous People and the Changing Direction of North American Cartography." *Cartographica* 28, no. 2 (1991): 1–12.

Saitō Gesshin. *Bukō nenpyō.* Edited by Kaneko Mitsuharu. 2 vols. Tokyo: Heibonsha, 1968.

Sakamoto Muneko, ed. *(Kyōho ikō) Hanmoto betsu shoseki mokuroku.* Osaka: Seibundō Shuppan Kabushiki Gaisha, 1982.

Sakuma Shōken. *Tachibana Nankei.* Yokkaichi: Tachibana Nankei Denki Kankōkai, 1971.

Santō Kyōden. "Edo umare uwaki no kabayaki." In *Kibyōshi, senryū, kyōka,* edited by Hamada Gi'ichirō, Suzuki Katsutada, and Mizuno Minoru, 117–37. Tokyo: Shōgakkan, 1971.

———. "Tsūgen sōmagaki." In *Kibyōshi, sharebon shū,* edited by Mizuno Minoru, 353–86. Tokyo: Iwanami Shoten, 1959.

Satō Yōjin. "Yoshiwara saiken shuppan jijō." *Bungaku* 49, no. 11 (1981): 114–24.

Schipper, Kristofer. *The Taoist Body.* Berkeley: University of California Press, 1993.

Screech, Timon. *Sex and the Floating World: Erotic Images in Japan 1700–1820.* Honolulu: University of Hawai'i Press, 1999.

———. *The Western Scientific Gaze and Popular Imagery in Later Edo Japan: The Lens Within the Heart.* Cambridge: Cambridge University Press, 1996.

Seigle, Cecilia Segawa. *Yoshiwara: The Glittering World of the Japanese Courtesan.* Honolulu: University of Hawai'i Press, 1993.

Shiba Keiko. *Kinsei onna tabi nikki.* Tokyo: Yoshikawa Kōbunkan, 1997.

Shiba Kōkan. *Kōkan saiyū nikki.* Edited by Haga Tōru and Ōta Rieko. Tokyo: Heibonsha, 1986.

Shigematsu Hiromi, ed. *Sōchō sakuhin shū: nikki, kikō.* Tokyo: Koten Bunkō, 1983.

Shikitei Sanba. <*Mata yakinaosu Hachikazuke-hime*> *Kusazōshi kojitsuke nendaiki.* In *Edo no gesaku ehon,* edited by Koike Masatane, Uda Toshihiko, and Tanahashi Masahiro, 229–63. Tokyo: Shakai Shisōsha, 1983.

Shirado Kinkichi. "Go-junkenshi gogekō ni tsuki shogoto kokoroe narabi ofuregaki." Ikarigaseki-mura: Shirado Shigemichi, 1985.

Shirane, Haruo. *Traces of Dreams: Landscape, Cultural Memory, and the Poetry of Bashō.* Stanford, Calif.: Stanford University Press, 1998.

Smith II, Henry D. "The Floating World in Its Edo Locale, 1750–1850." In *The Floating World Revisited,* edited by Donald Jenkins, 25–45. Portland, Ore.: Portland Art Museum and University of Hawai'i Press, 1993.

———. "The History of the Book in Edo and Paris." In *Edo & Paris: Urban Life and the State in the Early Modern Era,* edited by James L. McClain, John M. Merriman, and Ugawa Kaoru, 332–52. Ithaca, N.Y.: Cornell University Press, 1994.

———. *Ukiyōe ni miru Edo meisho.* Tokyo: Iwanami Shoten, 1993.

———. "World Without Walls: Kuwagata Keisai's Panoramic Vision of Japan." In *Japan and the World: Essays on Japanese History and Politics in Honour of Ishida Takeshi,* edited by Gail Lee Bernstein and Haruhiro Fukui, 3–19. London: Macmillan Press in Association with St. Antony's College, Oxford, 1988.

Smith, Richard J. *Chinese Maps.* Oxford: Oxford University Press, 1996.

Smith, Thomas C. "'Merit' as Ideology in the Tokugawa Period." In *Native Sources of Japanese Industrialization, 1750–1925,* 156–72. Berkeley: University of California Press, 1986.

Smits, Gregory. *Visions of Ryukyu: Identity and Ideology in Early-Modern Thought and Politics.* Honolulu: University of Hawai'i Press, 1999.

Stallybrass, Peter, and Allon White. *The Politics and Poetics of Transgression.* Ithaca, N.Y.: Cornell University Press, 1986.

Stefan, John J. *The Russian Far East: A History.* Stanford, Calif.: Stanford University Press, 1994.

Strassberg, Richard E. *Inscribed Landscapes: Travel Writing from Imperial China.* Berkeley: University of California Press, 1994.

Sugi Hiroshi. "Kasei ki no shakai to bunka: zaison no tenkai to kinseiteki bunka kōzō no kaitai." In *Chihō bunka no denryū to sōzō*, 17–70. Tokyo: Yūsankaku Shuppan, 1976.

Sugimoto Fumiko. "Kuniezu." In *Iwanami kōza Nihon tsūshi*, edited by Asao Naohiro et al., 303–25. Tokyo: Iwanami Shoten, 1994.

Suwa Haruo. *Shuppan kotohajime: Edo no hon*. Tokyo: Mainichi Shinbunsha, 1978.

Suzuki Toshio. *Edo no hon'ya*. 2 vols. Tokyo: Chūō Kōronsha, 1980.

Suzuki Toshiyuki. "Tsutaya-han saiken to sono fuzai kōkoku." In *Edo bijo kurabe: Yoshiwara saiken*, edited by Hiraki Ukiyōe Zaidan, 19–21. Yokohama: Hiraki Ukiyōe Foundation, 1995.

Tachibana Nankei. *Saiyūki*. In *Azuma ji no ki, Kishi kikō, Saiyūki*, edited by Itasaka Yōko and Munemasa Isoo. Tokyo: Iwanami Shoten, 1991.

———. *Tōyūki*. In *Tōzaiyūki*, edited by Munemasa Isoo. 2 vols. Tokyo: Heibonsha, 1974.

Takeuchi Makoto. *Edo to Osaka, Taikei Nihon rekishi*. Tokyo: Shōgakkan, 1989.

Takeuchi, Melinda. *Taiga's True Views: The Language of Landscape Painting in Eighteenth-Century Japan*. Stanford, Calif.: Stanford University Press, 1992.

Takizawa Bakin. "Kinsei mono no hon sakusha burui." In *Kinsei mono no hon sakusha burui*, edited by Kimura Miyogo. Tokyo: Hachigi Shoten, 1988.

Tanaka Yūko. *Edo no sōzōryoku: jūhasseiki no medeia to hyōchō*. Tokyo: Chikuma Shobō, 1986.

ten Grotenhuis, Elizabeth. *Japanese Mandalas: Representations of Sacred Geography*. Honolulu: University of Hawai'i Press, 1999.

Tenjiku Rōnin [Morishima Chūryō]. "Tōsei dōtsūki." In *Sharebon taikei*, edited by Takagi Kōji, Yamamoto Tetsuzō, and Watanabe Yoshi, 251–88. Tokyo: Rinpei Shoten, 1931.

Terajima Ryōan. *Wakan sansai zue*. Edited by Isao Shimada, Takeshima Atsuo, and Higuchi Motomi. 18 vols. Tokyo: Heibonsha, 1986.

Thomas, Julia Adeney. *Reconfiguring Modernity: Concepts of Nature in Japanese Political Ideology*. Berkeley: University of California Press, 2001.

Thompson, Sarah E. "The Politics of Japanese Prints." In *Undercurrents in the Floating World: Censorship and Japanese Prints*, edited by Sarah E. Thompson and H. D. Harootunian, 29–91. New York: Asia Society Galleries, 1991.

Thongchai Winichakul. *Siam Mapped: A History of the Geo-Body of a Nation*. Honolulu: University of Hawai'i Press, 1994.

Toby, Ronald P. "Carnival of the Aliens: Korean Embassies in Edo-Period Art and Popular Culture." *Monumenta Nipponica* 41, no. 4 (1986): 415–56.

———. "Contesting the Centre: International Sources of Japanese National Identity." *International History Review* 7, no. 3 (1985): 347–63.

———. "The 'Indianness' of Iberia and Changing Japanese Iconographies of Other." In *Implicit Understandings: Observing, Reporting, and Reflecting on the Encounters Between Europeans and Other Peoples in the Early Modern Era*, edited by Stuart B. Schwartz, 323–51. Cambridge: Cambridge University Press, 1994.

———. "Rescuing the Nation from History: The State of the State in Early Modern Japan." *Monumenta Nipponica* 56, no. 2 (2001): 197–237.

———. *State and Diplomacy in Early Modern Japan.* Princeton, N.J.: Princeton University Press, 1984.

Todorov, Tzvetan. *The Conquest of America: The Question of the Other.* New York: Harper Collins, 1985.

Tokyo Chigaku Kyōkai, ed. *Inō zu ni manabu.* Tokyo: Asakura Shoten, 1997.

Tokyo Daigaku Shiryō Hensanjo, ed. *Henshū chishi biyō tenseki kaidai.* Vol. 11, Pt. 1–6, *Dai Nihon kinsei shiryō.* Tokyo: Tokyo Daigaku Shuppankai, 1972.

Totman, Conrad. *Japan Before Perry.* Berkeley: University of California Press, 1981.

Tsujita Usao. *Nihon kinsei no chirigaku.* Tokyo: Yanagihara Shoten, 1971.

Tuan, Yi-Fu. *Space and Place: The Perspective of Experience.* Minneapolis: University of Minnesota Press, 1977.

Tucker, Mary Evelyn. *Moral and Spiritual Cultivation in Japanese Neo-Confucianism: The Life and Thought of Kaibara Ekiken (1630–1714).* Albany: State University of New York Press, 1989.

Turnbull, David. *Maps are Territories, Science Is an Atlas.* Chicago: University of Chicago Press, 1993.

Uda Toshihiko. "Daijin koku yobun—Hiraga Gennai to *Garibuaa ryokōki.*" *Edo bungaku* 13 (1994): 4–14.

Unno, Kazutaka. "Cartography in Japan." In *The History of Cartography: Cartography in the Traditional East and Southeast Asian Societies,* edited by J. B. Harley and David Woodward, 346–477. Chicago: University of Chicago Press, 1987.

———. "Government Cartography in Sixteenth-Century Japan." *Imago Mundi* 43 (1991): 86–91.

Unno, Kazutaka, ed. *Nihon kochizu taisei.* Tokyo: Kōdansha, 1979.

Van Den Abeele, Georges. *Travel as Metaphor: From Montaigne to Rousseau.* Minneapolis: University of Minnesota Press, 1992.

Vaporis, Constantine Nomikos. *Breaking Barriers: Travel and the State in Early Modern Japan.* Cambridge, Mass.: Harvard University Press, 1994.

Walker, Brett L. *The Conquest of Ainu Lands: Ecology and Culture in Japanese Expansion, 1590–1800.* Berkeley: University of California Press, 2001.

Walter, Lutz, ed. *Japan, A Cartographic Vision: European Printed Maps from the Early 16th to the 19th Century.* Munich: Prestel, 1994.

———. "Philipp Franz von Siebold." In *Japan, A Cartographic Vision: European Printed Maps from the Early 16th to the 19th Century,* edited by Lutz Walter, 69–76. Munich: Prestel, 1994.

Walthall, Anne. "Edo Riots." In *Edo & Paris: Urban Life and the State in the Early Modern Era,* edited by James L. McClain, John M. Merriman, and Ugawa Kaoru, 407–28. Ithaca, N.Y.: Cornell University Press, 1994.

———. *Social Protest and Popular Culture in Eighteenth-Century Japan.* Tucson: University of Arizona Press, 1986.

Watanabe Kenji. "Daimyo no kikōbun." *Sosho Edo bunkō geppō* 17, no. 20 (1991): 5–8.

———. *Edo yūri seisuiki.* Tokyo: Kōdansha, 1994.
———. *Kinsei daimyo bungeiken kenkyū.* Tokyo: Yagi Shoten, 1997.
———. "Kinsei kikō bungaku no saihyōka." *Kokubungaku: kaishaku to kanshō* 706, no. 3 (1990): 147–53.
Watson, Burton, ed. *Saigyō: Poems of a Mountain Home.* New York: Columbia University Press, 1991.
White, Hayden. "The Forms of Wildness: Archaeology of an Idea." In *The Wild Man Within,* edited by Edward Dudley and Maximillian E. Novak, 3–38. Pittsburgh, Penn.: Pittsburgh University Press, 1972.
Wigen, Kären. "The Geographic Imagination in Early Modern Japanese History: Retrospect and Prospect." *The Journal of Asian Studies* 51, no. 1 (1992): 3–29.
———. *The Making of a Japanese Periphery, 1750–1920.* Berkeley: University of California Press, 1995.
———. "Teaching About Home: Geography at Work in the Prewar Nagano Classroom." *The Journal of Asian Studies* 53, no. 3 (2000): 550–74.
Wood, Denis, with John Fels. *The Power of Maps.* New York: Guilford Press, 1992.
Yamashiro Yūkiko. "Yoshiwara saiken no kenkyū." *Komazawa shigaku* 24, no. 3 (1976): 111–34.
Yamori Kazuhiko. *Kochizu e no tabi.* Tokyo: Asahi Shinbunsha, 1992.
———. *Kochizu to fūkei.* Tokyo: Kōdansha, 1974.
———. *Toshizu no rekishi.* Vol. 1, *Nihon hen.* Tokyo: Kōdansha, 1974.
Yee, Cordell D. K. "Cartography in China: Chinese Maps in Political Culture." In *The History of Cartography: Cartography in the Traditional East and Southeast Asian Societies,* edited by J. B. Harley and David Woodward, 71–95. Chicago: University of Chicago Press, 1994.
———. *Space & Place: Mapmaking East and West.* Annapolis, Md.: St. John's College Press, 1996.
Yokota Fuyuhiko. "Imagining Women Working in Early Modern Japan." In *Women and Class in Japanese History,* edited by Hitomi Tonomura, Anne Walthall, and Wakita Haruko, 153–67. Ann Arbor: Center for Japanese Studies, University of Michigan, 1999.
Yonemoto, Marcia. "Envisioning Japan in Eighteenth-Century Europe: The International Career of a Cartographic Image." *Intellectual History Newsletter* 22 (2000): 17–35.
———. "*Het rijk in kaart gebracht: Bestuurlijke cartografie van het Tokugawashogunaat (1603–1868)* [Surveying the realm: Administrative mapmaking by the Tokugawa Shogunate (1603–1868)]." In *Staatsgevaar of sierobject. Japanse kaarten uit de collectie Von Siebold* [Classified material and ornament: Japanese maps from the Siebold Collection], edited by Matthi Forrer and Ivo Smits, 10–24. Leiden: Kleine publikaties Universiteitsbibliotheek Leiden, 2000.
———. "Maps and Metaphors of the 'Small Eastern Sea' in Tokugawa Japan (1603–1868)." *Geographical Review* 89, no. 2 (1999): 169–87.
———. "Nihonbashi: Edo's Contested Center." *East Asian History* 17/18 (1999): 49–70.

————. "The 'Spatial Vernacular' in Tokugawa Maps." *Journal of Asian Studies* 59, no. 3 (2000): 647–66.

Yonemoto, Marcia, Thongchai Winichakul, and Kären Wigen, eds. "Special Issue: Geographies at Work in Asian History." *The Journal of Asian Studies* 53, no. 3 (2000).

Yoneyama, Lisa. "Taming the Memoryscape." In *Remapping Memory: The Politics of Time/Space*, edited by Jonathan Boyarin, 99–135. Minneapolis: University of Minnesota Press, 1994.

Yoshiwara Ken'ichirō. "Edo chōnin bunka to hon'ya." *Komabaya* 37 (1987): 1–11.

Yū Koku Shi. *"[Ikoku kidan] Wasōbyōe."* In *Kokkeibon shū,* edited by Oka Masahiko, 5–51. Tokyo: Kokusho Kankōkai, 1990.

Index

Compositor: G&S Typesetters, Inc.
Text: Sabon
Display: Sabon